McGraw-Hill Education

PMP

Project Management Professional Exam

Henrique Moura

PMI-PMP, PMI-RMP, PMI-ACP

New York Chicago San Francisco Athens London Madrid
Mexico City Milan New Delhi Singapore Sydney Toronto

1 2 3 4 5 6 7 8 9 10   QVS/QVS   1 0 9 8 7 6 5 4

ISBN 978-0-07-183480-3
MHID   0-07-183480-X

e-ISBN 978-0-07-183178-9
e-MHID   0-07-183178-9

Library of Congress Control Number 2013957244

Interior artwork by MPS Limited

The following terms are registered trademarks of the Project Management Institute: PMP, Project Management Professional, Project Management Professional (PMP), PMI, *PMBOK Guide*, OPM3.

All efforts have been made to write a book that is technically accurate and able to successfully prepare readers for the PMP® exam. Nevertheless, the author will not accept any legal responsibilities regarding the book's content. The author also recommends readers use this book in combination with the *PMBOK Guide*®. Finally, the author warns that purchasing this book does not ensure that the reader will pass the PMP® exam and that the author will not accept any legal responsibility for the reader's exam results.

McGraw-Hill Education products are available at special quantity discounts to use as premiums and sales promotions or for use in corporate training programs. To contact a representative, please visit the Contact Us pages at www.mhprofessional.com.

This book is printed on acid-free paper.

To my wife, for her patience and support throughout the writing of this book.

To my parents, for their examples of honesty and humanity.

Contents

1 Guide to Your PMP Certification   1

2 Project Management Framework   5

3 Process Groups   29

4 Integration Management 41

5 Scope Management 73

6 Time Management 95

7 Cost Management 127

8 Quality Management 155

9 Human Resource Management 177

10 Communications Management 201

11 Risk Management 217

12 Procurement Management 253

13 Stakeholder Management 281

14 Full-Length Practice Exam 293

About This Book

I've managed projects my entire career. I love everything about project management: establishing direction, breaking down large complex objectives into smaller and more manageable elements, gathering people around a common objective, trying to build trust, preparing steering meetings, negotiating changes with the customer, closing open issues, and obtaining approvals.

If you want to have a Project Management Professional (PMP®) certification, then we probably share the same passion. Let me congratulate you on your decision. Not only do you believe that it is important to distinguish yourself from other professionals, but you have also chosen a highly reputable certification.

I designed *McGraw-Hill Education: Project Management Professional Exam* to support all those who wish to obtain the PMP certification, issued by the Project Management Institute (PMI). This book is a compilation of materials developed throughout years of experience as a project manager, thousands of hours preparing trainees for the PMP certification all over the world, and a continuous effort of collecting students' feedback.

McGraw-Hill Education: Project Management Professional Exam provides a consolidated source of project management knowledge. I designed it to combine technical accuracy with a didactical approach. For easier reading and more comprehensive learning, I used a combination of learning tools:

- Explanations for exercises
- Tips regarding the most common exam questions
- Examples to smooth the transition from theory to practice
- Tables and images
- Exam questions explained at the end of each chapter to test acquired knowledge
- Lists of the topics that must be learned for the exam
- Glossary of concepts
- Glossary of acronyms

McGraw-Hill Education: Project Management Professional Exam does not include a description of all the inputs, tools, techniques, and outputs of all project management processes. Such descriptions are already included in *A Guide to the Project Management Body of Knowledge (PMBOK® Guide)*. It does however complement the *PMBOK® Guide* with examples, exercises, and tips that help consolidate knowledge. To prepare for the PMP certification, you should combine this book with the *PMBOK® Guide*, fifth edition, and your experience.

About the Author

Henrique Moura is a project management professional with experience as project manager, trainer, and consultant. Over the past 13 years he has managed more than 25 projects crossing industries such as IT, automobile manufacturing, and ship repairing. He often managed complex projects with large implementation teams, multiple vendors, and multimillion-dollar budgets. These past few years, Henrique Moura has focused on managing troubled projects.

As a project manager trainer, he regularly works in Europe, America, the Middle East, and Asia, where he accumulated thousands of training hours. He also acts or acted as lecturer for several institutions in Europe, the Middle East, and America. As a project management consultant, he conducted project management offices and project management tools implementations.

In 2012 he was a speaker at the PMI International Congress in Marseille with a presentation on "dealing with troubled projects," and a speaker at the PMI Portugal congress. In 2011 he was a keynote speaker for the Project Management Institute—Portugal Chapter conference. He was part of the evaluating team of the 2011 Project Management Literature Award—PMI David I. Cleland. He was also a member of the volunteer team reviewing the *PMBOK Guide*, 5th edition, and the *Standard for Program Management*, 2nd edition.

Henrique Moura is a certified PMI-PMP, PMI-RMP, and PMI-ACP.

Guide to Your PMP Certification

Eligibility for the PMP credential has certain requirements of educational and professional experience. The following table highlights those eligibility requirements.

PMP Exam Eligibility Requirements

Category	Education	Project Management Education	Project Management Experience	Other
A	Bachelor's diploma or global equivalent	35 hours	4,500 hours (3 years)	Experience in all 5 process groups
B	High school diploma or equivalent	35 hours	7,500 hours (5 years)	Experience in all 5 process groups

Note that Project Management Institute (PMI) can change this information. Visit the PMI's website for official and complete information.

The Exam Application Process

The Project Management Professional (PMP) exam online application process includes the following steps:

1. Submit your application through the PMI website (http://www.pmi.org).
2. PMI will review your application, verifying its completeness.
3. Once your application has been successfully reviewed, you can submit payment of credential fees.
4. A sample of applicants who have submitted payment will be selected for an audit. If your application is selected, you must send the required information to PMI within 90 days.
5. Those who were not selected for an audit or have successfully completed it should receive an e-mail from PMI confirming that they are eligible to sit for the exam within one year.
6. The e-mail should also provide detail information regarding how to schedule the exam.

Again, note that this information can change. Please visit PMI's website for official and complete information.

About the Exam

The exam tests your knowledge regarding initiating, planning, executing, monitoring and controlling, and closing projects.

The exam consists of 200 multiple-choice questions to be completed within four hours. This means you have an average of one minute and 12 seconds per question. You should be able to complete most questions well within one minute and 12 seconds. However, some questions typically require more time because:

- They require diagram analysis.
- They require calculations.
- Their text is very long.

Only 175 questions of the 200 are testable. This means that there are 25 pretest questions, which are included in the exam as part of a control process that assesses whether they are ready to be included in future exams. Whether you get these 25 questions right will not impact your final score. Unfortunately, you will not know which questions are testable and which are nontestable.

Up to 2005, PMI used to publish the passing rates in the PMP handbook. The last known passing rate was 61 percent. PMI does not publish the passing mark any longer.

In the exam you may find different question types spread randomly throughout the exam:

- Knowledge questions
- Knowledge application questions
- Situational questions

Knowledge questions are typically the most straightforward, requiring you to identify a concept.

Question 1: Which document is used to formally approve the project start?
Answer: Project charter
Justification: The project charter is a formal document that authorizes the project start and provides the project manager the authority to apply resources to project activities.

Question 2: Which estimating technique is usually used during the initiating process group?
Answer: Analogous estimate
Justification: The analogous estimate is prepared using historical information accumulated in the organization. During the initiating process group, when detailed project information has not yet been identified, estimating based on analogies with previous projects is often the best alternative option.

Knowledge application questions require you not only to know the concept, but also to understand its multiple perspectives and applications.

Question 3: Which of the following is the most likely cause of experiencing constant scope changes?
Answer: The project does not have an approved project charter.
Justification: There are many potential reasons why a project could be experiencing constant scope changes, including the lack of an approved project charter. The project charter authorizes the project start. It also establishes a common project vision among stakeholders. Someone, with enough authority, uses the project charter to establish high-level objectives and project

constraints. These objectives and constraints should provide a sense of direction and help to prevent erratic scope changes.

Question 4: Which of the following is an advantage of using an analogous estimate?

Answer: The project management team is able to understand management's expectations.

Justification: The analogous estimate is prepared using historical information accumulated in the organization. Often, this analogous estimate is prepared by management during initiation, when the project manager and the team have not been assigned to the project yet. Later, during planning, the project manager and the team will be able to prepare more accurate estimates based on more detailed information. Any existing analogous estimate may then be used as a basis for comparison to understand what management is expecting.

Situational questions test which approach to adopt in specific project situations.

Question 5: How should the project manager proceed if the sponsor insists on proceeding with the project without a project charter?

Answer: Explain to the sponsor why the project charter is critical for project success.

Justification: The project manager should adopt the right process, explaining in a pedagogical way the importance of having a project charter.

Question 6: The project manager has prepared a detailed cost estimate that is significantly higher than the analogous estimate prepared during initiation. The sponsor is now asking for a 20 percent reduction on the detailed cost estimate. How should the project manager proceed?

Answer: Provide the sponsor with potential scenarios of scope, quality, and schedule that can support a 20 percent reduction of project costs.

Justification: Reducing the cost estimate without redefining other project constraints, such as scope or quality, is not an acceptable project management alternative. Project objectives should remain integrated, feasible, and credible.

During the Exam

The exam starts with a tutorial about the exam software. You can use this time to become familiar with the software and to write down all information that may help you during the exam. In a four-hour exam, these notes can prove to be important when your memory shows signs of fatigue.

There is no negative marking, so you should attempt each and every question, even if you have to guess. All exam questions are worth the same. Do not waste time with questions that you don't know how to answer or have strong doubts about. Simply mark the question for review and move on. Later you can easily retrieve questions marked for review.

Project Management Framework

Learning Topics	▸ Project ▸ Temporary, unique, and progressive elaboration ▸ Operation ▸ Project management, project success, and project failure ▸ Knowledge areas and process groups ▸ Constraint and triple constraint ▸ Application area ▸ Project life cycle and product life cycle ▸ Project phase and phase review ▸ Organization types (projectized, functional, matrix, and composite) ▸ Program, portfolio, and sub-project ▸ Organizational Project Management Maturity Model (OPM3) ▸ Project management office (PMO) ▸ Stakeholders (project manager, project management team, sponsor, steering committee, customer, project team, functional manager, program manager, portfolio manager, project expediter, project coordinator, and performing organization)

Let's start building the foundations for your PMP exam preparation. This chapter is about key project management concepts that will be systematically used throughout the book, such as *project*, *knowledge areas*, *organization types*, and *stakeholders*. Read through the chapter, and complete the exercises and exam to become familiar with these topics.

Projects and Operations

For the PMP exam, it is important to clearly understand the concept of ***project***, as well as distinguish it from ***operational work***.

Projects

A project is a temporary initiative carried out with the aim of producing a unique product. With this definition, two characteristics can be highlighted: **temporary** and **unique**.

Temporary means that the project has a specific beginning and end. Its beginning occurs when the organization establishes the objectives and authorizes resources to be mobilized for the project. Its end occurs when the objectives are met or when the project is cancelled. Are you comfortable with the meaning of *temporary*? Let's examine the concept further:

- *Temporary* does not mean that the scheduled duration may not change. Factors such as uncertainty, lack of change control, bad processes, and inadequate project management often lead to project schedule delays.
- *Temporary* does not mean that the project has a short duration. Some projects have short durations, while others have longer durations.
- *Temporary* does not refer to the project's product longevity. Often projects deliver products with lasting characteristics.

Developing a *unique* product means that there is a certain degree of uncertainty. Doubts regarding what product should be developed, what work should be performed, how much time is required, what level of quality is needed, and how many resources should be allocated are frequent examples of project uncertainty. This uncertainty does not mean that all project components are unique. Projects often deliver components with known and recurrent characteristics. For example, a project may include training sessions with a predictable content and duration.

Projects develop products, but this generic expression may in fact be referring to creating, enhancing, or discontinuing products or services. It may also be referring to results. For example, a project may be required to be able to make an important and complex business decision.

Being unique, projects often lead to situations where there is not enough information to plan in detail future phases. For example, during a project set to develop an information system, the team may not have enough information to plan in detail the development phase until the requirements definition phase is finished. To deal with this uncertainty, the project should be progressively elaborated. **Progressive elaboration** is the third key characteristic of projects. It represents the process of providing greater levels of planning detail as the project moves toward completion and as more and better information becomes available.

The concept of *progressive elaboration* might not be intuitive, as people often feel more comfortable working with a detailed plan. However, in a project environment, progressive elaboration can help deal with the lack of information. Let's look at some examples of progressive elaboration:

- Product requirements can be detailed in the beginning of each new project phase, as team and customer increase their level of understanding.
- A breakdown of the work required to complete a specific product component might only be prepared after contracting an external supplier.
- To plan the next few weeks, the team can decompose work packages into detailed activities.
- A quality metric might only be detailed when more precise product information becomes available.
- The human resource management plan can be revised at the end of the design phase to detail resources needed, along with the skills required.

> Rolling wave planning is a progressive elaboration planning technique (see Chapter 6). (See Figure 2.1.)

Operations

Work is divided into two major categories: projects and operations. As you have seen, projects are temporary, unique, and progressively elaborated. Operations tend to be permanent and instead of being unique, they often repeat the same process. The permanent nature of operations is

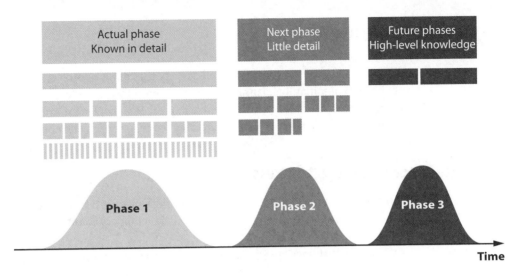

Figure 2.1 Progressive elaboration

frequently a consequence of having objectives directly related to the organization's main purpose. For example, a household appliances factory has a daily operation of distributing its products through the distribution chain. The operation's repetitive nature reduces the uncertainty over scope, schedule, and costs, supporting a more detailed planning.

There are, however, shared characteristics among projects and operations. Both initiatives have a purpose, use constrained resources, and may require planning, executing, and controlling.

On the exam, be careful not to apply project management approaches to operations.

Differences Between a Project and an Operation

Project	Operation
Temporary	Permanent
Unique	Recurrent work
Progressively elaborated	May be planned in detail

Similarities Between a Project and an Operation

Project	Operation
Has a purpose	Has a purpose
Requires planning and controlling	Requires planning and controlling
Uses constrained resources	Uses constrained resources

Project Management

Project management is a professional activity that pursues project success through a structured application of initiating, planning, executing, monitoring and controlling, and closing processes. Using a combination of technique and art, project management processes try to keep the project aligned with its objectives, while delivering value to project stakeholders.

The Concept of Project Success

If project management is about pursuing project success, it is important to better understand the concept of project success. Asking different stakeholders about the meaning of "project success" will likely garner very different answers.

From a customer's perspective, project success can mean:

- The product meets the approved requirements.
- The product is fit for use. It meets the need for which it was created, even if such need was not accurately reflected by the approved product requirements. As you probably know, this can happen often.
- The product is available to its market or internal organization in an acceptable time frame.
- The project adheres to changes in the organization, market, or economy.
- The final cost does not jeopardize the project business case.

From a supplier's perspective, project success can mean:

- The project is performed within budget and is able to deliver a financial return.
- The customer is satisfied.
- There are no negative impacts to the company's reputation.
- There are no legal actions.

From a management's perspective, project success can mean:

- The project implements the organization's strategy.
- The product is successful and sustainable.
- The organization's profitability is increased.

How can project success be defined in a way that is compatible with such different perspectives? Standard project management uses a combination of project objectives and value to define project success. A successful project should meet objectives that deliver value to project stakeholders. See Figure 2.2, where the circles represent customer value and supplier value.

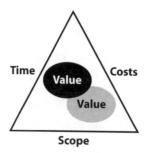

Figure 2.2 Objectives and value

To meet objectives, project management must follow a few rules:

- During planning, it is important to establish objectives that are feasible, can be clearly verified by the project stakeholders, and are integrated and achievable during the project life cycle. Thus planning must translate needs and expectations into specific scope, schedule, costs, and quality requirements. This translation effort can help avoid acceptance criteria that are subjective, volatile, or only able to be assessed after the project ends.
- During controlling, try to keep the project aligned with its objectives. Maintaining this alignment can lead to correcting or preventing variances to the agreed-upon plan. For example, a preventive action can be issued to avoid an anticipated schedule delay. Maintaining an alignment can also mean managing changes should they occur.

A second dimension of project success concerns the value delivered to stakeholders. To align project objectives to value, project management should follow a few rules:

- During planning, define objectives that deliver value to project stakeholders.
- During controlling, manage changes whenever the project is not delivering the expected value.

Managing value does not mean accepting changes without considering their impact. Project objectives should remain integrated, feasible, and credible. Managing value means understanding potential changes, analyzing their impact, and requesting their approval. For example, if the customer requests a new product functionality that was not included in the approved requirements, there is an integration problem between the approved scope and the required scope. The team should identify the required change, analyze its impact on the schedule and on the budget, and if it is acceptable, issue a formal change request.

Project Failure

Projects fail when accumulated or estimated variances go beyond a tolerance limit, when they no longer deliver an acceptable level of value to one or more key stakeholders. Some of the most common reasons for project failure include:

- Lack of management support
- Poor management of key stakeholders
- Ambiguous goals and requirements
- Poor project management
- Unfeasible estimates
- Inadequate risk management
- Lack of qualified resources
- Poor change control
- The project not being aligned with the organization's strategy

Knowledge Areas

Knowledge areas are a logical organization of project management processes according to their nature. According to *A Guide to the Project Management Body of Knowledge* (*PMBOK Guide*), fifth edition, there are ten project management knowledge areas:

- Integration management
- Scope management

- Time management
- Cost management
- Quality management
- Human resource management
- Communications management
- Risk management
- Procurement management
- Stakeholder management

Process Groups

Process groups are another logical organization of project management processes. They are used to group processes according to their purpose. According to the *PMBOK Guide*, fifth edition, there are five project management process groups:

- **Initiating**   Authorizes the start of the project or phase
- **Planning**   Defines project objectives and the actions required to attain them
- **Executing**   Integrates all the necessary resources to execute the plan
- **Monitoring and controlling**   Assesses performance, issues corrective and preventive actions, and manages project changes
- **Closing**   Leads the project or phase to a controlled end

Constraint

Managing a project can be complex. Such complexity is a result not only of permanent uncertainty, but also of existing limits to project management decisions. These limits can include scope, schedule, budget, quality, resources, and risk constraints. Examples of constraints can be:

- The organization has chosen a specific technology.
- There is a deadline to deliver the project.
- There is a limit of project funds.
- The developed system must meet a specific performance.
- There is only one available resource with a specific skill.
- The organization is averse to schedule risks.

Constraints also create additional challenges for project management. Examples of these challenges are:

- Constraints require constant planning iterations until feasible and integrated objectives can be defined.
- When identifying variances to the agreed-upon plan, it is important to identify corrective actions that do not compromise the existing constraints.
- When identifying a variance, it may not be possible to issue a corrective action without sacrificing one or more project constraints. Correcting that variance requires a choice among different project constraints. For example, correcting a schedule delay by sacrificing a cost constraint is based on a choice that the schedule is more important than the budget.
- The project manager does not have autonomy to make decisions that compromise one or more constraints. These decisions should be made by the sponsor or management.
- Management or the sponsor may define a priorities structure to guide options whenever there is a conflict among project constraints. For many projects, scope is the key constraint,

often defined within a contract, while schedule may be the second priority due to penalties for late delivery. For other projects, the urgency of delivering a product to the market makes schedule the main priority. Other projects have quality as their main priority.

- When a change occurs, project constraints may have to be revised. For example, to change the project scope, management may revise the funds available for the project.

Triple Constraint

Triple constraint is a term used to describe three concurrent project constraints that must be simultaneously accomplished. These constraints are scope, schedule, and budget. The term *triple constraint* does not mean that there are no other relevant constraints, such as quality, resources, and risks.

Application Area

An application area is a category of projects that share specific characteristics. For example, construction projects are different from research and development projects.

Life Cycles

For the PMP exam, you should be able to distinguish a project life cycle from a product life cycle. Additionally, make sure you understand the difference between project life cycle and project management process groups (initiating, planning, executing, monitoring and controlling, and closing).

Project Life Cycle

The project life cycle is the collection of phases that the project must go through from its beginning to its closing. The project life cycle may be represented as a methodology that groups deliverables by phases. Each deliverable may then be used as an input into future phases.

There isn't just one project life cycle. Different projects may adopt different project life cycles, according to their industry, product, risks, and organization culture.

> It is generally accepted that most projects follow a pattern where few resources are consumed at the beginning, more resources are used at intermediate phases, and fewer resources are used at the project end.

There are different families of project life cycles:

- **Waterfall** Work development is seen as constantly flowing forward (waterfall) through sequential and different phases. Objectives are defined at the beginning of the project and may be changed only through formal change control. This model is often recommended when the product must be delivered in full to have value.
- **Iterative and incremental** *Iterative* means that the product is developed through cycles, or constant iterations. Each iteration builds on top of the previous product

version, benefiting from previous lessons learned. *Incremental* means that the product components may be developed in parallel and be integrated whenever they are built.

- **Adaptatives or agile**   Work development is performed through small iterative and incremental cycles, usually with fixed duration and resources. This approach is recommended when the scope is not completely defined and the product can be delivered in short cycles.

You will probably not be tested on these families of project life cycles. Nevertheless, understanding these concepts might help you bridge the concept of life cycle to your own project experience.

Product Life Cycle

The product life cycle is the complete history of a product, extending through its idea, definition, development, operation, and disposal phases. A product development project might be more intuitive and common. Still, projects can occur at any moment of the product life cycle, and a product can spawn many projects over its life cycle. Examples of projects interacting in the product life cycle are:

- A project to determine if a product is feasible
- A project to develop a new product
- A project to enhance an existing product
- A project to discontinue an existing product

> Product life cycle is not the same as project life cycle.

Project Phases

Project work can be grouped into phases for easier planning and controlling. Each phase tends to group logically related work, which usually leads to the completion of a major deliverable and is frequently linked to a project milestone. For example, the definition phase of an information systems project may include defining system requirements, training requirements, and data conversion requirements.

If you are managing a project without a previously established methodology, you might need to decide which phases to adopt. A phase can be determined for a number of reasons:

- The end of a major deliverable
- Significant changes to resources and skills needs
- The need to implement a control point before advancing on the project
- The involvement of an external organization

> The end of a phase is usually linked to a project milestone.

Phases are usually completed sequentially, with the deliverables of one phase being used as inputs into the activities of future phases. It is, however, common that some overlapping exists, with a phase starting before the end of the previous phase. This overlapping relationship can reduce the project duration, but will typically increase its risk.

> Project phases are not process groups.

On simpler projects there is only one cycle of initiating, planning, executing, monitoring and controlling, and closing. On more complex projects, process groups may be repeated in each phase to guide the project toward completion. Therefore, initiating, planning, executing, monitoring and controlling, and closing can be applied to a project or to a phase.

Stage Gate, Kill Point, Phase Gate, or Phase Review

A stage gate, also known as a kill point, phase gate, or phase review, is a predefined event in the project, typically at the end of a phase, where the sponsor and steering committee have the opportunity to review the project performance and major deliverables, as well as decide whether to proceed to the next phase. For example, a stage gate can be implemented at the end of an initial design phase of a large industrial project, before moving on to the procure phase and involving external suppliers. A stage gate assessment can also be used to terminate the project, if it is no longer required or if the actual performance compromises the value delivered to stakeholders.

REVIEW EXERCISE

The advantages of organizing projects into phases are:

1. _____

2. _____

3. _____

4. _____

5. _____

Projects and the Organization

Most of your PMP exam preparation will be focused on the project manager's perspective over the project. You will learn how a combination of processes, tools, techniques, and skills can help to deliver value for a single project. There is, however, a different perspective on project management that will also strongly influence project success, and it is also relevant for the exam. Organizational project management perceives project management from the organization's perspective. How can an organization influence the project performance and return on investment by changing its structure, policies, procedures, governance bodies, tools, or even culture?

This topic is focused on organizational project management, with a particular emphasis on the different types of organizational structures. It will also address how projects and operations can be combined into programs and portfolios in order to maximize the value delivered to the organization. Finally, this topic addresses the role of the project management office (PMO) as the body accountable for project management throughout the organization.

Organization Types

The organizational structure will strongly influence the project's performance. Different organizations will have different answers for critical questions such as: Who controls the resources? Who determines the schedule and budget? What is the reporting structure? How complex is it to manage communication? How stable is the resource allocation during the project? Are project resources working within a single physical location?

PMI distinguishes organization types according to the level of the project manager's authority. Basic organization types are functional, projectized, and matrix.

Functional Organization, Hierarchical or Vertical

In a functional organization, also known as hierarchical or vertical, staff are grouped hierarchically by functions, such as marketing, sales, and human resources. (See Figure 2.3.) The authority of the functional managers over the project is clear, with each employee having only one clear boss. When a project manager is assigned to a project, he or she assumes the role of a **project coordinator** or a **project expediter** (see the section on stakeholders).

In functional organizations, projects normally occur inside a single department. If the project spans different functions, the information and the decisions go through the functional managers involved. This distribution of project authority through multiple managers tends to slow down decisions and fragment the project into different interests, schedules, and priorities. Additionally, because people are organized by functions, the team is typically physically separated, which constrains the team development process and leads to the development of silos.

Projectized Organization

A projectized organization is structured around and oriented toward projects. (See Figure 2.4.) Authority over each project is exclusively assigned to a project manager who has full control over the budget, schedule, resources, and work assignments. Resources are usually allocated full time to a single project and are frequently collocated in a common physical space. Unlike in most organizations, resources in a projectized organization do not belong to a department or business function. At the end of each project, resources are mobilized for another project, allocated to a resource pool, or released from the organization.

Figure 2.3 Functional organization

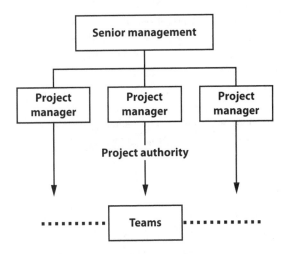

Figure 2.4 Projectized organization

Matrix Organization

The matrix organization is the most common organization type. It is a multidimensional organization that combines the functions' vertical lines with the projects' horizontal lines to better adapt to a project's challenges. (See Figure 2.5.)

Similar to a functional organization, functional managers remain responsible for their vertical functions, developing and providing the project with resources as well as technical expertise. Similar to a projectized organization, the project manager in the matrix organization is accountable for project success.

There is, however, a shared authority over the projects in the matrix organization. This sharing will naturally lead to conflicts of authority over who is responsible for:

- Estimating work
- Selecting resources
- Managing resources
- Recognizing and rewarding resources
- Prioritizing the work of the different projects and operations
- Justifying unfavorable costs variances

Depending whether the authority is more concentrated on the functional manager or on the project manager, the matrix organization may be classified as weak, balanced, or strong.

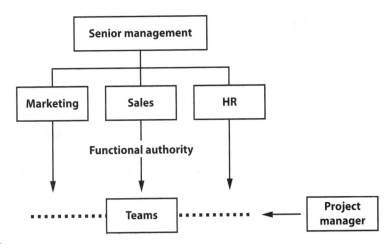

Figure 2.5 Matrix organization

15

In a **weak matrix**, most of the authority belongs to the functional manager. In a **balanced matrix**, the authority is evenly shared between the functional manager and the project manager. In this organization, the project manager has to work with the functional managers to recruit, manage, and reward the team members. Finally, in a **strong matrix**, most of the authority over project decisions belongs to the project manager.

> In all matrix organizations, including the strong, the authority over the project and resources is shared between the project manager and the functional manager.

Composite Organization

After reading about functional, projectized, and matrix organizations, you may have thought of organizations that can fit more than one of the types described. Some organizations adopt composite structures with characteristics of different organization types. For example, a matrix organization may adopt a projectized type for a specific business line that is developing projects on the customers' sites.

Functional Organization

Advantages	Disadvantages
Clear authority over the project	Fragmented approach because no one is fully responsible for the project
Clear communication channels	Possibly slow project decisions
Flexibility on resource utilization	Functional areas often adopt a silo mentality, showing a lack of loyalty to the project's interests
Organized around resources' functional expertise, making it easier to develop and share knowledge	Challenge to control the project due lack of project accountability from the functional areas
Easier communication and sharing because the team is physically grouped according to their functions	

Projectized Organization

Advantages	Disadvantages
Clear authority over the project	Inefficient resources utilization because resources are often duplicated across different projects
Clear communication channels	Challenge to transfer accumulated knowledge to future projects because organization is not oriented toward technical specialization
Team physically grouped on same location	Lack of a clear career path
High loyalty toward the project	Possibility of team members losing their jobs at the end of the project

Matrix Organization

Advantages	Disadvantages
Resources shared among different projects and operations	Conflict of interests between the project and the functional managers
Project possibly crossing different functional areas and having a single project manager accountable for its success	Tendency for a complex and unstable resource allocation
Higher loyalty toward the project than the functional organization	Frequent authority conflicts over projects and resources
Project cost possibly optimized by sharing resources	Complex communication channels
	Prone to constant shifts in priorities

Project Alignment Toward Strategy

Projects are not independent events within an organization. The projects that an organization undertakes should be oriented toward a strategy. As such, they should be prioritized so that the most important projects are given the opportunity to succeed. Likewise, they should be regularly assessed as to their impact on the overall corporate vision. Managing projects, programs, and portfolios in a coordinated approach allows the organization to increase the value delivered by its initiatives.

Programs

A program is a set of related projects and operations that when managed in a coordinated way address a common business objective. Program management adds value to the organization, coordinating the dependencies between the different projects and operations to maximize the organizational benefits.

Portfolios

A portfolio is a group of projects or programs coordinated to implement the business strategy. (See Figure 2.6.) Projects and programs inside a portfolio may not be directly related. They are managed in an integrated way because the portfolio's different initiatives are under the same constraints. Examples of constraints shared within the portfolio are a single resource pool, a common limit for risk exposure, and common funds.

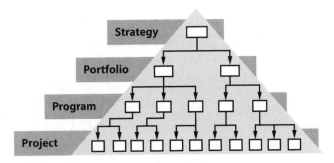

Figure 2.6 Projects, programs, and portfolio

Subproject

A subproject is a decomposition of a project into more easily manageable components. A subproject may be established to manage a large deliverable, a phase, or a work component developed by a supplier.

Project Management Office (PMO)

A project management office (PMO) is the organizational unit responsible for project management throughout the organization. Its responsibilities may include defining methodologies, organizing training, mobilizing project managers for projects that require assistance, providing tools and templates, guiding, facilitating communication and negotiation, reporting project performance to management, and assisting in defining project priorities.

> PMOs typically exist on strong matrix and projectized organizations.

There are different PMOs, according to their level of project control and organizational influence:

- A PMO with a consultative and support role. Its responsibilities may include providing guidance, helping solve and escalate problems, providing templates, organizing project management training, and maintaining projects' historical information.
- A PMO that not only provides support and guidance, but also establishes project standards, specifies methodologies, templates, and tools. It may also perform periodical project performance reviews.
- A PMO that can assume direct control over a project or over the resources shared among projects.

> The project manager may request support and guidance from the PMO.

Organizational Project Management Maturity Model (OPM3)

The Organizational Project Management Maturity Model (OPM3) is the PMI's globally recognized best-practice standard for assessing the maturity of the organization's practices for managing projects, programs, and portfolios. By assessing management maturity, OPM3 can prepare organizations for enhancing their management practices.

Stakeholders

A stakeholder is a person or group who can be positively or negatively impacted by the project. A stakeholder can also be someone who has a positive or negative influence over the project.

The level of interest and power of different stakeholders can range significantly. Identifying stakeholders, understanding their interests and power, and managing their "stakes" are critical for project success. Chapter 13 will discuss how to identify and proactively manage stakeholder engagement.

Typical stakeholders include the project manager, the project management team, the sponsor, the steering committee, the customer, the team, the PMO, the functional manager, the portfolio manager, and the program manager.

Project Manager

With authority delegated by the sponsor, the project manager is accountable for managing the project and meeting project objectives. Responsibilities include coordinating the team, negotiating and optimizing resource utilization, managing the project interfaces, and reporting on project performance. Depending on the organizational structure, the project manager may report to a functional manager, program manager, portfolio manager, or PMO.

To systematically lead the project to its objectives, the project manager will need specific professional knowledge regarding project management processes, techniques, and tools. But this knowledge is far from being sufficient. Project managers must have the required personal skills to lead the team and establish meaningful relationships with different stakeholders. These personal skills can include communicating, leading, motivating, influencing, negotiating, organizing, and solving problems.

Project Management Team

The project manager is not the only member of the project team who performs project management work. Other team members can participate regularly in the planning and controlling efforts, developing planning components, coordinating teams, and reporting performance. The complete set of team members directly involved in project management work is known as the project management team.

Sponsor

The sponsor is the manager who provides the financial resources and promotes the project. The sponsor, and often other high-level managers, also plays a significant role on the project charter development, approving the project start, providing authority to the project manager, and helping establish a preliminary understanding of the project scope.

At critical moments, the sponsor may become directly involved in the project, deciding on significant changes and risks and validating key deliverables. The sponsor can also provide a route for the project manager to escalate and influence issues.

As was previously discussed, the project manager is accountable for meeting project objectives. However, when accumulated variances cannot be corrected without compromising existing constraints, the decisions should be escalated to the sponsor.

Steering Committee

The steering committee is an advisory group that includes the sponsor and other high-level stakeholders from the organization, or organizations, involved. The steering committee provides project management guidance, makes key decisions, monitors progress, arbitrates conflict, approves key deliverables, and facilitates resources allocation.

Customer

The customer is the person or group who receives the project's product, using it to create value for the organization. The customer is also frequently responsible for defining requirements and verifying if the product meets these requirements. When the product under development is destined to be used outside the organization, the customer is not the future user of the product, but can represent its interests on the project.

Project Team

The team includes everyone who is involved with project activities and may include the project management team, experts, customers, users, suppliers, and partners. Team members may be fully allocated to the project or be working on a part-time basis. In some projects, the team is physically colocated in the same physical space. In others, each team member works from his or her own organizational unit. The availability of communication technology, such as e-mail and online meetings, makes it easier to create virtual teams, where cooperation is possible without physically meeting.

Team members are responsible for technical execution. They may also be involved in project management activities, engaging in planning, helping identify and solve problems, providing work performance information, and sharing knowledge.

Functional Manager or Line Manager

The functional manager is a manager responsible for the work of a business function, business line, or organization unit. For example, a functional manager may be a marketing manager or the head of sales. The functional manager may provide resources to the project, negotiating with the project manager regarding which resources to allocate. The functional manager may also be involved in planning and controlling project activities that concern his or her functional area.

Project interests will not always be aligned with the functional manager's interests. For example, a project resource may be needed in a different project or operation. This conflict of interests is common within the relationship between the project manager and the functional manager in a matrix organization.

> Project managers negotiate project resources with the functional managers.

Program Manager

A program manager coordinates a set of related projects and operations that address a common business objective. The program manager's role is to manage the dependencies between the different projects and operations in order to maximize the organizational benefits. Additionally, he or she should oversee and support the project managers of the projects comprised in the program.

Portfolio Manager

A portfolio manager is an executive who coordinates a group of projects or programs in order to implement the business strategy. The portfolio manager is responsible for selecting the appropriate mix of projects and programs that maximizes the organization value, while working under resource constraints and an acceptable level of risk exposure. The portfolio manager should also oversee the projects and programs to ensure that their performances do not compromise the expected return on investment.

Project Expediter

A project expediter is a type of project management role in a functional or a weak matrix organization. The project expediter has a very low level of authority. The project expediter does not make decisions and acts as an assistant to management, helping transmit information and directions to the team.

Project Coordinator

A project coordinator is another type of project manager in a functional or weak matrix organization. The project coordinator has a low level of authority, but has a higher level of project authority than the project expeditor, with some level of coordination authority over the team.

The authority of the project coordinator does not usually derive from any formal assignment. It is often an indirect result of the coordinator's technical and personal skills.

Performing Organization

The performing organization is the organization responsible for performing the work and for managing the required resources. A project establishes a relationship between the performing organization (or supplier) and the requesting organization (or customer).

MEMORIZATION EXERCISE

> Assign the following definitions to a project management concept.

1. Responsible for technical execution and may also be involved in project management activities

   _____

2. Category of projects that share common and specific characteristics

   _____

3. Collection of phases that the project must go through from its beginning to its closing

   _____

4. Group of projects or programs coordinated to implement the business strategy

   _____

5. Manager responsible for the work of a business function, business line, or organization unit

   _____

6. Manager who provides the financial resources, promotes the project, and plays a significant role on the project charter development

   _____

7. Matrix organization where the authority is evenly shared between functional manager and project manager

   _____

8. Members of the project team directly involved in project management work

   _____

9. Multidimensional organization that combines the functions' vertical lines with the project's horizontal lines to better adapt to the project's challenges

_____

10. Organization structured around and oriented toward projects: authority over each project is exclusively assigned to a project manager who has full control over the budget, schedule, resources, and work assignments

_____

11. Organization where the staff is grouped hierarchically by functions: authority of the functional managers over the project is clear, with each employee having only one clear boss

_____

12. Organizational unit responsible for project management across the organization

_____

13. Person or group who receives the project's product, using it to create value for the organization

_____

14. Person or group who can be positively or negatively impacted by the project

_____

15. Process of providing greater levels of planning detail as the project moves toward completion and as more and better information becomes available

_____

16. Set of related projects and operations that when managed in a coordinated way address a common business objective

_____

17. Temporary initiative carried out with the aim of producing a unique product

_____

18. Term used to describe three concurrent project constraints that must be simultaneously accomplished: scope, time, and costs

_____

19. The complete history of a product, extending through its idea, definition, development, operation, and disposal phases

_____

20. Work with permanent characteristics, frequently repeating the same process

_____

CHAPTER 2 EXAM

> The following questions were designed to test your knowledge on this chapter's topic. Read each question carefully, and choose the option that most accurately answers the question. Once you have completed the exam, compare your answers with the solution and read through the justification provided. Note the topics where you have the most difficulty, and make sure that you dedicate enough study time to them.

1. Which of the following does NOT distinguish a project from an operation?
   A. It produces a unique product or service.
   B. It has a specific beginning and end.
   C. It should be planned and controlled.
   D. It's progressively elaborated.

2. The quality department is performing regular inspections on an engine assembly line. The quality department is involved in:
   A. A project
   B. An operation
   C. A program
   D. A subproject

3. You are managing a critical project for your organization with a brand-new technology. The customer has given you a brief scope of work, and management is requiring a project schedule. What should you do NEXT?
   A. Ask for a better scope definition.
   B. Delay planning until more information is available.
   C. Provide a basic project schedule, with considerable schedule flexibility, and detail future work when more and better information becomes available.
   D. Refuse to do the project until the level of risk is controlled.

4. Which of the following statements regarding progressive elaboration is NOT TRUE?
   A. Project deliverables are often progressively elaborated.
   B. Progressive elaboration is closely related to project uncertainty.
   C. Progressive elaboration should be avoided once baselines have been approved.
   D. Rolling wave planning is a progressive elaboration technique.

5. The project manager is responsible for:
   A. Delivering above expectations
   B. Determining the project business need
   C. Adapting the project management approach to project needs
   D. Prioritizing projects

6. The project manager should recommend corrective action when detecting a project variance. What should be the project manager's priority when correcting project variances?
   A. Scope, schedule, quality, costs
   B. Schedule, scope, costs, quality
   C. Scope, schedule, costs, quality, risk
   D. Constraints are equally important unless priorities were previously defined.

7. A software company is developing a new application dedicated to the media industry. Before finishing the application development project, the sales team managed to make the first sale. The application development team agreed to incorporate some of the requirements of the first customer into the scope of the development project. Meanwhile, the sales team is being trained to increase their ability to sell the application. What BEST describes the work the company is doing?
    A. Project
    B. Operation
    C. Program
    D. Portfolio

8. Portfolio management aims to:
    A. Manage ongoing work
    B. Coordinate benefits of related projects and programs
    C. Improve program management focus
    D. Select projects and programs that are aligned with the organization's strategic objectives

9. The _____ is the complete history of a product, extending through its idea, definition, development, operation, and disposal phases.
    A. Project life cycle
    B. Product life cycle
    C. Business plan
    D. Life cycle costing

10. All of the following are advantages of adopting a project life cycle EXCEPT:
    A. To adopt a progressive elaboration approach
    B. To promote confidence regarding project success
    C. To detect project variances sooner
    D. To approve major deliverables

11. All of the following are examples of projects interacting with the product life cycle EXCEPT:
    A. Initiating a project to launch a new IT system
    B. Closing a factory site
    C. Upgrading an assembly line
    D. Adding a new work shift to increase production throughput

12. A product development project is facing resource allocation problems. Team members often abandon their project activities to respond to their operational work priorities. Other times, late management decisions stall the team's progress. The project has been constantly delayed, but the project manager argues that he does not have enough authority to act and all he can do is adjust the schedule. What is the MOST likely cause of such delays?
    A. Poor human resource management planning
    B. Poor communications management planning
    C. The project being managed in a functional organization
    D. The project manager not implementing a change control system

13. Senior management held a meeting to discuss the project scope validation approach and then directed the project manager to implement it. The project manager must be working _____.
    A. With the steering committee
    B. In a strong matrix organization
    C. With the project management office
    D. As a project expediter

14. Why is ambiguous authority more common in a matrix organization than in a functional organization?
    A. A functional organization provides more coercive authority to project managers.
    B. Matrix organizations' projects are usually more complex.
    C. In a matrix organization the project's responsibilities are defined ambiguously.
    D. In a matrix organization team members have two bosses.

15. Who is responsible for the recognition and rewards system in a weak matrix organization?
    A. Sponsor
    B. Project manager
    C. Human resources department
    D. Functional manager

16. Which of the following statements regarding the difference between a weak and a strong matrix organization is NOT TRUE?
    A. In a strong matrix, the project manager negotiates resources with the functional managers.
    B. In a strong matrix, team members do not report to functional managers.
    C. In a strong matrix, the project manager has more authority to manage the schedule and the budget.
    D. Project management offices are more common in strong matrix organizations.

17. In which type of organization would a critical project best fit where the project manager would need to exercise maximum control over resources?
    A. Strong matrix
    B. Projectized
    C. Weak matrix
    D. Project management office

18. All of the following can be performed by the project management office EXCEPT:
    A. Assigning a project manager to a critical project
    B. Defining project management methodologies
    C. Defining the business need
    D. Helping prioritize projects according to company strategy

19. Which of the following BEST describes a stakeholder in a highway construction project?
    A. Project team member and project manager
    B. Team member, project manager, and customer
    C. Environmental organization
    D. All of the above

20. The project manager does not have sufficient authority to manage the project. Who is responsible for managing the situation?
    A. Project manager
    B. Sponsor
    C. Functional manager
    D. Team

21. In a matrix organization, the project manager should address resource requirements with the:
    A. Functional manager
    B. Sponsor
    C. HR department
    D. Customer

22. A team member has just detected an inconsistency in the change management plan. What is the BEST thing for her to do?
    A. Correct the change management plan.
    B. Do nothing. The project manager is responsible for the change management plan.
    C. Recommend corrective action.
    D. Inform the project manager immediately.

23. A project manager has moved from a functional to a matrix organization. The project manager is now responsible for:
    A. Negotiating contracts
    B. Selecting the change requests that should be implemented
    C. Negotiating resources
    D. Approving the project management plan

ANSWERS

Review Exercise

1. Improve planning by facilitating the adoption of a rolling wave approach.
2. Detect potential variances earlier, in time for correction.
3. Reduce project risk by performing intermediate validations.
4. Promote confidence by achieving intermediate closures.
5. Create control points at the end of each phase.

Memorization Exercise

1. Project team
2. Application area
3. Project life cycle
4. Portfolio
5. Functional manager or line manager
6. Sponsor
7. Balanced matrix organization
8. Project management team
9. Matrix organization
10. Projectized organization
11. Functional organization, hierarchical or vertical

12. Project management office
13. Customer
14. Stakeholder
15. Progressive elaboration
16. Program
17. Project
18. Triple constraint
19. Product life cycle
20. Operation

Chapter 2 Exam

1. **C** Projects, just as many operations, require planning and controlling. Unlike operations, projects are temporary, unique, and progressively elaborated.

2. **B** Regular inspections on an engine assembly line have a repetitive nature and are relatively certain. Thus the quality department is performing an operation. There is no information to suggest that the quality department is involved in a project, a program, or a subproject.

3. **C** The question may suggest that something is wrong with this particular project because the customer has provided a brief scope of work. However, the very definition of *project* indicates that projects are uncertain, particularly during their early stages. How should you approach this uncertainty? Answers A, B, and D may be tempting, but they are not realistic. Your approach to uncertainty cannot be to require information that does not exist (A), plan the project later (B), or refuse to do the project (D). With a brief scope of work, you only can provide a high-level project schedule, with considerable flexibility to account for existing uncertainty. The scope and the schedule can be progressively elaborated when more information becomes available.

4. **C** Progressive elaboration may occur throughout the project and does not necessarily lead to a change to project baselines. All the other statements are correct.

5. **C** Adapting the project management approach is part of planning and should therefore be part of the project manager's responsibility. Answer A is not correct because project management is about translating expectations into requirements and then meeting those requirements (not exceeding them). Answers B and D are not correct because management is responsible for determining the project business need and prioritizing projects.

6. **D** There is no preestablished structure of priorities common to every project. In some projects, scope is the most important constraint because it was agreed upon within a contract. Other projects may have a rigid schedule or be subject to contractual penalties for late delivery. Others have costs or even quality as their key constraint. When the project manager needs to recommend a corrective action, he does not have the authority to choose among different priorities. Instead, he should follow the priorities previously defined by the sponsor for that specific project. When those priorities haven't been defined, all the constraints are equally important and the project manager should request guidance from the sponsor.

7. **C** The company is dealing with projectized work (application development) and operational work (sales team work). The company is managing a program because projects and operations are being managed in a coordinated way to meet a common business objective. Answers A and B would not fully describe the organization's work.

8. **D** A portfolio is a group of projects, programs, or operations that may be managed in a coordinated way to implement the business strategy. Projects, programs, and operations within the portfolio may not be directly related.

9. **B** The product life cycle is the complete history of a product, extending through its idea, definition, development, operation, and disposal phases.

10. **D** Approving major deliverables is not a consequence of adopting a project life cycle. Major deliverables may be approved even when the project is not structured into phases. All other options describe advantages of adopting a project life cycle.

11. **D** Increasing or decreasing the operational throughput does not typically require a project. All other options represent projects interacting with the product life cycle, by developing, closing, or enhancing products.

12. **C** If the project manager does not have any control over resources, all the authority is at the functional managers' level. This type of organization is known as a functional organization. The lack of project manager's authority in a functional organization cannot be solved with human resource management planning, communications planning, or a change control system.

13. **D** The project expediter has an extremely low level of authority. The project expediter does not make decisions but acts as an assistant to management, helping transmit information and directions to the team. The steering committee (answer A) and the project management office (answer C) are not responsible for defining the project scope validation approach. A project expediter is a type of project management role within a functional or weak matrix organization (answer B).

14. **D** In every matrix organization, including the strong matrix, the authority over projects and resources is shared between the project manager and the functional manager. The difference between a weak, a balanced, and a strong matrix lies on how the authority is distributed between them. Answers A, B, and C are incorrect statements.

15. **D** In a week matrix organization, most of the project's authority belongs to the functional manager.

16. **B** In every matrix organization, including the strong, the authority over the project is shared between the project manager and the functional manager. All other statements are true.

17. **B** In a projectized organization, resources report exclusively to a project manager, who has full authority over the project.

18. **C** Management should be responsible for establishing the business need. All other options may be performed by the project management office.

19. **D** Stakeholders are individuals or groups who can be positively or negatively impacted by the project. Thus D is the best option.

20. **B** The sponsor is responsible for formally delegating authority to the project manager.

21. **A** The functional manager provides human resources to the project. The project manager should negotiate the assigned resources with the functional manager.

22. **C** Team members should be involved in project management activities. Although they are not accountable for project management activities, they should support them with their experience and knowledge. Recommending corrective action is about more than just informing the project manager of the error (answer D). Doing nothing (answer B) or correcting the plan without the project manager's validation (answer A) would not be appropriate actions.

23. **C** Negotiating resources with the functional manager is part of the project manager's responsibility within a matrix organization. Answer A is not correct because the project manager is not usually responsible for negotiating contracts. Answers B and D are not correct because the project manager does not have the authority to select the change requests or to approve the project management plan.

Process Groups

Learning Topics	
	▸ Process
	▸ Input
	▸ Tool and technique
	▸ Output
	▸ Initiating
	▸ Planning
	▸ Executing
	▸ Monitoring and controlling
	▸ Closing

Process

A **process** is a set of related activities that generates a desired output by using specific inputs, techniques, and tools. Need an example? The **define scope** process delivers a scope statement as an output, using the project charter as an input and expert judgment as a technique.

Projects are performed through product-oriented and project-management-oriented processes. Product-oriented processes are specific to each application area and are not covered in the *PMBOK Guide*. Regarding project management, there are 47 processes. Every process has specific inputs, tools, techniques, and outputs. Each process also belongs to one, and only one, of the five process groups and one, and only one, of the 10 knowledge areas.

Project management processes are usually performed in sequence, so the outputs from one process can act as inputs to another. Processes may also have inputs that were not generated in the project (e.g., organizational procedures and historical information).

> For the exam, you should be able to identify a process based on the description of one or more of its activities. For example, if the project manager is estimating the schedule reserve, he is in the **estimate activity durations** process. To learn how to identify the processes, read each process description and complete the process exercises found at the end of each chapter.

You should also be able to identify the logical sequence of the processes. For example, if the project manager is determining the budget, the **estimate costs** process was already initiated. To learn how to identify the process's logical sequence, read the process description and complete the Process Exercise 2 at the end of the next chapters.

Input

An input is an item required by the process to produce its output. An input may be external to the project (e.g., a business case) or be the output of another project management process (e.g., a project schedule).

Tool

A tool is a tangible item used in a process to develop an expected output. For example, the develop schedule process uses scheduling software as a tool.

Technique

A technique is a group of systematic steps required to obtain a specific outcome, using specific tools. For example, the develop schedule process uses the critical path method as a technique.

Output

An output is an item developed by a project management process. This item may be a tangible deliverable, such as a project schedule, or may be an intangible result, such as a procurement closure.

Initiating

The initiating process group includes all the processes required to authorize the start of a project or phase, as well as to establish a common vision. Let's look at some of the key initiating activities:

- Selecting the project manager
- Delegating to the project manager the authority to use organizational resources on the project
- Identifying stakeholders and understanding their influence over the project
- Determining the project business need
- Analyzing the project feasibility and comparing it with existing alternatives
- Translating stakeholders' expectations and needs into high-level requirements
- Providing a high-level project description
- Identifying high-level risks
- Defining acceptance criteria
- Defining initial high-level plans such as a schedule, a budget, and an organization chart
- Formally authorizing the start of the project or phase

Projects should be initiated. Still, many organizations incorrectly skip initiation and jump straight into planning. Some of the symptoms of lack of project initiation are unrealistic constraints, lack of stakeholders' involvement, and constant project changes.

Planning

The planning process group includes all the processes required to define, refine, and formalize objectives, as well as to determine the necessary actions to attain them. Planning activities cross all project management knowledge areas and may include:

- Defining the rules on how the project will be managed, which processes will be used, and how they will be implemented
- Identifying constraints and assumptions
- Collecting product requirements

- Defining the project scope, identifying and describing the project deliverables
- Decomposing the work into smaller elements (work breakdown structure [WBS]) and describing the work elements for future reference (WBS dictionary)
- Identifying and sequencing activities
- Estimating resource requirements
- Estimating durations
- Developing the schedule
- Estimating costs and determining budget
- Determining quality standards and metrics, and establishing quality management processes
- Defining how resources will be acquired, controlled, and released
- Planning roles and responsibilities, establishing hierarchical relationships and recognition and rewards criteria
- Defining communication requirements and determining who can provide such information
- Defining what, when, and how to procure
- Preparing procurement documents
- Determining how stakeholders will be managed
- Identifying, analyzing, and responding to risks
- Performing the necessary iterations to develop a coherent and integrated plan
- Managing conflicts with existing constraints, initial objectives, and expectations
- Obtaining a project management plan formal acceptance and establishing project baselines
- Holding a project kickoff meeting

Planning starts with the development of a project management plan, which establishes the rules on how to manage the project. Once these rules are established, all knowledge areas can be planned, according to their natural dependencies. For example, scope should be addressed immediately after the rules are established, because establishing the scope statement and WBS is required to plan other knowledge areas. As another example, risks should only be identified, analyzed, and responded to once all other knowledge areas are planned.

> Project risks should not be identified until all knowledge areas are planned.

Uncertainty, lack of information, existing constraints, and dynamic environments push the project management team to complete planning iterations. Within each iteration, different plans may be updated to respond to project requirements. Iterations will be performed during these early planning stages to find a balance among plans and existing constraints. Planning iteration can also occur throughout project execution as more and better information becomes available.

Under pressure to establish definitive scope, schedule, and costs objectives, the initial planning effort cannot occur indefinitely. The project management team will have to commit to specific objectives by determining project baselines. The moment when those baselines are defined will depend on the application area and on the existing project management culture. Once the baselines have been established, the project management plan should be approved and communicated to stakeholders through a project kickoff meeting.

> Involving stakeholders in the planning process tends to increase satisfaction, decrease the volume of future change requests, and facilitate acceptance.

REVIEW EXERCISE 1

> **Number the following planning activities to show the most natural order:**

1. Decompose the work into smaller components (WBS) _____
2. Define the rules on how the project will be managed _____
3. Define how resources will be acquired, controlled, and released _____
4. Define the project scope _____
5. Develop the schedule _____
6. Estimate durations _____
7. Estimate resource requirements _____
8. Identify and sequence activities _____
9. Identify, analyze, and respond to risks _____
10. Obtain a project management plan formal acceptance _____
11. Perform a project kickoff meeting _____
12. Perform the necessary iterations to develop a coherent and integrated plan _____

Executing

The executing process group includes all the processes required to execute the plan, complete the project deliverables, and coordinate the resources required to carry out the plan. Examples of executing activities include:

- Completing the project deliverables
- Providing work performance data
- Requesting changes
- Issuing corrective and preventive actions
- Documenting lessons learned
- Performing quality audits
- Analyzing processes to identify improvement opportunities
- Acquiring human resources
- Obtaining the team necessary training
- Assessing the team's performance
- Performing team-building activities
- Solving problems and disputes
- Distributing information according to the communications management plan
- Managing the involvement and commitment of project stakeholders
- Reviewing suppliers' proposals and negotiating contracts

> Most of the project resources are spent on the executing process group.

Monitoring and Controlling

The monitoring and controlling process group includes all the processes required to compare the actual performance with the plan, identify potential variances, issue corrective or preventive actions, and manage changes. Examples of monitoring and controlling activities include:

- Assessing project performance
- Comparing actual performance with planned performance to identify variances
- Recommending corrective or preventive actions
- Managing project changes
- Managing product configuration
- Controlling the project scope to prevent the team from completing unplanned work
- Validating project deliverables
- Analyzing schedule and cost variances
- Determining the project actual costs
- Determining the schedule and costs forecasts
- Performing quality inspections
- Recommending and validating defect repairs
- Responding to changes on communication requirements
- Monitoring and reassessing risks
- Identifying risks throughout the project
- Assessing the effectiveness of risk responses
- Monitoring the supplier's performance

Closing

The closing process group includes all the processes required to bring a formal and controlled end to the phase, project, or contract. Among all closing activities, it is particularly important to formally accept the project or phase. While closing, the project management team may:

- Verify if the product was delivered as required
- Verify if the phase or project acceptance criteria were met
- Decide on whether to advance to the next project phase
- Obtain the formal acceptance to close the project or phase
- Transfer the product to stakeholders
- Manage the project termination before completion
- Issue final payments
- Close contracts
- Collect final lessons learned
- Update organizational process assets with the acquired lessons learned
- Produce a final project performance report
- Archive project documentation
- Release resources

REVIEW EXERCISE 2

> There may be some overlapping within closing activities, but they are usually completed in a logical sequence. Use numbers from 1 to 5 to order the following activities.

Activity	Sequence
1. Archive project documentation	_____
2. Collect final lessons learned	_____
3. Release resources	_____
4. Obtain the formal acceptance to close the project or phase	_____
5. Verify if the product was delivered as required	_____

PROCESS EXERCISE

> Assign each activity to a process group and a knowledge area.

Activity	Area	Process Group
1. Acquire human resources	_____	_____
2. Analyze processes to identify improvement opportunities	_____	_____
3. Analyze schedule variances	_____	_____
4. Archive project documentation	_____	_____
5. Assess the team's performance	_____	_____
6. Close contracts	_____	_____
7. Collect final lessons learned	_____	_____
8. Collect product requirements	_____	_____
9. Complete the project deliverables	_____	_____
10. Decide on whether to advance to the next project phase	_____	_____
11. Decompose the work into smaller elements (WBS)	_____	_____
12. Define the project scope, identifying and describing the project deliverables	_____	_____
13. Define the rules on how the project will be managed	_____	_____
14. Describe what, when, and how to procure	_____	_____
15. Determine communication requirements	_____	_____
16. Determine how stakeholders will be managed	_____	_____

Activity	Area	Process Group
17. Determine quality standards	_____	_____
18. Determine the project actual costs	_____	_____
19. Determine the project business need	_____	_____
20. Develop a high-level schedule and budget	_____	_____
21. Develop the schedule	_____	_____
22. Distribute information according to the communications management plan	_____	_____
23. Estimate activity durations	_____	_____
24. Estimate costs and determine budget	_____	_____
25. Establish project baselines	_____	_____
26. Estimate resource requirements	_____	_____
27. Identify, analyze, and respond to risks	_____	_____
28. Identify and sequence activities	_____	_____
29. Identify stakeholders and understand their influence over the project	_____	_____
30. Manage scope changes	_____	_____
31. Manage the involvement and commitment of project stakeholders	_____	_____
32. Manage the project termination before completion	_____	_____
33. Monitor and reassess risks	_____	_____
34. Monitor the suppliers' performance	_____	_____
35. Obtain the formal acceptance of the project or phase	_____	_____
36. Perform quality audits	_____	_____
37. Perform quality inspections	_____	_____
38. Plan roles and responsibilities	_____	_____
39. Prevent the team from completing unplanned work	_____	_____
40. Produce a final project performance report	_____	_____
41. Respond to changes on communication requirements	_____	_____
42. Review proposals	_____	_____
43. Select the project manager	_____	_____
44. Update organizational process assets with the acquired lessons learned	_____	_____
45. Validate project deliverables	_____	_____

CHAPTER 3 EXAM

The following questions were designed to test your knowledge on this chapter's topic. Read each question carefully, and choose the option that most accurately answers the question. Once you have completed the exam, compare your answers with the solution and read through the justification provided. Note the topics where you have the most difficulty, and make sure that you dedicate to them enough study time.

1. Which of the following is NOT part of project initiation?
   A. Providing formal authority to the project manager
   B. Identifying stakeholders
   C. Establishing expectations
   D. Establishing project baselines

2. A project manager is working with senior management identifying stakeholders' influence. In which project management process group is the project manager working in?
   A. Initiating
   B. Planning
   C. Executing
   D. Stakeholder management

3. The project manager has just completed a high-level risk identification. What should be done NEXT?
   A. Perform a qualitative risk analysis.
   B. Plan risk responses.
   C. Identify detailed risks.
   D. Develop the project management plan.

4. A project manager is meeting with functional managers to define when and how team members will be acquired. In what project management process group is the project manager working in?
   A. Initiating
   B. Planning
   C. Executing
   D. Stakeholder management

5. The project manager and the team have just developed a preliminary project schedule. Which of the following should be completed NEXT?
   A. Begin iterations.
   B. Establish project baselines.
   C. Develop the project management plan.
   D. Develop the quality management plan.

6. The project team has just completed a detailed risk identification, analysis, and response. What should be done NEXT?
   A. Begin planning iterations.
   B. Establish project baselines.
   C. Plan communications management.
   D. Plan procurement management.

7. Which of the following would be the MOST appropriate definition of planning?
   A. Starts the project and authorizes the project manager to use organizational resources in project activities
   B. Defines and formalizes objectives and plans the actions required to attain them
   C. Compares the actual performance against the plan, identifies potential variances, and issues corrective actions
   D. Defines the work required to complete the deliverables

8. Planning iterations result in updates to the:
   A. Project charter
   B. Project management plan
   C. Change request log
   D. Performance reports

9. Which process group spends most of the project's funds?
   A. Integration
   B. Planning
   C. Executing
   D. Closing

10. A project manager is working with her team to determine corrective actions to an identified cost variance. Which project management process group is the project manager in?
    A. Corrective action
    B. Planning
    C. Executing
    D. Monitoring and controlling

11. The monitoring and controlling process group includes which of the following processes' sets?
    A. Control communications and validate scope.
    B. Develop project team and identify stakeholders.
    C. Manage communications and control procurements.
    D. Manage stakeholder engagement and manage project team.

12. All of the following are part of monitoring and controlling EXCEPT:
    A. Measure progress.
    B. Manage change.
    C. Manage stakeholder engagement.
    D. Identify corrective action.

13. The project has successfully completed all technical deliverables according to the project management plan and is now entering closing. The last activity performed during closing should be:
    A. The customer formally accepting the project's product
    B. Documenting lessons learned
    C. Archiving project documentation
    D. Releasing resources

14. All of a project's technical deliverables have been completed and validated. What is the NEXT step?
    A. The customer formally accepting the project's product
    B. Gathering final lessons learned
    C. Archiving project documentation
    D. Releasing resources

15. As a policy, your company checks if the project matches the phase exit criteria before issuing a formal acceptance. Your company policy is performing a _____ activity.
    A. Closing
    B. Product management
    C. Monitoring and controlling
    D. Planning

16. Which of the following is NOT performed during closing?
    A. Archive project records.
    B. Obtain sign-off.
    C. Hand over the product.
    D. Approve the project management plan.

ANSWERS

Review Exercise 1

1. 3
2. 1
3. 8
4. 2
5. 7
6. 6
7. 5
8. 4
9. 9
10. 11
11. 12
12. 10

Review Exercise 2

1. 4
2. 3
3. 5
4. 2
5. 1

Process Exercise

1.	Human resources	Executing
2.	Quality	Executing
3.	Time	Controlling
4.	Integration	Closing
5.	Human resources	Executing
6.	Procurement	Closing
7.	Integration	Closing
8.	Scope	Planning
9.	Integration	Executing
10.	Integration	Closing
11.	Scope	Planning
12.	Scope	Planning
13.	Integration	Planning
14.	Procurement	Planning
15.	Communication	Planning
16.	Stakeholders	Planning
17.	Quality	Planning
18.	Cost	Controlling
19.	Integration	Initiating
20.	Integration	Initiating
21.	Time	Planning
22.	Communication	Executing
23.	Time	Planning
24.	Cost	Planning
25.	Integration	Planning
26.	Time	Planning
27.	Risk	Planning
28.	Time	Planning
29.	Stakeholders	Initiating
30.	Scope	Controlling
31.	Stakeholders	Executing
32.	Integration	Closing
33.	Risk	Controlling
34.	Procurement	Controlling
35.	Integration	Closing
36.	Quality	Executing
37.	Quality	Controlling
38.	Human resources	Planning
39.	Scope	Controlling
40.	Integration	Closing
41.	Communication	Controlling
42.	Procurement	Executing
43.	Integration	Initiating
44.	Integration	Closing
45.	Scope	Controlling

Chapter 3 Exam

1. **D** Establishing project baselines is part of planning. All other options are part of initiating.
2. **A** Identifying stakeholders' influence is part of the initiating process group.
3. **D** A high-level risk identification is performed during initiation. Because all available options are performed during planning, select the option that is performed first. The first activity performed in planning is developing the project management plan.
4. **B** Meeting with functional managers to define when and how team members will be acquired is part of planning human resource management. Thus answers A and C are not correct. Answer D is not correct, because stakeholder management is not a process group.
5. **D** The project management plan should already have been initiated before developing the schedule (answer C). Beginning iterations (answer A) and establishing baselines (answer B) will always be performed after developing the quality management plan. Thus developing the quality management plan is the best option.
6. **A** Iterations should only be performed after risk identification, analysis, and response. Project baselines should only be established after completing planning iterations (answer B). Risk identification analysis and response should only be performed once all other knowledge areas have been planned (answers C and D). Thus beginning iterations is the best option.
7. **B** Planning includes all the processes required to define and formalize objectives, as well as determine the actions required to attain them.
8. **B** Planning iterations frequently results in project management plan updates.
9. **C** Most project resources are spent during the executing process group.
10. **D** Corrective actions are part of the monitoring and controlling process group.
11. **A** Developing project team, managing communications, managing stakeholder engagement, and managing project team are all part of the executing process group. Identifying stakeholders is part of the initiating process group.
12. **C** Managing stakeholder engagement is part of the executing process group.
13. **D** Resources are required to perform the closing activities. Therefore, releasing resources is the best option.
14. **A** Gather final lessons learned (answer B) should occur after formal acceptance. Archiving documentation (answer C) and releasing resources (answer D) should occur after gathering final lessons learned.
15. **A** The closing process group verifies if the project or phase acceptance criteria are met before issuing a formal acceptance.
16. **D** Approving the project management is part of planning. All other options are performed during closing.

Integration Management

While the need to manage scope, schedule, and costs is self-explanatory, the need to manage integration may not be obvious. **Integration management** includes all the processes required to ensure the coordination of the different project management knowledge areas, protecting their consistency and alignment with project constraints and stakeholders' expectations.

This definition is still too theoretical. What exactly needs to be integrated? Let's look at some practical examples of integration:

- Integrate the project with the business need.
- Integrate the product scope with the stakeholders' expectations.
- Integrate the project work with the product specifications.
- Integrate the scope with the schedule.
- Integrate the schedule with the resources available.

- Integrate the budget with the schedule and with the available funds.
- Integrate the quality metrics with the scope.
- Integrate the project resource requirements with the existing resource skills.
- Integrate the suppliers' schedules with the project master schedule.
- Integrate the risks with the scope definition.
- Integrate accumulated lessons learned in the organization knowledge base.
- Integrate the developed product with the organization operations.

Integration management should be performed continuously throughout the project. The following table provides specific examples of this continuous effort of integration management:

Examples of Integration Throughout the Project

Initiating	Approve a project charter that aligns the project with the business need
Planning	Define integrated, coherent, and realistic baselines
Executing	Provide performance data regarding different project dimensions
Monitoring and controlling	Analyze the impact of a project change on baselines
Closing	Verify if the project's or phase's acceptance criteria were met

> The most important role of the project manager is managing integration. Managing integration is done through communication.

Project communication may be written or oral, formal or informal. In the integration management area, communication tends to be formal and written. For example, documents such as the project charter or a change request are usually formal and written.

The following table shows the integration management processes with their specific process group:

Integration Management Processes

Process	*Process Group*
Develop project charter	Initiating
Develop project management plan	Planning
Direct and manage project work	Executing
Monitor and control project work	Monitoring and controlling
Perform integrated change control	Monitoring and controlling
Close project or phase	Closing

Develop the Project Charter

Develop the project charter is the first process performed in the project. A project charter is a formal document that:

- **Formally initiates the project**   Have you ever worked on projects unknown to the rest of the organization? The project charter is the document in which management should formally launch the project, announcing its objectives, providing support, and clarifying the expected resource allocations for the project.
- **Provides formal authority to the project manager**   Authority is necessary to correctly perform project management work—authority to acquire, manage, and release team members; to implement new approaches; and to manage stakeholders' engagement and expectations. Management should use the project charter to formally delegate authority to the project manager during the project life cycle.
- **Provides resources**   Have you ever felt that team members did not have enough time to dedicate to your project? Did your projects get delayed due to lack of resource availability? The project charter helps reduce resource utilization conflicts between the project manager and functional managers, assigning the project manager the authority to use organizational resources.
- **Establishes expectations**   The project charter creates a common vision on the project that will guide the planning effort, avoiding entropy and erratic decisions. Expectations are established through high-level objectives, priorities, assumptions, and constraints.
- **Makes decisions to reduce risk**   Although a significant part of the risk management effort is performed during planning, it is possible to proactively respond to risks during initiation. For example, if previous projects failed due to lack of engagement by some of the organization's functions, the sponsor may use the project charter to specify the level of dedication expected of each organizational unit.

A typical project charter may specify:

- Business need at the root of the project
- Project objectives and acceptance criteria
- High-level requirements
- High-level project description
- High-level schedule and budget
- High-level risks
- Acceptance criteria
- Project manager and his or her level of authority

The project manager can, whenever possible, participate in the project charter development. Nevertheless, the responsibility for approving the project charter belongs to the sponsor, senior management, program manager, portfolio manager, or project management office (PMO). Whoever approves the project charter should have the ability to finance the project and have enough authority for key decision making.

> If there is no approved project charter, the project manager should insist on its development, demonstrating the advantages of a project charter.

Direct the work
Procedures
Templates
Processes
Policies

Reuse knowledge
Historical information
Lessons learned
Databases

Figure 4.1 Organizational process assets

The project charter may have as inputs the organizational process assets, the enterprise environmental factors, a project statement of work, a business case, and existing contracts.

> On projects where there is more than one organization involved, each organization should have its own project charter, according to its needs, scope, and interests.

Organizational Process Assets

Organizational process assets are assets accumulated in the organization, which can be used to guide and improve the project management effort. These assets may include procedures, templates, processes, and policies that establish a formal guidance. (See Figure 4.1.) They can also include accumulated knowledge, such as historical information, lessons learned, and databases. Typical examples of **historical information** or **historical data** are:

- Scope planning documents from previous projects, such as a scope statement, a work breakdown structure (WBS), and a WBS dictionary
- Records of durations, actual costs, and resource utilization
- Description of the risks and the effectiveness of the adopted risks responses
- Problems and their resolutions
- Change requests

> It is usually preferable to base project decisions on objective data, available through historical information, than to base them on the subjectivity of experts' opinions.

Enterprise Environmental Factors

Enterprise environmental factors are elements that exist around the project and may influence its performance. These factors include organizational elements such as infrastructure, organizational structure and culture, risk tolerance, human resources skills, and project management information system. Environmental factors may also be external to the organization, such as market competitiveness, economic environment, and political stability. (See Figure 4.2.)

> Organizational process assets and enterprise environmental factors are inputs for project management processes within all process groups, but are particularly relevant during the initiating and planning process groups.

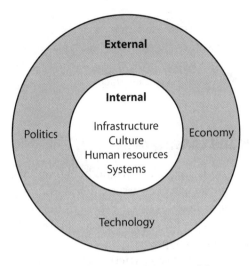

Figure 4.2 Enterprise environmental factors

Project Statement of Work (SOW)

A project statement of work (SOW) is a formal document that describes the products and services that should be provided by the project. This narrative description of the work allows the performing organization to assess whether it has the capacity to perform the project. It also provides enough information to prepare a high-level estimate of the required work.

> When the project involves an external acquisition, the project SOW is prepared by the customer and sent to the supplier as part of the procurement documents.

At minimum, an SOW should include:

- The project purpose or business need
- A description of the product scope

Additionally, an SOW may include information regarding how the project fits the organizational strategy.

Business Case

The business case is the document used to analyze the project feasibility and justify its selection. A typical business case may include a description of the project business need and a cost-benefit analysis, as well as frame the project within the organization strategy.

The stimulus that may justify the project launch may have different natures, including:

- A customer need
- A corporate decision
- A legal requirement
- A market opportunity
- A process improvement opportunity
- A political decision

The business case is typically created before the start of the project and its development is not explicitly considered as a project management activity. However, in some organizations, project managers might be involved in the business case development to help build a bridge from the business to the project side.

Assumptions and Constraints

Assumptions are factors that, although uncertain, are considered as givens for planning purposes. An example of an assumption is assuming a future price for procured materials. Because assumptions hold a certain degree of uncertainty, they should be recorded within a project assumptions log for improved traceability. This log may be part of the scope statement or an independent assumptions log.

Constraints are restrictions to project management decisions that limit the available options. For example, the sponsor may establish that the project may use only internal resources while preparing a human resource management plan.

Project Selection Methods

Projects are initiated when someone with enough authority within the organization decides to mobilize resources for the project. To make such a decision, the organization must have concluded that the project is favorable and better than other available options. Sometimes this decision is based on an empirical analysis of the project. Other times, the organization adopts structured methods to identify, select, and prioritize projects.

There are several types of project selection methods. Each method has a different perspective on project feasibility. To prepare for the exam, you will analyze the most relevant financial and economic methods, including the net present value, the internal rate of return, the payback period, the benefit-cost ratio, and the opportunity cost.

The logic behind these methods is that the value of the project to the organization may be quantified financially. This financial evaluation allows the organization to make a structured decision regarding whether to accept or reject a potential project, or choose among alternative projects.

Net Present Value (NPV)

The net present value (NPV) is the present value of the project future cash flows. To better understand this concept, let's clarify the meaning of *present value* and *cash flows*. The concept of present value is based on the economic theory of the time value of money. This theory recognizes that if you deposit $1,000 in the bank today and hold the deposit for a year, you will receive a value greater than $1,000. Moreover, if a project has an expected return of $1,000 within one year, the present value of such return is less than $1,000.

Cash flows represent money flowing in and out of the project throughout time. For example, the cash flow of a project established to redesign the store's layout of a major retailer can be determined by the initial investment on equipment, by the expected increase on revenue, and by the expected change in shop maintenance costs.

The NPV is used to compare cash flows generated in different periods. Expected future cash flows are discounted to the present period, considering the cost of time. This cost of time is represented by a discount rate. The discount rate will vary from one organization to the other, depending on factors such as rate of return of previous projects and interest rate of bank loans.

Once calculated, the NPV supports a rapid interpretation of the project return. If the NPV is greater than zero, the project is favorable, adding value to the organization. If the NPV is less than zero, the project is unfavorable.

> Analyzing the project feasibility is not the same as analyzing the project performance. A project may have a negative NPV and be aligned with its baselines. A project may have a positive NPV and have a poor cost performance.

Let's say that projects A and B have the same investment and the same financial return. In project A, most of the return will happen in the first two years. In project B, most of the return will occur in the last two years. As a consequence, project A has a more favorable NPV.

Year	Cash Flow	Present Value (Discount Rate = 10%)
0	(36,000)	(36,000)
1	20,000	18,182
2	20,000	16,529
3	5,000	3,757
NPV		2,467

Project A adds value.

Year	Cash Flow	Present Value (Discount Rate = 10%)
0	(36,000)	(36,000)
1	5,000	4,545
2	10,000	8,264
3	30,000	22,539
NPV		(651)

Project B does not add value.

You do not need to know how to calculate the NPV. You just need to understand the concept. However, if you are curious about the subject, the NPV formula is shown in Figure 4.3, where r stands for *discount rate* and n for *number of years*.

Internal Rate of Return (IRR)

The internal rate of return (IRR) measures the project return on a percentage basis. (See Figure 4.4.) It is determined by calculating at which discount rate the NPV equals zero. If the IRR is greater than the discount rate, the initiative adds value. If project A has an IRR of 15 percent and a discount rate of 10 percent, it adds value to the organization.

$$\text{NPV} = \text{cash flow year 0} + \frac{\text{cash flow year 1}}{(1 + r)^1} + ... \frac{\text{cash flow year } n}{(1 + r)^n}$$

Figure 4.3 Net present value (NPV)

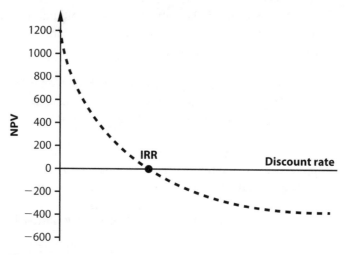

Figure 4.4 Internal rate of return (IRR)

You do not need to know how to calculate the IRR. You just need to understand the concept. However, if you are curious about the subject, the NPV formula is shown in Figure 4.5:

$$\mathbf{NPV = 0} = \text{cash flow year } 0 + \frac{\text{cash flow year 1}}{(1 + \text{IRR})^1} + \dots \frac{\text{cash flow year } n}{(1 + \text{IRR})^n}$$

Figure 4.5 IRR formula

Payback Period

The payback period is the period of time required for the project to repay the original investment. If the payback period is greater than a limit of time set by the organization, the project may not be accepted.

Year	Cash Flow	Present Value (Discount Rate = 10%)	Accumulated Present Value
0	(36,000)	(36,000)	(36,000)
1	20,000	18,182	(17,818)
2	20,000	16,529	(1,289)
3	5,000	3,757	2,467
NPV		2,467	
Project A repays itself during the third year.			

Benefit-Cost Ratio (BCR)

A benefit-cost ratio (BCR) is the ratio of the project benefits, relative to its costs. (See Figure 4.6.) Benefits and costs should be expressed in discounted present values. Once again, you do not need to know how to calculate the BCR. Still, the BCR formula is:

$$BCR = \frac{Benefits}{Costs}$$

Figure 4.6 Benefit-cost ratio (BCR)

Benefit-Cost Ratio Examples

Value	Meaning
2	Benefits are twice the costs.
1	Benefits equal the costs (project hit its breakeven).
0.5	Benefits represent 50 percent of the costs.

Opportunity Cost

The opportunity cost is the cost of losing the best available alternative to the project. The concept of opportunity cost assumes that choices are mutually exclusive. In the following example, the best available alternative to project 1 is project 3. Therefore, the opportunity cost of project 1 equals the NPV of project 3.

Project	NPV	Opportunity Cost
1	10,000	30,000
2	20,000	30,000
3	30,000	20,000

Develop the Project Management Plan

Are you familiar with the expression, "Do not use a cannon to kill a mosquito"? A project management plan sets the rules regarding how the project will be managed, including which processes will be used and how they will be implemented. This **tailoring** of rules adapts the project management processes to the project needs and environment.

Project management rules are documented in the project management plan through a set of subsidiary plans, such as a scope management plan or a schedule management plan. Rules are also set through integration plans, such as a change management plan or a configuration management plan.

Baselines are another critical element of the project management plan (see the section on baselines). A typical project management plan includes a scope, schedule, and cost baseline.

The project manager should adapt the project management processes to the project needs.

Developing the project management plan is naturally the first process performed during planning, to establish the rules that will be used to guide the project through planning, executing, monitoring and controlling, and closing. The project management plan, as any other plan, is developed iteratively, as other knowledge areas are planned. These iterations are a result of the uncertainty inherent to the projects and the need to balance concurrent constraints.

> A project management plan is not the same as a schedule.

The project management plan is a formal document that requires formal approval. Only when all knowledge areas have been planned, defining an integrated and coherent whole, should the plan be approved. The project management plan may be approved by the project key stakeholders, including the sponsor, other managers, the customer, suppliers, and team representatives. Once the baselines are established, the project management plan can only be changed through an approved change request.

The project management plan may be communicated through a **project kickoff meeting**, where the stakeholders have an opportunity to familiarize themselves with the project baselines, management approach, and team members. The kickoff meeting can also be used as an event where stakeholders publically demonstrate their commitment to the project management plan.

> If the project exists as part of a program, the project management plan should be aligned with the procedures adopted within the program.

Subsidiary Plans

Subsidiary plans are elements of the project management plan used to establish management rules for a specific area. Some examples of subsidiary plans are:

- Scope management plan
- Schedule management plan
- Cost management plan
- Human resource management plan
- Communications management plan
- Risk management plan
- Procurement management plan
- Process improvement plan
- Requirements management plan

REVIEW EXERCISE 1

Examples of project management plan elements that may be defined on subsidiary plans are:

1. _____

2. _____

3. _____

4. _____

5. _____

6. _____

7. _____

8. _____

9. _____

10. _____

11. _____

12. _____

13. _____

14. _____

15. _____

16. _____

Integration Plans

Integration plans are elements of the project management plan that establish product and project change management rules. Examples of integration plans are:

- **Change management plan**   Rules on how to manage project changes
- **Configuration management plan**   Rules on how to identify, document, and change the product of the project

Baseline and Performance Measurement Baseline

A baseline is a formally approved version of project objectives used to assess performance. By establishing a baseline, you create a reference for comparing actual performance. When a variance to the baseline is identified or forecasted, a corrective or preventive action should be issued. If these actions are not enough to correct the variance, the sponsor and the customer may choose to reassess the baselines. This process is known as **rebaselining**.

> A baseline may not be changed without a written and formally approved change request.

A baseline may be applied to:

- **Scope baseline**   Approved version of the scope statement, WBS, and WBS dictionary
- **Schedule baseline**   Approved version of the project schedule
- **Cost baseline**   Approved version of the authorized time-phased budget

Collectively the scope, schedule, and cost baseline are known as the **performance measurement baseline** by the earned value management technique (discussed in Chapter 7).

Direct and Manage Project Work

Direct and management project work is the execution process that prepares the project deliverables. It is also the process that spends most of the project resources. Another important role of directing and managing project work is the routine activity of feeding the control cycle with detailed work performance data.

> The project manager's main responsibility in this process is to coordinate resources.

Examples of activities performed by the **direct and manage project work** process include:

- Complete project deliverables.
- Use the project management information system to provide work performance data.
- Request changes to baselines, subsidiary plans, or formally controlled project documents.
- Implement change requests.
- Implement corrective and preventive actions.
- Use the work authorization system to authorize the team to start working on a work package.
- Update the project management plan.
- Update project documents that are not part of the project management plan.

Project Information

Have you thought about all the information required to monitor and control the project? Work performance information may include:

- **Work performance data**   Data that were not processed by the project management team, such as activity physical progress, actual dates, planned start and finish dates, technical performance assessments, resource utilization, and actual costs.
- **Work performance information**   Data that were processed by the project management team while performing the control activities, such as forecasts for completion, earned value metrics, and information regarding the deliverables status.
- **Work performance reports**   Documented project control information used to report performance to relevant stakeholders.

Project Management Information System (PMIS)

The project management information system (PMIS) includes the tools required to collect, record, process, and disseminate information across project stakeholders. This system is part of enterprise environmental factors and may include:

- Project management software
- Information repositories used to store information
- Collaboration tools use to facilitate communication
- Work authorization system
- Configuration management system
- E-mail system

Work Authorization System

A work authorization system authorizes, formally and in writing, the start of work packages or activities. You might not be familiar with a work authorization system because it is not used in every application area. Think of a work authorization system as traffic lights that ensure that work flows at the right time and at the right sequence. In large projects, a work authorization system can help to coordinate a large number of contractors. In some smaller projects, the bureaucracy introduced by the system can be compensated by the additional control over the complexity and dynamism of the work dependencies. A work authorization system can also help to exercise control over the budget, ensuring that expenses will only be charged to a work package once it has been properly funded and authorized, and limiting the amount of resources that can be expended.

A work authorization system is a subsystem of the project management information system.

Project Documents

Some documents are permanently updated as you plan, execute, and monitor the project. To prevent unnecessary change management effort, these dynamic documents should not be part of the project management plan. Examples of project documents are:

- Risk register
- Issue log
- Change log
- Stakeholder register
- Assumptions log
- Quality control measurements
- Requirements documentation
- Quality metrics
- Checklists
- Performance reports
- Suppliers' proposals

Lessons Learned

Stakeholders can generate lessons learned, capturing what went well and also what could have been done better. To improve future performance, these lessons should be shared within the organization so that everyone understands the root causes of prior successes and failures.

Indirectly, generating lessons learned can also foster a project team's development, by encouraging people to acknowledge what was positive and less positive in the past.

The main purpose of lessons learned is to improve future performance.

Ideally lessons learned should be generated throughout the project. As a minimum requirement, these lessons should be issued during project closing. There may also be postmortem lessons learned, issued after the project is finished.

Lessons learned are transferred to organizational process assets in the closing process group. But they are not merely a project output. As part of the organizational process assets, they are inputs to multiple project management processes, influencing decisions during the initiating, planning, executing, monitoring and controlling, and closing process group.

Initiating Lessons Learned

- **Input**   Accumulated lessons learned can influence project selection decisions and project charter development.

Planning Lessons Learned

- **Input**   Organizational process assets such as checklists, templates, record of activity lists, duration and cost estimates, quality metrics, communication problems, risks, and risk responses may influence planning decisions.

Executing Lessons Learned

- **Output**   Lessons learned are collected and documented as part of the direct and manage project work process. Lessons learned documents are distributed through the manage communications process.
- **Tools and techniques**   Meetings and expert judgment are used to generate lessons learned.

Monitoring and Controlling Lessons Learned

- **Output**   Updates to organizational process assets to record variances and their root causes, effectiveness of corrective and preventive actions, and history of project changes.
- **Tools and techniques**   Meetings and expert judgment are used to generate lessons learned.

Closing Lessons Learned

- **Output**   Updates to organizational process assets transfer lessons learned to the organizational historical information.
- **Tools and techniques**   Meetings and expert judgment are used to generate final lessons learned on the project and the procurement process.

Monitor and Control Project Work

The **monitor and control project work** process compares the actual performance with the planned performance, determining whether corrective or preventive actions are required. The following activities are part of this process:

- Analyze variances between actual and planned performance.
- Recommend corrective and preventive actions.
- Recommend repair for defects.
- Forecast future performance.
- Request changes to baseline, subsidiary plans, or documents that are formally controlled.
- Issue performance reports.
- Update the project management plan.
- Update project documents that are not part of the project management plan.

Corrective Actions

A corrective action is an action required to correct an existing variance to the project management plan. Before issuing the corrective action, the team should analyze the variance cause to determine the best solution. Examples of corrective actions are:

- Correct a deliverable that was not completed according to its requirements.
- Add new members to the team to recover from a schedule delay.
- Correct a product defect.
- Organize training for the team regarding a topic where existing knowledge is insufficient.
- Change a team member with a performance systematically below expectations.

Preventive Actions

A preventive action is an action required to avoid an anticipated variance to the project management plan. Examples of preventive actions are:

- Increase the involvement of a stakeholder in the project to prevent future scope changes.
- Augment the team to gain some slack against future complex and risky activities.
- Change a technical solution to prevent product defects.
- Review the recognition and rewards system to prevent performance issues due to low morale.

Perform Integrated Change Control

Changes happen in almost every project. Some changes will imply changes to scope, schedule, and cost baselines. Others will lead to changes in subsidiary plans. Finally, some changes result in modifications to documents that the project chose to control formally.

Some change requests are requested directly by the customer. Others are an indirect consequence of a corrective or preventive action. Others may result from changes in technology, market, economy, or political environment.

REVIEW EXERCISE 2

| What are the most likely causes of a project plagued with changes? |

1. _____

2. _____

3. _____

4. _____

5. _____

6. _____

7. _____

8. _____

Not surprisingly, lack of control over changes is one of the most common causes of project failure. How should you approach change? How can the project manager protect the coherence and integrity of the project?

Some project managers choose to accept changes without control, neglecting to formally validate their impacts. The result is a progressive accumulation of unfavorable variances. Changes should always go through a change control system, even when they don't apparently have an impact on the project baselines. A more comprehensive analysis may reveal an impact on baselines, subsidiary plans, risks, human resources, or other project constraints.

Other project managers choose to avoid changes to prevent entropy and an increase in work volume. This approach does not usually lead to good results. Often changes add value to the project and can even be critical to project feasibility. Changes should be managed, regardless of their timing or their virtues. If the potential change is not favorable to the project, its adversity should be reflected in the change impact analysis.

> Managing a change does not mean to accept or avoid the change. Managing a change means submitting it into an integrated change control system.

You have seen how project management is a combination of technique and art, promoting integrated and realistic objectives, while delivering value to stakeholders. Change management performs these two roles by:

- **Protecting the credibility of the project baselines** Without change management, it is not possible to understand all the implications of the adopted changes.
- **Managing stakeholders' expectations** Change management prevents future performance problems due to unmanaged expectations or obstacles.
- **Influencing the project** Encourages favorable changes and discourages unfavorable changes. This influence may be established by documenting the impacts of the change and managing the expectations of the stakeholders involved.

> The main advantage of adopting a **change management** process is the ability to influence project changes.

Examples of **change requests** include those issued by the:

- Project manager after identifying a variance to the baseline
- Team after identifying an inconsistency in the scope statement
- Sponsor to anticipate the schedule baseline in one week
- Customer to include a new functionality in the product scope
- Sponsor triggered by a change in legislation

REVIEW EXERCISE 3

Advantages of performing an integrated change management can be to:

1. _____

2. _____

3. _____

4. _____

5. _____

6. _____

7. _____

8. _____

9. _____

Change Management System

The rules used to manage changes are defined in the change management plan. This plan specifies what change control system should be adopted, including procedures, tools, and responsibilities. It also identifies what baselines, subsidiary plans, and project documents are subject to formal change control.

A **change request** is a formal written request that supports the change management process. To keep track of all change requests, the project should maintain an updated **change log**.

A change request may be analyzed in a **change control meeting**, reviewing its impact and making a decision on whether to move forward or not. The project may also include a **change control board (CCB)**, as a formal board established to review and validate changes requests.

The stakeholders accountable for approving the change requests are defined in a change management plan.

The project manager may have authority to approve changes when they do not impact project baselines. There can also be procedures that allow the project manager to implement urgent changes. This urgency procedure does not exempt a future change request.

> A change to the project charter should be approved by the sponsor.

The change management process may be simple or more complex, but it usually includes the following steps (see Figure 4.7):

- **Identify**   The need for change is identified by any of the stakeholders and a change request is created.
- **Assess**   The impact of the change is analyzed. The team also looks for alternative solutions that may minimize the impact of the change.
- **Complete**   A change request is documented, recording the impact information and the alternative available.

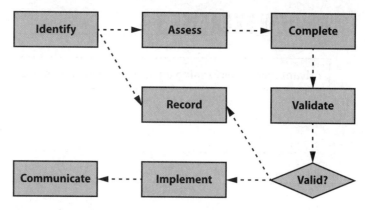

Figure 4.7 Example of change management flow

- **Validate**   A change request is submitted for approval and may be approved or rejected.
- **Record**   Throughout the whole process, the change request status should be documented in the change log for improved traceability.
- **Implement**   The baselines, subsidiary plans, or project documents are updated.
- **Communicate**   The change is communicated to the stakeholders to improve their project engagement and commitment.

Configuration Management System

Some projects require a special control over the development of their product components. For example, controlling the development of software functionalities, a weaponry system, or project documents may require significant control over the product details. The configuration management system defines formal and specific guidelines and tools to control the product, specifying how the project will:

- Identify and document the product characteristics
- Control the product development
- Record, control, and report changes to product elements
- Verify the conformance of product specific elements to its requirements

> The change management system is part of the configuration management system.

The configuration management system may also use the concept of a baseline. This type of baseline refers to the product version used as a logical basis for comparison. Changes to this baseline imply a formal change to the product. Examples of configuration management system baselines are:

- **Functional baseline**   Defined by the functional specifications
- **Development baseline**   Defined when the product development phase is completed
- **Product baseline**   Defined when the product is delivered to the customer

Close Project or Phase

Close project or phase is the closing process of the integration management knowledge area. It includes the activities required to close the project or phase in a controlled manner, avoiding situations where the projects remain open due to unmanaged issues.

Closing naturally implies verifying that the project and product meet their requirements and obtaining a formal acceptance. Another key element of closing is making sure that the organization and the customer capture the project benefits. Capturing benefits means ensuring a smooth product transition to the next project phase or to operations. Capturing benefits also means updating the organizational historical information with lessons learned, project documents, and other records.

> This process is one of the two processes of the closing process group (the other is close procurements, discussed in Chapter 12).

As you probably know from your own experience, closing a project or phase is challenging work. Close project or phase activities may include:

- Verifying if the project or phase acceptance criteria were met
- Closing outstanding issues
- Obtaining the formal acceptance to close the project or phase
- Deciding on whether to advance to the next project phase
- Transferring the product to the operations or the next project phase
- Performing administrative activities
- Managing the project termination before completion
- Collecting final lessons learned
- Updating organizational process assets with the acquired lessons learned
- Producing a final project performance report
- Archiving project documentation
- Releasing resources

> The project is not finished until all deliverables, including project management deliverables, are completed.

MEMORIZATION EXERCISE

> **The following exercise was designed to facilitate the memorization of the main concepts on this chapter. Assign the following definitions to an integration management concept.**

1. A formal written request for a change to a baseline, subsidiary plan, or formally controlled document

_____

2. Action required to avoid an anticipated variance to the project management plan

_____

3. Action required to correct an existing variance to the project management plan

_____

4. Assessment performed by stakeholders to capture what went well and what could have been done better, in order to improve future performance

_____

5. Assets accumulated in the organization that can be used to guide and improve the project management effort

     _____

6. Elements of the project management plan used to establish management rules for a specific area

     _____

7. Elements that exist around the project and may influence its performance, such as infrastructure, organizational structure and culture, human resources skills, and project management information system

     _____

8. Factors that, although uncertain, are considered as givens for planning purposes

     _____

9. Formal document that authorizes the beginning of the project and provides the project manager with the authority to apply resources to project activities

     _____

10. Formal document that describes the products and services that should be provided by the project

     _____

11. Formally approved version of project objectives used to assess performance

     _____

12. Includes all the processes required to ensure the coordination of the different project management knowledge areas, protecting their consistency and alignment to project constraints and stakeholders' expectations

     _____

13. Plan that sets the rules on how to manage project changes

     _____

14. Plan that sets the rules regarding how to identify, document, and change specific product components

     _____

15. Project documentation accumulated by the organization that can be used as planning inputs on future projects

     _____

16. Restrictions to project management decisions that limit the available options

     _____

17. Scope, schedule, and cost baseline for the earned value management technique

     _____

18. Sets the rules regarding how the project will be managed, including which processes will be used and how they will be implemented; also includes scope, schedule, and cost baseline

   _____

19. System that includes the tools required to collect record, process, and disseminate information across project stakeholders

   _____

20. System used to authorize, formally and in writing, the start of work packages or activities

   _____

Process Exercises

The following exercises were designed so you could learn how to recognize the processes and understand their logical sequence. Integration management processes are listed next, including their unique numbers in the *PMBOK Guide*:

- 4.1 Develop project charter
- 4.2 Develop project management plan
- 4.3 Direct and manage project work
- 4.4 Monitor and control project work
- 4.5 Perform integrated change control
- 4.6 Close project or phase

PROCESS EXERCISE 1

Assign processes to the following activities.

1. Analyze variances between actual and planned performance. _____
2. Archive project documentation. _____
3. Collect and document lessons learned. _____
4. Complete a change request. _____
5. Complete the project deliverables. _____
6. Create a change management system. _____
7. Decide whether to advance to the next project phase. _____
8. Establish project baselines. _____
9. Forecast schedule and costs performance. _____
10. Identify the project business or justification. _____
11. Manage the project termination before completion. _____
12. Meet with the change control board. _____
13. Obtain the formal acceptance to close the project or phase. _____

14. Prepare the subsidiary plans that establish the project procedures. _____

15. Present a high-level schedule and budget. _____

16. Provide work performance data. _____

17. Recommend corrective and preventive actions. _____

18. Recommend defect repairs. _____

19. Request changes to baselines, subsidiary plans, or documents formally controlled. _____

20. Select the project manager and specify his or her level of authority. _____

21. Update organizational process assets with the acquired lessons learned. _____

22. Update project documents that are not part of the project management plan. _____

23. Update the project management plan. _____

24. Use the project management information system to automate the collection, processing, and distribution of information. _____

25. Verify if the phase or project acceptance criteria were met. _____

PROCESS EXERCISE 2

> **Assign processes to the following inputs.**

Inputs   **Processes**

1. Business case   _____

2. Contract   _____

3. Project statement of work   _____

4. Accepted deliverables   _____

5. Project management plan   _____

6. Project charter   _____

CHAPTER 4 EXAM

> The following questions were designed to test your knowledge on this chapter's topic. Read each question carefully, and choose the option that most accurately answers the question. Once you have completed the exam, compare your answers with the solution and read through the justification provided. Note the topics where you have the most difficulty, and make sure that you dedicate enough study time to them.

1. Who is accountable for project integration management?
   A. Senior management
   B. Customer
   C. Project manager
   D. Change control board

2. Integration management is critical to project success. When should most of the integration management effort occur?
   A. During initiation, by approving a project charter that integrates the project with the organization's business need
   B. During planning, by defining integrated, coherent, and realist baselines
   C. During monitoring and controlling, by analyzing the impact of changes on project baselines
   D. Throughout the project

3. To manage project integration, the project manager should be focused on:
   A. Establishing credible baselines
   B. Obtaining customer sign-off
   C. Maintaining constant and appropriate communication
   D. Following the change control procedure

4. You have received a phone call from a senior manager nominating you as the project manager for a new important company initiative. You have also received a copy of the business case. Which document should be developed NEXT?
   A. Contract
   B. Project management plan
   C. Project charter
   D. Requirements documentation

5. Which process formally initiates the project?
   A. Initiating
   B. Develop project management plan
   C. Project kickoff meetings
   D. Develop project charter

6. Your company is implementing an e-commerce solution. The sponsor has requested that all products sold online should be delivered within three days. This is an example of:
   A. Assumption
   B. Quality planning
   C. Quality policy
   D. Project constraint

7. A stakeholder requested a scope change that is not aligned with the project charter. Who should approve the change request?
   A. Project manager
   B. Change control board
   C. Customer
   D. Sponsor

8. Your project has just completed the initiating processes. Which process should be performed NEXT?
   A. Collect requirements
   B. Define scope
   C. Develop project charter
   D. Develop project management plan

9. What does a project management plan establish?
   A. Procedures used to manage the project and the performance measurement baselines
   B. Project justification
   C. The start and finish dates of project activities
   D. Project charter

10. Which of the following options is NOT part of the project management plan?
    A. Requirements documentation
    B. Requirements management plan
    C. Process improvement plan
    D. Scope statement

11. Which of the following statements regarding baselines is NOT TRUE?
    A. Project management baselines are used to assess variances.
    B. Baselines are a part of the project management plan.
    C. Baselines should not be changed.
    D. Configuration management establishes product baselines.

12. Which of the following options is NOT part of the performance measurement baseline?
    A. Quality metrics
    B. Project schedule
    C. Scope statement
    D. Time-phased budget

13. The project scope includes a deliverable that has been the cause of major schedule delays in previous projects. What should the project manager do FIRST?
    A. Determine the deliverable's priority with project stakeholders.
    B. Discuss the root cause of previous schedule delays with the project management office.
    C. Recommend a scope change.
    D. Analyze the organization's historical information.

14. In which of the following processes would the use of historical information be LEAST relevant?
    A. Define scope.
    B. Develop project charter.
    C. Close project or phase.
    D. Develop project management plan.

15. Which of the following types of historical information is LEAST reliable?
    A. Commercial databases
    B. Lessons learned records
    C. Project files
    D. Team knowledge

16. _____ are factors that, although uncertain, are considered as givens for planning purposes.
    A. Objectives
    B. Constraints
    C. Assumptions
    D. Risks

17. What is the project manager's main responsibility during the direct and manage project work process?
    A. Coordinating resources
    B. Producing project deliverables
    C. Analyzing performance variances
    D. Analyzing the impact of change requests

18. Which of the following is an output of the direct and manage project work process?
    A. Work performance data
    B. Change requests issued while performing the work
    C. Project deliverables
    D. All of the above

19. The project manager receives regular information about the status of scheduled activities, including physical completion, technical performance measures, and actual costs. This is an example of:
    A. Communications control
    B. Work authorization system
    C. Work performance data
    D. Good team spirit

20. The supplier has received instructions that each work package can only initiate after a written approval. Which project management tools is the project adopting?
    A. Quality auditing
    B. Scope inspection
    C. Work authorization system
    D. Configuration management system

21. Which of the following is part of the monitor and control project work process?
    A. Approve project changes.
    B. Forecast future performance.
    C. Implement corrective actions.
    D. Manage conflict.

22. How frequently should monitoring and controlling be performed?
    A. Weekly
    B. Each two weeks
    C. At the end of each phase
    D. Continuously

23. An action required to correct an existing variance to the project management plan is known as a:
    A. Preventive action
    B. Corrective action
    C. Variance analysis
    D. Baseline revaluation

24. All of the following are examples of preventive actions EXCEPT:
    A. Use less-expensive materials to prevent a cost overrun
    B. Increase the size of the team to gain float in a complex and risky activity
    C. Change a technical solution to prevent future defects
    D. Organize team training to deal with a problem of inadequate team performance

25. Which of the following activities is NOT part of the perform integrated change control process?
    A. Identifying changes
    B. Approving changes
    C. Avoiding changes
    D. Following the configuration management system

26. Which of the following should be the project manager's main concern when managing changes?
    A. Documenting changes
    B. Keeping the project baselines integrated
    C. Making sure that changes are approved or rejected
    D. Influencing changes

27. Management informed the project manager that some of the resources assigned to the project would be transferred to another project within the next week. How should the project manager proceed?
    A. Procure external resources.
    B. Try to redo the plan without the resources, and document the decision and impact in the next performance report.
    C. Issue a change request.
    D. Fast track the project.

28. Your company has just announced a change in corporate strategy. What should you do as project manager of an ongoing project that might be negatively impacted by lack of resources?
    A. Issue a change request to review the project schedule
    B. Wait until management confirms the change
    C. Fast track your project to finish sooner
    D. Meet with the sponsor to confirm the change and discuss its impacts on your project

29. The project manager realized that functionality was informally added to the product scope. What is the FIRST thing to do?
    A. Evaluate the impact of the added functionality.
    B. Review the change control system to prevent further scope creep.
    C. Find out how the functionality was added.
    D. Prepare a change request, and ask the customer to approve it.

30. Which of the following statements regarding integrated change control is FALSE?
    A. Change requests can occur in every project phase.
    B. Change requests do not have to be written.
    C. The team can request changes.
    D. Project changes should be formal and written.

31. Which of the following changes is NOT managed by the change management system?
    A. Corrective action with impact on the scope statement
    B. Preventive action with impact on the project management plan but no impact on baselines
    C. Update to the risk register reassessing the probability of a previously identified risk
    D. Change to the schedule management plan

32. Which of the following options is the LEAST likely cause of constant project changes?
    A. The project charter has not been formally approved.
    B. The project does not have a change management plan.
    C. To avoid conflicts, the team did not analyze all stakeholders' requirements.
    D. Stakeholders were not managed.

33. Two weeks before the project scheduled finish date, one team member informs you that a key stakeholder is not happy and is requesting a product change. What should you do FIRST?
    A. Issue a change request.
    B. Meet with the key stakeholder.
    C. Finish the project before discussing future product improvements.
    D. Analyze the impact of the change.

34. Close to the due date for delivering a critical deliverable, the customer requested a change. After analyzing the customer requirement, the team believes that it has no impact on costs and schedule. Knowing that meeting the schedule is critical for project success, the project management team should:
    A. Follow the change control system
    B. Inform the customer that no changes can be implemented because the deliverable is almost due
    C. Obtain an approval for the change before implementing it
    D. Implement the change because it has no impact on schedule and costs

35. The project manager issued a change request regarding a customer request. However, the customer is refusing to approve the change, claiming he does not agree with its schedule impact. The customer is also insisting that the change is critical and that delaying its implementation can compromise the project's purpose. What should the project manager do?
    A. Only implement the change if there is enough time available.
    B. Do not implement the change.
    C. Implement the change, but document the risk of schedule delay caused by the adopted change.
    D. Explain the importance of managing changes.

36. The team is having trouble keeping control over product changes. What could have prevented this situation?
    A. A communications management plan
    B. A clear scope statement
    C. A configuration management plan
    D. A change control board

37. All technical deliverables have been completed and approved, but the project manager is still waiting for the customer to schedule a meeting where the final performance report will be prepared. The project is considered to be:
    A. Complete because deliverables have been accepted
    B. Complete because the contract was breached
    C. Incomplete until all deliverables are completed and accepted
    D. Terminated

38. Which of the following options is NOT part of the close project or phase process?
    A. Decide whether to move further to the next phase
    B. Manage an early project termination
    C. Transfer the product to operations
    D. Establish final acceptance criteria

39. In which process group are lessons learned transferred to organizational process assets?
    A. Planning
    B. Executing
    C. Monitoring and controlling
    D. Closing

40. Which of the following statements regarding lessons learned is NOT TRUE?
    A. Lessons learned should only be generated after project closure.
    B. Lessons learned from similar projects should be used throughout the project.
    C. Lessons learned should be shared with all relevant stakeholders.
    D. Lessons learned should be stored in the corporate knowledge base.

ANSWERS

Review Exercise 1

1. Adopted life cycle
2. How to document scope
3. How, who, and when to validate scope
4. What schedule formats should be used
5. How to use and report schedule and costs contingencies
6. Rules to assess performance
7. Rules to forecast future performance
8. Report formats
9. Criteria to initiate an audit
10. Units of measure
11. Checklists
12. Adopted communication technology
13. Categories used to group risks
14. Criteria used to assess risks' probability and impact
15. Stakeholders' risk tolerance
16. Types of contracts to use

Review Exercise 2

1. Some stakeholders were not identified.
2. Some stakeholders were not involved in project decisions.
3. The scope management approach was not appropriate.
4. To avoid a conflict among stakeholders, the team did not define a clear scope.
5. There is no project charter.
6. The project purpose or justification was not clearly established.
7. There are constant organizational changes.
8. There is a lack of management support.

Review Exercise 3

1. Reduce the cost impact of changes through their early identification.
2. Influence changes, encouraging favorable changes and discouraging unfavorable changes.
3. Identify alternatives that can minimize the impact of changes.
4. Manage stakeholders' expectations.
5. Analyze the impact of the changes.
6. Ensure that changes are approved or rejected.
7. Document changes for future reference.
8. Update documentation, reviewing the baselines, subsidiary plans, or project documents in accordance with the approved changes.
9. Protect the integrity of project baselines throughout the change process.

Memorization Exercise

1. Change request
2. Preventive action
3. Corrective action
4. Lessons learned
5. Organizational process assets
6. Subsidiary plans
7. Enterprise environmental factors
8. Assumption
9. Project charter
10. Project statement of work (SOW)
11. Baseline
12. Integration management
13. Change management plan
14. Configuration management plan
15. Historical information or historical data
16. Constraint
17. Performance measurement baseline
18. Project management plan
19. Project management information system (PMIS)
20. Work authorization system

Process Exercise 1

1. 4.4
2. 4.6
3. 4.3, 4.6
4. 4.5
5. 4.3
6. 4.2
7. 4.6
8. 4.2
9. 4.4
10. 4.1
11. 4.6

12. 4.5
13. 4.6
14. 4.2
15. 4.1
16. 4.3
17. 4.3, 4.4
18. 4.3, 4.4
19. 4.3, 4.4
20. 4.1
21. 4.6
22. 4.3, 4.4, 4.5
23. 4.3, 4.4, 4.5
24. 4.3
25. 4.6

Process Exercise 2

1. 4.1
2. 4.1
3. 4.1
4. 4.6
5. 4.3, 4.4, 4.5, 4.6
6. 4.2

Chapter 4 Exam

1. **C** The project manager is accountable for managing the integration of the different knowledge areas.
2. **D** Answers A, B, and C refer to important moments in integration management. Integration is performed throughout the project. Therefore, D is the best option.
3. **C** Establishing credible baselines, obtaining customer formal acceptance, and following the change control processes are all integration management activities. However, maintaining constant and appropriate communication is a wider answer because all integration management activities require communication.
4. **C** You are in the initiating process group, and you should prepare a project charter. The contract may be used as an input into initiation but is not an output (answer A). The project management plan (answer B) and the requirements documentation (answer D) will only be prepared later, during planning.
5. **D** Develop the project charter is the process that formally initiates the project. Initiating (answer A) is not a process.
6. **D** The maximum number of delivery days is a constraint limiting the project's options. Answer A is not correct, because the number of delivery days was not assumed by the project management team. It was imposed by the sponsor. The sponsor's constraint might impact quality, but it is not quality planning (answer B) or a quality policy (answer C).
7. **D** A change that impacts the project charter should be approved by the project sponsor.
8. **D** Developing the project management plan is the first planning process to be performed, establishing the rules by which the project will be managed. Collecting requirements (answer A) and defining scope (answer B) should only start once the project management rules are defined. The project charter should be developed during the initiating process group (answer C).

9. **A** A project management plan sets the rules regarding how the project will be managed and establishes the project baselines. The project justification is typically part of the business case or project charter (answer B). The project management plan is more than a project schedule (answer C). A project management plan is not a project charter (answer D).

10. **A** Requirements documentation is the only available option that is not part of the project management plan. Answers B and C are subsidiary plans, and answer D is part of the scope baseline.

11. **C** Baselines can be changed with approved change requests. These change requests can add value to the project and even be critical to project feasibility. All other statements are correct.

12. **A** Collectively, the scope, schedule, and cost baselines are known as the performance measurement baseline. Therefore, quality metrics are not part of the performance measurement baseline.

13. **D** Any action required to prevent a future schedule delay should be based on the cause of previous failures. These causes may be found within accumulated historical information. All other options may eventually be performed once the cause is known.

14. **C** Historical information is particularly relevant as an input into the initiating and planning process groups. Close project or phase is a closing process. The remaining options are part of the initiating or planning process groups.

15. **D** Databases, project files, and lessons learned are usually more reliable than expert judgment. Opinions are often biased by personality characteristics, personal agendas, or recent experiences.

16. **C** Assumptions are elements that, although uncertain, are considered as givens for planning purposes. Answer D may look tempting because assumptions are a common source of risk. However, there are many risks that do not derive from assumptions.

17. **A** Analyze performance variances (answer C) and analyze the impact of change requests (answer D) are not part of the direct and manage project work process. Producing project deliverables (answer B) is part of the direct and manage project work process, but it would not be the project manager's main responsibility. The project manager's main responsibility should be to coordinate.

18. **D** All the options available are an output of the direct and manage project work process.

19. **C** During the executing process group, work performance data are collected to support the monitoring and controlling effort.

20. **C** A work authorization system is used to formally authorize the team to start working on a work package.

21. **B** Forecast future performance is part of the monitor and control project work. Approve project changes (answer A) is part of the perform integrated change control process. Implement corrective actions (answer C) is part of the direct and manage project work process. Manage conflict (answer D) is part of the manage project team process.

22. **D** Monitoring and controlling should be performed continuously, as the project requires the project manager's attention to analyze variances, identify corrective actions, repair defects, and manage changes.

23. **B** Corrective actions are actions needed to correct existing variances to the project management plan.

24. **D** Organize team training to deal with a problem of inadequate team performance is an example of corrective action. All other options are examples of preventive actions.

25. **C** Changes should not be avoided. Some changes are favorable. Others, although potentially unfavorable, should be analyzed regarding their impact and alternatives. By managing changes, instead of avoiding them, the project manager can effectively manage stakeholders' expectations. All other options are part of the perform integrated change control process.

26. **D** All the available options are important. However, the project manager's main concern should be to influence project changes, seeking to encourage favorable changes and discourage unfavorable changes.

27. **C** The project manager should try to exert influence, showing the impact of the change on human resources. In all other options, the project manager accepted the change without managing it. The result of accepting the change may be an increase in costs (answer A), in schedule (answer B), or in risks (answer D).

28. **D** Problems should be managed proactively. The project manager should confirm that the change does exist in order to manage it. Answers A and C should only be performed once the change is understood. Waiting for management to confirm the change (answer B) is not a proactive approach to the situation.

29. **A** To solve the problem, the project manager must first understand the change in the functionality. Answer D will always be performed after answer A. Answers B and C are not directly related to the main problem (functionality was added to the scope) and therefore should not be the first priority.

30. **B** The integration management knowledge area is particularly formal. A change request should be formal and written. All other statements are true.

31. **C** The update to the risk register is the only option that updates a project document instead of the project management plan. Due to its dynamic nature, project documents are less subject to integrated change control than the project management plan.

32. **B** The absence of a change management plan may create some confusion when managing each change, but it does not lead to new changes. If the project charter is not approved, its ability to establish direction and prevent unnecessary changes is limited (answer A). Delaying requirements analysis may lead to future changes (answer C). Poor stakeholder management usually leads to project changes (answer D).

33. **B** Expectations should always be managed, even when the project is nearly over. The project manager should manage expectations following the problem solve technique discussed in Chapter 9. The project manager should identify the problem before looking for a solution.

34. **A** Changes should always follow the change control system, even when they apparently have no impact on schedule and costs. A thorough impact analysis may reveal an impact on other project constraints, such as scope, quality, resources, and risks.

35. **D** Even though the change is critical, it still has to be analyzed and validated. The project manager's role is to follow the right process, explaining in a pedagogical way the importance of such a process.

36. **C** A configuration management plan provides formal guidance on how to identify, document, and change the project's product.

37. **C** The project is not closed until all deliverables, including project management deliverables, are completed.

38. **D** Establishing acceptance criteria is a planning activity. All other options are part of the close project or phase process.

39. **D** Lessons learned are transferred to organizational process assets in the closing process group.

40. **A** Lessons learned should be generated throughout the project. Only postmortem lessons learned are identified after project closure. All other statements are correct.

Scope Management

Scope management ensures that all the required work is performed and only the required work is performed. What are the consequences of this definition? You must plan all the necessary work to fulfill customer requirements. You must verify that all the work planned has been completed. You cannot go beyond the agreed-upon work. If the customer requires additional work that is outside the project scope, you must manage the requirement as a project change. Scope management key activities include:

- Plan scope management.
- Collect requirements.
- Define project scope with stakeholders.
- Prepare a work breakdown structure (WBS) with the team.
- Prepare a WBS dictionary.
- Validate whether the deliverables were developed according to requirements.
- Manage scope changes.

There is frequently some confusion regarding the meaning of *scope*. The term *scope* may refer to project scope or product scope. **Project scope** describes all the work required to deliver the project's product, as well as meet other project objectives. The project scope is established through a combination of a scope statement, a WBS, and a WBS dictionary. **Product scope** describes the product functionalities or specifications and is established through product requirements.

The following table displays the scope management processes with their respective process group:

Scope Management Processes

Process	Process Group
Plan scope management	Planning
Collect requirements	Planning
Define scope	Planning
Create WBS	Planning
Validate scope	Monitoring and controlling
Control scope	Monitoring and controlling

Plan Scope Management

The **plan scope management** process defines a common understanding of how the scope should be managed. To reach such understanding, you can prepare a scope management plan and a requirements management plan.

Scope Management Plan

The scope management plan specifies the procedures, tools, techniques, and responsibilities required for managing scope. A typical scope management plan may define rules, approaches, techniques, and responsibilities concerning:

- Collect requirements techniques
- Adopted WBS templates
- Methods used to develop the WBS
- Work inspection
- Deliverables validation
- Scope management changes

Requirements Management Plan

The requirements management plan is an element of the project management plan that sets the rules regarding how to analyze, prioritize, document, approve, develop, verify, change, and trace requirements. These rules should be specific for the project, depending on its dimensions, complexity, product, number of stakeholders involved, culture, and organizational history.

Collect Requirements

Consider the **collect requirements** process as a translation effort. The needs and expectations of the customer, sponsor, management, and other stakeholders must be translated into product and project scope requirements. This translation is critical, because—unlike needs

	Requirement	Priority	Effort	Risk
Requirements	A	Critical	Medium	Low
	B	Critical	High	Medium
	C	Important	Medium	Medium
	Deliver above this line			
	D	Useful	High	Low

Figure 5.1 Prioritize requirements

and expectations—requirements are specific and measurable elements upon which you can set acceptance criteria.

The team should attempt to identify all the requirements from all the stakeholders. Some of the requirements might fall outside the project objectives set within the project charter. Others might not be feasible or applicable. Others might not be compatible with existing scope, schedule, costs, quality, and risks constraints. Therefore, not all collected requirements can be part of the project scope. During the collect requirements process, customer and team members should carefully analyze and prioritize requirements (see Figure 5.1). An agreement on definitive requirements will be done later during the define scope process.

Using a stakeholder register and a project charter as inputs, the team can then prepare requirements documentation and a requirements traceability matrix.

Requirements Documentation

Requirements should be documented along with a description of how the project business need will be addressed. Documentation should include functional, nonfunctional, and quality requirements, as well as identified acceptance criteria, assumptions, and constraints. Once approved, requirements documentation will be used as input by other scope planning processes.

Documentation should be comprehensive, defining requirements in a verifiable, consistent, clearly understandable, and easily controlled way. Requirements should also be defined in terms of the "what is required" instead of the "how it will be delivered." In other words, requirements should not be defined in terms of solutions.

Establishing verifiable requirements is critical for project success. **Verifiable** means that there is no ambiguity during validation. For an easier verification, requirements should use quantitative criteria whenever possible.

Requirements Traceability Matrix

The collect requirements process also develops a requirements traceability matrix. (See Figure 5.2.) This document, typically in a tabular form, connects each requirement to one business need, a project objective, and a deliverable. This matrix also leads to improved control over the

Need	Functional requirement	Technical requirement	Module	Test document	Tested on	Approved on	Status

Figure 5.2 Requirements traceability matrix

requirements management, tracing the requirements implementation throughout the project life cycle.

Collect Requirements Techniques

There are several collect requirements techniques. Some of the most widely used include:

- **Interviews**   Information is collected through direct questions to project stakeholders.
- **Focus groups**   Stakeholders discuss ideas and generate a solution with the help of a moderator.
- **Workshops**   Stakeholders from multiple areas meet to discuss ideas with the help of a facilitator. The interactive nature of workshops enables a swift collection of information and generates consensus.
- **Questionnaires and surveys**   Requirements are generated using previously defined questions. This approach is appropriate for large populations.
- **Observation**   Requirements are collected by examining individuals within their work environment.
- **Prototypes**   Requirements are generated by presenting a model to stakeholders and requesting feedback.

Some techniques collect requirements by exploring creativity. **Group creativity techniques** can include:

- **Brainstorming**   This creative technique is based on an unconstrained and informal exchange of ideas. A facilitator should incentivize all participants to contribute. When the participants have run out of ideas, existing ideas are organized and structured in requirements.
- **Nominal group technique**   This technique reaches a decision quickly through vote. Each member ranks each opinion and the highest ranked opinion is selected. Therefore, the group's decision is reached by taking into account everyone's opinion.
- **Delphi technique**   A consensus is reached by repeatedly consulting experts, usually through an anonymous process. A facilitator requests ideas from and within a group of experts. Inputs are collected, summarized, and sent back to the experts, without information regarding who generated what idea. The process is repeated until a reasonable consensus is achieved. The main advantage of this technique is reaching a consensus, letting everyone contribute without the influence of group pressure. Indirectly, this technique also leads to greater involvement and commitment of the project team to the project decisions. The Delphi technique may also be useful when experts are geographically scattered.
- **Mind maps**   These diagrams help generate and organize ideas.
- **Affinity diagrams**   For improved manageability, existing ideas are organized into groups according to their similarities.
- **Multicriteria decision analysis**   This assessment technique is based on weighting multiple criteria.

Define Scope

Define scope is the scope planning process where the project and product are described in detail. When defining scope, the team works with the customer and other stakeholders, creating a common basis of understanding. Define scope is possibly the most critical project management process. An incorrect scope definition will almost certainly lead to inadequate planning and performance problems within all knowledge areas.

REVIEW EXERCISE 1

Scope management greatest challenges can be:

1. _____

2. _____

3. _____

4. _____

5. _____

6. _____

7. _____

8. _____

9. _____

10. _____

Scope Statement

The scope statement is the main output of the scope definition. This document establishes a common understanding among different stakeholders over the project and product scope and may include:

- Product scope
- Deliverables identification
- Assumptions and constraints
- Acceptance criteria
- Elements specifically excluded from the project

The scope statement will be used as a key element of the scope baseline, determining whether the project performance conforms to the defined scope objectives.

One of the core elements of the scope statement is the deliverable. A **deliverable** is a tangible and verifiable item that must be produced to complete the project. Deliverables may represent elements directly related to the product but can also be subsidiary elements, such as project management documentation.

The development of the scope statement is also a translation effort. The team and the stakeholders should attempt to translate the project charter, which establishes the purpose and high-level objectives, into a specific project and product description. Additionally, the product's descriptions included in the statement of work and project charter, should be translated into specific project deliverables. This translation effort will use tools and techniques such as expert judgment, workshops, and product analysis.

Product Analysis

Product analysis is a scope definition technique that translates the product into specific deliverables. Product analysis aggregates techniques such as:

- **Product breakdown**   The product is decomposed into deliverables to facilitate agreement among project stakeholders. For example, a documentation element included in the product scope may be decomposed into functional and technical documentation.
- **Value analysis**   Technique focused on reducing the cost of developing the product without changing the scope.
- **Value engineering**   Systematic and quantitative method that examines the product's high-level requirements looking for alternatives to increase the product's value. Value can be increased by improving the product's functionalities or by reducing its cost.

Create Work Breakdown Structure (WBS)

Create WBS is a scope planning process that has the WBS as its main output. A WBS is a deliverable-oriented treelike representation of all the work required to achieve the project objectives. Deliverables identified in the scope statement will be progressively decomposed into smaller and more manageable work packages. A WBS defines the total scope of the project. (See Figure 5.3.)

> Work that is not in the WBS is outside the scope of the project.

There are different approaches for developing a WBS. You can adopt a top-down approach, decomposing each deliverable into smaller components. You can use a bottom-up approach, developing the WBS by integrating other previously planned WBS for different subcomponents of the project. Finally, you can accelerate planning by using **WBS templates** previously established in the organization.

The WBS is one of the planning structural elements. It will be used as a key input during activity definition, cost estimating, cost budgeting, quality planning, procurement planning, and risk identification.

> A WBS does not establish scope objectives. The WBS establishes all the work required to achieve objectives.

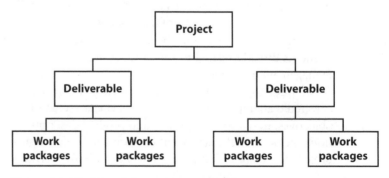

Figure 5.3 Work breakdown structure (WBS)

Unlike the scope statement, which establishes a common understanding between the team and the stakeholders, the WBS is primarily developed within the project team.

> Do not confuse the WBS with the organization breakdown structure or product breakdown structure.

The advantages of using a WBS are that it:

- Prevents scope creep by clearly defining the required work
- Increases the team's commitment to the plan
- Develops team spirit because the team is involved in the WBS creation
- Facilitates the internal and external project communication
- Enables more accurate estimates
- Identifies scope incoherencies
- Facilitates the responsibilities assignment
- Can be reused through WBS templates
- Allows a unique code identifier to be assigned to each work element to facilitate reporting and reusing historical information (see section on code of accounts)

Decomposition

The **decomposition** process breaks down project deliverables into smaller, more manageable components, known as "work packages." This decomposition is critical for project planning. It leads to an increased understanding over scope, to more precise estimates, and to more clearly defined responsibilities.

> Once a WBS deliverable has been decomposed into smaller elements, the sum of those elements must be exactly the same as the deliverable.

The right level of WBS detail will depend on the context and can change throughout the project. Usually, more detail will help clarify the work required, improve estimates, define more clear responsibilities, and increase visibility over performance. However, a very detailed WBS may lead to an excessive level of plan maintenance effort as well as lack of information accuracy. Throughout the project, you should adopt the level of detail that effectively facilitates estimation, control, and responsibility assignment.

For the exam, make sure you are able to distinguish between product, deliverables, and work packages. Additionally, you should be able to understand the purpose of product analysis and decomposition. During the **define scope** process, product analysis can translate the product (e.g., new customer care application) into tangible and verifiable items known as deliverables (e.g., requirements definition, application configuration, and reports). Later, in the **create WBS** process, the team decomposes the deliverables into smaller and more manageable components known as work packages (e.g., reports, previously identified as project deliverables, can be decomposed into reports design, reports development, and unit tests). (See Figure 5.4.)

Figure 5.4 Product analysis versus decomposition

Work Packages

As was previously discussed, deliverables will be decomposed into smaller and more manageable elements. Thus work packages will be represented at the lowest level of the WBS. These work packages will be used to develop time and cost estimates and will provide a basis for a detailed project performance control.

Work packages can also be used to assign work responsibilities to individuals or organizational units. This responsibility assignment is not, however, exclusively done at the work package level. Responsibility assignment can also be performed at higher levels of the WBS.

The following table prevents confusing the WBS with other project management documents:

Element	Objective
Business case	Document used to analyze the project feasibility and justify its selection
Statement of work	Formal document that describes the products and services that should be provided by the project, typically developed by the customer before scope definition and frequently a basis for a contractual relationship
Project charter	Formal document that authorizes the beginning of the project and provides the project manager with the authority to apply resources to project activities
Scope statement	Document that establishes a common understanding among different stakeholders over the project and product scopes
WBS	Deliverable-oriented treelike representation of all the work required to achieve the project objectives; deliverables identified in the scope statement will be progressively decomposed into smaller and more manageable work packages; defines the complete project scope

WBS Dictionary

A WBS may be complemented with a dictionary, allowing you to store additional information regarding each work package. Specific information may include work descriptions, applicable responsibilities, detailed requirements, identified activities, reference technical documents, relevant assumption and constraints, resource requirements, estimates, performance assessment criteria, acceptance criteria, pertinent risks, code of accounts, and chart of accounts.

> By documenting in detail each WBS element, the WBS dictionary helps the team avoid performing work that is outside the scope.

The **code of accounts** is a numerical system used to assign a unique number to each WBS element. This numerical system can facilitate the reporting of specific performance information to specific stakeholders. It can also help organize and reuse organizational historical information.

The project **chart of accounts**, based on the organization chart of accounts, is a numerical system used for accounting purposes. By using a chart of accounts, the project costs may be categorized according to their nature (e.g., work, traveling, and external supplies).

REVIEW EXERCISE 2

A WBS dictionary may include:

1. _____

2. _____

3. _____

4. _____

5. _____

6. _____

7. _____

8. _____

9. _____

10. _____

11. _____

12. _____

Scope Baseline

A scope baseline aggregates three distinct documents: approved version of the scope statement, WBS, and WBS dictionary. There may be changes at the lowest level of the WBS that do not modify the scope statement. For example, the team can decide that an additional test is required before handing the deliverable to the customer. This type of WBS update does not imply a scope baseline change. When an update to the WBS modifies a deliverable established in the scope statement, the scope baseline must be changed.

> The project manager is not necessarily responsible for reviewing and validating modifications to work packages that do not imply a scope baseline change. Often, the team has enough authority to decide on such modifications.

The WBS and the Level of Cost Control

Controlling at the most detailed level of the WBS does not necessarily mean better control. Excessive detail can often lead to too much control effort. It can also produce sensitive and volatile data that may distract stakeholders' attention from the real project performance. To overcome this problem, some organizations choose to control at a higher level of the WBS than that of the work package. The **control account** level establishes the level of WBS detail where the project performance will be assessed by the earned value management method (see Chapter 7). Each control account may group several work packages. For accounting purposes, each control account may be linked to the organization's chart of accounts. In the long run, where work packages are not yet identified, the control accounts are defined around large blocks of work, known as **planning packages**.

Validate Scope

Validate scope determines whether each deliverable has been completed according to requirements and obtains a formal acceptance from the customer or sponsor. Scope validation is performed through work results **inspections**. Depending on the application area, these inspections might be known as revisions, product revisions, audits, or walkthroughs.

The **validate scope** process is similar to the **quality control** process because both involve verifying the work results. However, the goal of scope validation is to accept the deliverable, while the goal of quality control is to obtain the correct results. Validate scope is frequently performed after quality control, but both processes may be performed in parallel.

> The validate scope process may be performed throughout the project, although it tends to be performed at the end of the project phases, when the main deliverables are handed out for customer validation.

REVIEW EXERCISE 3

The similarities between the validate scope process and the close project or phase process are:

1. _____

2. _____

3. _____

REVIEW EXERCISE 4

The differences between the validate scope process and the close project or phase process are:

1. _____

_____

2. _____

_____

3. _____

_____

Control Scope

Controlling scope means delivering all the project and product scope requirements and managing changes to the requirements baseline and scope baseline. Controlling the scope can include the following activities:

- Comparing actual scope performance with the baseline
- Preventing the team from completing work that is not included in the project scope
- Recommending corrective or preventive actions to deal with scope variances
- Identifying scope changes
- Assessing the impact of changes
- Encouraging positive scope change and discouraging negative change
- Ensuring that changes go through a formal authorization system
- Maintaining a change log
- Protecting the baselines' integrity
- Communicating the changes

Scope control should help the team avoid **scope creep**. This term refers to uncontrolled additions to project and product scopes. This control effort should also avoid changes that compromise the project charter, unless these changes are approved by the sponsor.

REVIEW EXERCISE 5

The difference between control scope and validate scope is:

_____

_____

_____

MEMORIZATION EXERCISE

The following exercise was designed to facilitate the memorization of the main concepts in this chapter. Assign each of the following definitions to a scope management concept.

1. Consensus reached by repeatedly consulting experts, usually through an anonymous process

   _____

2. All the work required to deliver the project's product as well as meet other project objectives

   _____

3. Approved version of the scope statement, WBS, and WBS dictionary

_____

4. Deliverable-oriented treelike representation of all the work required to achieve the project objectives

_____

5. Document that establishes a common understanding among different stakeholders regarding the project and product scopes

_____

6. Document that stores additional information regarding each work package

_____

7. Document, typically with a tabular form, that connects each requirement to one business need, a project objective, and a deliverable

_____

8. Element of the project management plan that sets the rules on how to analyze, prioritize, document, approve, develop, verify, change, and trace requirements

_____

9. Elements at the lowest level of the WBS, used to facilitate estimation, assign responsibility to individuals or organizational units, and improve performance control

_____

10. Knowledge area that ensures that all the required work is performed and only the required work is performed

_____

11. No ambiguity while validating the requirements

_____

12. Numerical system used for accounting purposes

_____

13. Numerical system used to assign a unique number to each WBS element

_____

14. Product functionalities or specifications established through product requirements

_____

15. Scope definition technique that translates the product into specific deliverables

_____

16. Tangible and verifiable item that must be produced to complete the project

_____

17. Technique focused on reducing the cost of developing the product without changing the scope

_____

18. Technique that quickly reaches a decision through vote, taking into account everyone's opinion. Each member ranks each opinion and the highest-ranked opinion is selected.

_____

19. The process of breaking down a project deliverable into smaller, more manageable components that can be scheduled, budgeted, and assigned to an individual or group

_____

20. Work and deliverables examination to verify if they conform to requirements

_____

Process Exercises

The following exercises were designed so you could learn how to recognize the processes and understand their logical sequence. Scope management processes are listed next, including their unique numbers in the *PMBOK Guide*:

- 5.1 Plan scope management
- 5.2 Collect requirements
- 5.3 Define scope
- 5.4 Create WBS
- 5.5 Validate scope
- 5.6 Control scope

PROCESS EXERCISE 1

Assign processes to the following activities

1. Avoid scope creep. _____
2. Complete a prototype to collect product requirements. _____
3. Decompose the product to facilitate an agreement among stakeholders. _____
4. Decompose the work into smaller and more manageable elements. _____
5. Describe the work in the WBS dictionary. _____
6. Identify stakeholders' project requirements. _____

7. Manage scope changes. _____

8. Prepare a requirements management plan. _____

9. Prepare a requirements traceability matrix. _____

10. Prepare a scope statement. _____

11. Prepare the requirements documentation. _____

12. Verify whether the deliverables meet acceptance criteria. _____

PROCESS EXERCISE 2

Assign processes to the following inputs.

Inputs	Processes
1. Scope statement	_____
2. Requirements documentation	_____
3. Stakeholders management plan	_____
4. Requirements management plan	_____
5. Project charter	_____

CHAPTER 5 EXAM

The following questions were designed to test your knowledge on this chapter's topic. Read each question carefully, and choose the option that most accurately answers the question. Once you have completed the exam, compare your answers with the solution and read through the justification provided. Note the topics where you have the most difficulty and make sure that you dedicate enough study time to them.

1. All of the following are part of scope management EXCEPT:
   A. Defining all the work required to meet project objectives
   B. Preventing changes that fall outside the project charter
   C. Performing all the work required and only the work required
   D. Preventing scope changes

2. The team is not sure how deliverables should be validated. Which document should they check?
   A. Requirements documents
   B. Scope statement
   C. Scope management plan
   D. WBS dictionary

3. Which of the following is NOT part of the collect requirements process?
   A. Establishing requirements acceptance criteria
   B. Completing prototypes
   C. Preparing a requirements traceability matrix
   D. Defining high-level product requirements

4. Which of the following statements regarding requirements collection is TRUE?
   A. The project manager cannot exclude requirements from the project scope.
   B. The project manager should try to identify all stakeholders' requirements.
   C. All collected requirements will be included in the scope baseline.
   D. Only high-level requirements should be identified in the collect requirements process.

5. The team is working with the customer trying to prioritize project requirements. They are, however, having trouble remembering where and why those requirements were collected. What scope management tool would be of MOST help?
   A. Requirement traceability diagram
   B. Mind map
   C. Affinity diagram
   D. WBS

6. The team is working with a number of stakeholders to establish a clear understanding of the project's needs. They are defining what should and should not be included in the project scope, as well as establishing a clear set of deliverables. What are they creating?
   A. WBS
   B. Project charter
   C. WBS dictionary
   D. Scope statement

7. You have received a project from another project manager that left the company. If the scope statement is already complete, what should you do NEXT?
   A. Create a WBS.
   B. Submit the project management plan for approval.
   C. Identify activities.
   D. Confirm that stakeholders are committed to the project scope.

8. A tangible and verifiable item that must be produced to complete the project is:
   A. An objective
   B. A work package
   C. A deliverable
   D. A milestone

9. Product analysis includes:
   A. Decomposing project deliverables into work packages
   B. Turning project and product objectives into deliverables
   C. Describing the product
   D. Defining the rules that will be used for managing scope

10. How would you describe a work breakdown structure (WBS)?
    A. A narrative description of products or services that should be supplied by the project
    B. A technique used to decompose the project's product
    C. A document that establishes agreement on objectives, product characteristics, deliverables, exclusions, constraints, assumptions, and product acceptance criteria
    D. A deliverable-oriented treelike representation of project work where each deliverable is decomposed into smaller, more manageable work packages

11. Which of the following is NOT an advantage of using a WBS?
    A. Prevents scope creep
    B. Promotes team buy-in
    C. Makes the communication simpler
    D. Defines project objectives

12. Which of the following is NOT included in the scope baseline?
    A. WBS
    B. Requirements documentation
    C. WBS dictionary
    D. Scope statement

13. Which of the following statements regarding WBS decomposition is correct?
    A. The right level of WBS detail might change throughout the project.
    B. WBS decomposition is a product analysis technique.
    C. The greater the level of WBS detail, the greater the accuracy of the estimates.
    D. The project manager should always validate WBS decomposition.

14. Which of the following statements regarding work packages is NOT correct?
    A. A change in a work package is not necessarily a scope baseline change.
    B. The project manager must approve all changes to work packages.
    C. Work packages can be used to assign work to organizational units.
    D. Work packages are found at the lowest level of the WBS.

15. A deliverable was completed without some of its planned work packages. The project manager should:
    A. Change the project WBS
    B. Issue a change request
    C. Change the communications management plan
    D. Direct the project team to complete the remaining work packages

16. A team member needs access to detailed information regarding a project deliverable, including a description of the work required, estimates, resources required, constraints, assumptions, and acceptance criteria. You should direct the team member to the:
    A. Scope statement
    B. WBS dictionary
    C. RAM
    D. Project schedule

17. Which of the following statements regarding a WBS is NOT TRUE?
    A. Defines the total scope of the project
    B. Work that is not in the WBS is outside the project's scope
    C. Should include information regarding resources
    D. Is deliverable oriented

18. You are about to start developing the project schedule. Most of the scope validation effort occurs _____.
    A. When all the project work is completed
    B. When the project management plan is ready for approval
    C. At the end of every project phase
    D. Immediately after scope definition

19. What is the difference between scope validation and quality control?
    A. Scope validation is performed by the team, while quality control can be performed by other stakeholders.
    B. Quality control may be applied to any project deliverable, while scope validation can only be applied to project management deliverables.
    C. Scope validation is performed throughout the deliverable's development, while quality control is only performed once the deliverable is completed.
    D. None of the above

20. A team member completed a deliverable that is different from what you expected. As project manager, how should you proceed?
    A. Correct the deliverable.
    B. Discuss the issue with the team member.
    C. Perform scope validation.
    D. Ask the team member to correct the deliverable and then review your change management system.

21. While working with the customer to get a deliverable accepted, the customer argues that the deliverable does not meet project objectives. Which project management process can help redefine the deliverable?
    A. Define scope
    B. Validate scope
    C. Control scope
    D. Scope management

22. The project is having trouble measuring the accomplished work. Which of the following is the LEAST likely cause of the problem?
    A. Poor scope definition
    B. Deliverables that were not decomposed into work packages
    C. Poor integrated change control
    D. Lack of a WBS numbering system

23. The customer informed you that a key functionality should be added to the project's scope. How should you proceed?
    A. Notify management.
    B. Include the functionality in the project scope so the plan can be progressively elaborated.
    C. Obtain an approval for the change request.
    D. Analyze the change's impact.

24. Which of the following is NOT part of controlling scope?
    A. Compare actual scope performance with the baseline.
    B. Determine actions required to correct scope variances.
    C. Work with the customer to obtain formal approval of project deliverables.
    D. Discourage unnecessary changes to the scope baseline.

25. During the construction of a sports arena, the team detected an inconsistency in the project technical documentation. Correcting the documentation inconsistency will likely cause a schedule delay, leading to contract penalties for late delivery. You are also aware that the customer will not be able to detect the inconsistency and that the construction quality will not be affected. How should you proceed?
    A. Complete the arena construction as scheduled, and correct the documentation once the arena is complete.
    B. Correct the documentation, and inform the customer.
    C. Complete the arena construction as scheduled, and leave the document as is.
    D. Understand the impact of correcting the documentation, and discuss the issue with the customer.

26. Which of the following statements regarding scope changes is correct?
    A. An unfavorable cost variance cannot be justified with an approved scope change.
    B. Once approved, the scope baseline cannot be changed.
    C. Scope changes should be approved by the team.
    D. Scope changes should be accepted as the natural consequence of scope progressive elaboration.

ANSWERS

Review Exercise 1

1. Some stakeholders were not identified or were insufficiently involved.
2. There is a lack of stakeholders' commitment.
3. There are constant changes due to lack of management support or ineffective project initiation.
4. No acceptance criteria have been established.
5. The team and the customer use different terminologies.
6. Scope was not documented.
7. Methodology is not adequate.
8. Scope definition was delayed to avoid conflict.
9. There is a lack of business knowledge.
10. There are changes in the organizational environment.

Review Exercise 2

1. Work description
2. Identification of the organization responsible for performing the work
3. Related activities
4. Assigned resources
5. Times and cost estimates
6. Risks
7. Performance assessment criteria
8. Acceptance criteria
9. Reference documents
10. Unique code of accounts
11. Detailed requirements
12. Required authorizations

Review Exercise 3

1. Both deal with formal acceptance.
2. Both tend to be performed at the end of the phase or project.
3. Both are performed with the customer or sponsor.

Review Exercise 4

1. Validate scope validates deliverables. Close the project or phase validates the project or phase as a whole.
2. Validate scope may be performed throughout the project because there are often deliverables completed during a phase that require approval.
3. Validate scope is a monitoring and controlling process. Close the project or phase is a closing process.

Review Exercise 5

Control scope avoids unauthorized changes and manages scope changes. Validate scope determines whether the deliverables were performed according to requirements, in order to obtain formal acceptance.

Memorization Exercise

1. Delphi technique
2. Project scope
3. Scope baseline
4. Work breakdown structure (WBS)
5. Scope statement
6. WBS dictionary
7. Requirements traceability matrix
8. Requirements management plan
9. Work packages
10. Scope management
11. Verifiable
12. Chart of accounts
13. Code of accounts
14. Product scope
15. Product analysis
16. Deliverable
17. Value analysis
18. Nominal group technique
19. Decomposition
20. Inspection

Process Exercise 1

1. 5.6
2. 5.2
3. 5.3

    4. 5.4
    5. 5.4
    6. 5.2
    7. 5.6
    8. 5.1
    9. 5.2
  10. 5.3
  11. 5.2
  12. 5.5

Process Exercise 2

1. 5.4
2. 5.3, 5.4, 5.5, 5.6
3. 5.2
4. 5.2
5. 5.1, 5.2, 5.3

Chapter 5 Exam

1. **D** Scope management is about managing potential changes instead of avoiding them. All other statements are correct.
2. **C** The scope management plan specifies the procedures, tools, and techniques adopted for managing scope.
3. **D** Defining high-level product requirements is performed during the develop project charter process. All other options are part of the collect requirements process.
4. **B** The team should try to identify all stakeholder' requirements and meet those that are within project objectives. If there is a conflict among requirements, customer and team members should try to prioritize them and pursue a different balance between scope requirements, schedule, costs, quality, resources, and risks. The project manager can exclude requirements that were excluded from the project charter (answer A). Not all collected requirements will be part of the scope baseline (answer C). Detailed requirements can be identified in the collect requirements process (answer D).
5. **A** The requirements traceability matrix tracks requirements from their identification to their delivery. The mind map (answer B) and the affinity diagram (answer C) could help in collecting requirements, but would not help the team in keeping control over them. The WBS documents the project work, not the requirements (answer D).
6. **D** The team is defining the scope with stakeholders. Thus the result should be a scope statement. Answers A and C are not correct because the WBS and the WBS dictionary should be prepared by the team after defining the scope statement. Answer B is not correct because the project charter should already have been prepared.
7. **D** The project manager should have confidence regarding the scope's consistency in order to be accountable for project objectives. Thus he or she should confirm that the stakeholders are committed to the project scope. All remaining options may be required, but they would always be performed after answer D.
8. **C** A deliverable is a tangible and verifiable item that must be produced to complete the project.
9. **B** The define scope process transforms project and product objectives into deliverables through the product analysis technique. Answer A refers to the decomposition technique used during the WBS development. Answer C refers to the statement of work. Answer D refers to the scope management plan.

10. **D** A WBS is a deliverable-oriented treelike representation of project deliverables. Answer A refers to the statement of work. Answer B refers to the decomposition technique. Answer C refers to the scope statement.

11. **D** The WBS does not establish project objectives. The WBS establishes all the work required to achieve those objectives. All other options are advantages of using a WBS.

12. **B** The scope baseline is the approved version of the scope statement, WBS, and WBS dictionary. Therefore, requirements documentation is not part of the scope baseline.

13. **A** The work is decomposed progressively, as more and better information becomes available. The WBS level of detail may change throughout the project. All other statements are not correct.

14. **B** Statement A is correct because a change in a work package is always an update to the project management plan, but is not necessarily a change to the scope baseline. Statements C and D are correct because work packages are frequently used to assign work to organizational units and are at the lowest level of the WBS. Statement B is not correct because the team may find an alternative solution to perform the agreed-upon scope, without requiring the project manager's approval.

15. **A** If there are no changes to the project deliverable, there is no need for a change request. Therefore, the project manager only needs to update the project WBS to reflect the change in the required work packages.

16. **B** The WBS dictionary would store additional information about each work package.

17. **C** A WBS does not include information regarding resources. All other statements are correct.

18. **C** Validate scope means validating deliverables, which tends to coincide with the end of project phases. Statements A and D are not true because scope validation occurs throughout the project. Statement B is not true because scope validation is not specific to project management plan validation.

19. **D** Statement A is not correct because scope validation may or may not be performed by the team. Statement B is not correct because scope validation is not restricted to validating project management deliverables. Statement C is also incorrect because quality control may be performed throughout the development of the deliverable.

20. **C** Before assuming that the deliverable is not conformant to requirements and correcting it (answer A) or asking a team member to correct it (answer B), the project manager should first verify if the deliverable was developed according to requirements. Answers B and C try to make such verification. However, performing a scope validation would be the most structured choice because it would follow the agreed-upon procedure to validate the deliverable. Discussing the problem with the team member may not be enough to verify whether the deliverable can be accepted. Frequently, such verification requires more thorough analysis and tests.

21. **C** The control scope process can manage the deliverable's change. Define scope and validate scope are not valid options, since the question is not referring to defining or accepting the deliverable. Scope management is not an option because it is not a process.

22. **D** A WBS code of accounts may be used to report performance, but not to assess it. All other options may lead to performance assessment problems.

23. **D** Changes should go through a change control process where the change is analyzed. Answers A and B are not managing the change; answer C would always be performed after answer D.

24. **C** Working with the customer to get a formal acceptance of the deliverables is part of the validate scope process. All other options are part of the scope control process.

25. **D** Technical documentation is part of the project scope. Hence, the project should deliver the technical documentation without inconsistencies. The project manager does not have the authority to decide if the project should sacrifice the schedule (answer B) or sacrifice the scope (answers A and C). The project manager should analyze the impact of correcting the documentation and discuss the issue with the customer.

26. **A** An approved change with impact on costs should have resulted in a change to the cost baseline. Therefore, an unfavorable cost variance cannot be justified with a scope change. All other statements are correct.

Time Management

The first thing that comes to mind when addressing time management is preparing a project schedule. But managing time entails much more than just using a scheduling tool. **Time management** is about delivering the project on schedule, and its activities can include:

- Preparing a schedule management plan
- Defining activities
- Identifying the project milestones
- Documenting the activity attributes
- Sequencing activities

- Using leads and lags to optimize the network diagram
- Defining resource requirements
- Developing a resource breakdown structure
- Defining the resource calendars
- Estimating activity durations
- Estimating the schedule contingency reserve
- Calculating the activities' start and finish dates
- Analyzing the project's floats to understand its risk
- Compressing the schedule
- Leveling the resources to adapt to existing constraints
- Analyzing the project's global risk with a Monte Carlo simulation
- Analyzing schedule variances by using bar charts
- Managing changes to the project schedule

The following table displays the time management processes with their respective process group:

Time Management Processes

Process	Process Group
Plan schedule management	Planning
Define activities	Planning
Sequence activities	Planning
Estimate activity resources	Planning
Estimate activity durations	Planning
Develop schedule	Planning
Control schedule	Monitoring and controlling

Plan Schedule Management

Plan schedule management establishes a common understanding on how to manage the time knowledge area. Unsurprisingly, its outcome is a **schedule management plan** that specifies the procedures, tools, and techniques used for managing the schedule, including:

- Metrics used to assess the status, progress, and variances, and to forecast performance
- Approach used to develop estimates
- Rules used to measure the performance of ongoing work
- Methods used to forecast future performance
- Level of detail where the control and reporting is performed
- Reports used for controlling
- Adopted software
- Tolerated variances
- Schedule changes, procedures, and authorities
- Roles and responsibilities

Define Activities

While managing scope, people use terms such as *deliverables* and *work packages*. These terms refer to tangible elements that are developed throughout the project. While managing time, people think about the actions required to develop the deliverables and the work packages. This is because it is simpler to sequence and estimate verbs than to sequence and estimate the outcome of those verbs. For example, you may decompose a document into such activities as "meet with the customer," "prepare the document," and "validate the document" to more easily schedule the document elaboration.

In defining activities, each work breakdown structure (WBS) work package may be broken down, or decomposed, into smaller components known as activities. The decomposed activities may then be organized into an **activity list**.

> The technique used to decompose work packages into activities is similar to the decomposition technique used on scope management to decompose deliverables into work packages.

Define activities also includes documenting relevant information that may be used by the team while completing the work. This additional information, known as **activity attributes**, may include activity-unique identifiers, work descriptions, dependencies, resource requirements, deadlines, estimates, constraints, and assumptions.

To more easily reuse the knowledge accumulated in the organization, historical information regarding activities and their attributes may be standardized in **activity templates**.

Project Milestones

The **define activities** process also defines a list of **milestones**. A milestone is a significant project event, like the completion of a phase or a major project deliverable.

> Milestones have zero duration. Hence, they do not represent project work.

The project manager may use a milestone chart to report schedule performance, concentrating stakeholders' attention on the project main events. In other words, milestones are used for schedule planning and controlling, but also to model communication with the stakeholders.

In many organizations, the milestones are already identified on the standardized project methodology. When they have not been previously defined, the project manager may ask the main stakeholders to identify the most relevant events that they want to have greater schedule visibility over.

Rolling Wave Planning

A detailed plan is not necessarily more accurate or useful. Rolling wave planning is a progressive elaboration planning technique that plans for the short term in detail and prepares a high-level plan for the long run. The plan is detailed as more and better information becomes available.

> Define activities is the process most subject to rolling wave planning, due to the level of detail required to plan the activities.

REVIEW EXERCISE 1

> **The inputs for the define activities process are:**

1. _____

2. _____

3. _____

4. _____

5. _____

6. _____

Sequence Activities

Once the activities have been identified, the next step is to define their sequence by observing their characteristics and organizing them in the order that they must be performed. For example, it is not possible to install software until the hardware is available.

The main output of sequencing activities is a network diagram that graphically represents the activities, milestones, and dependencies. In a network diagram, the activities and milestones should converge from the project start to its end. Therefore, with the exception of the first and the last activity, each activity and milestone should have at least a predecessor and a successor activity.

Historical information regarding activities, milestones, and dependencies may be standardized in **network diagrams templates**, supporting the reuse of accumulated knowledge.

There are two methods for representing activities graphically: the precedence diagramming method (PDM) and the arrow diagramming method (ADM).

Precedence Diagramming Method (PDM) or Activity on Node (AON)

PDM is the main technique used to sequence activities, representing activities by nodes and dependencies by arrows. (See Figure 6.1.)

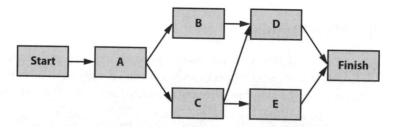

Figure 6.1 Precedence diagramming method (PDM)

In this method, the logical relationships between activities may be of the following types:

- **Finish to start**   The predecessor activity has to finish before the successor activity starts. (See Figure 6.2.) For example, the wall construction must be finished before painting of the wall starts.

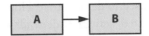

Figure 6.2 Finish to start dependency

- **Finish to finish**   The predecessor activity has to finish before the successor activity finishes. (See Figure 6.3.) For example, product testing mush finish before correcting the errors finishes.

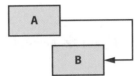

Figure 6.3 Finish to finish dependency

- **Start to start**   The predecessor activity has to start before the successor activity starts. (See Figure 6.4.) For example, repairing the machine must start before controlling the quality of the repair starts. Note that both activities do not have to start at the same time.

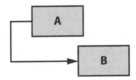

Figure 6.4 Start to start dependency

- **Start to finish**   The predecessor activity has to start before the successor activity finishes. (See Figure 6.5.) For example, the maintenance of an application version can stop only when the next software version is available.

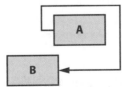

Figure 6.5 Start to finish dependency

Arrow Diagramming Method (ADM) or Activity on Arrow (AOA)

ADM is used to sequence activities, with the arrows representing activities and the nodes, or circles, representing dependencies. This approach has two limitations, when compared with PDM. The first is that it can represent only finish to start dependencies. The second is that the method may have to use dummy activities to represent dependencies. Dummy activities are zero duration activities used to demonstrate a logical relationship that cannot be described with a regular node. In Figure 6.6, activity D depends on activities B and C. Because activity E also depends on activity C, this project may only be represented with a dummy activity between C and D.

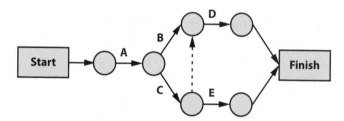

Figure 6.6 Arrow diagramming method with dummy activity

Determine Dependencies

Regarding their obligatoriness, dependencies may be classified as:

- **Mandatory dependency or hard logic**   Inherent to the physical nature of the work, or results from a contract or legal requirement. For example, you must open the door before entering the room.
- **Discretionary dependency or soft logic**   Optional dependency, frequently recommended as part of a methodology but may be changed at the behest of the project manager and team decisions. For example, the technical documentation must be finished before initiating construction. A discretionary dependency should be documented because it may be necessary to review the network diagram and its dependencies in order to compress the schedule.

Dependencies may also be grouped as:

- **External dependency**   Dependency from actions and decisions from external entities. For example, before the construction starts, a construction permit from a public entity is required.
- **Internal dependency**   Dependency from actions, decisions, or results generated within the project. For example, documentation needs to be completed before the development starts.

Apply Leads and Lags

Leads and lags can be applied to the project logical network to determine dependencies with increased accuracy. A lead is used when you need to accelerate the schedule by overlapping activities. For example, you may start developing software one week before the technical design is approved. A lag is usually used when there is a waiting time between the predecessor activity and the successor. For example, you must wait two days for the paint on the wall to dry before you can hang the painting on the wall.

Estimate Activity Resources

So far, the previous time management processes enabled us to define a schedule management approach, identify project activities, and prepare a network diagram. There are still some steps remaining before being able to develop a schedule. Naturally, we still need to estimate activity resources, as well as durations. We might not know exactly how many resources we will have, but establishing some assumption on the number and type of resource requirements is needed in order to estimate durations.

Resource Requirements

Before preparing time and cost estimates, it is important to identify the resources required to perform the project activities, including people, materials, services, and equipment. These resource requirements should specify not only the type of resource required, but also its skills, characteristics, quantity, and planned occupation throughout time.

> Estimating resource requirements is not about identifying specific individuals. It is about identifying required profiles, as well as quantities.

Resource requirements are also used as an input to plan human resource management. (See Figure 6.7.) The staffing management plan (see Chapter 9) will determine whether the organization has the ability to supply the identified resource requirements. Finally, assumptions on resources requirements will be needed in order to establish what the project will procure externally during procurement management planning.

Resource Breakdown Structure (RBS)

Estimating activity resources can also include the development of a **resource breakdown structure (RBS)**. This hierarchical graphic shows the relationship between work and the resources types, to facilitate their management. For example, you can use an RBS to understand the planned utilization of resources requiring a particular skill or to prepare a report on the scheduled utilization of resources from an external organization.

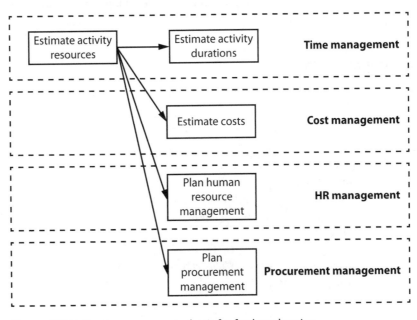

Figure 6.7 Estimate resources as a basis for further planning

Estimate Activity Durations

Estimate activity durations is the process that estimates the time periods necessary to complete the project activities, based on the available resources.

> The estimate activity durations process estimates the duration of the activities. It does not estimate the project duration.

The duration estimates are strongly constrained by the resource capacity and available skills. However, other factors may constrain the estimate, such as external factors and historical information regarding similar activities.

The activity estimates should be developed within the team to increase its accuracy and generate commitment. Additionally, it may be necessary to use published estimating data as a reference, such as productivity indexes and resource unit costs.

Duration estimates should consider the schedule risk, estimating the schedule contingency reserve that should be included in the project (see the sections on reserve analysis in this chapter and Chapter 7). While controlling the schedule throughout the project, the project manager should monitor whether the available reserve suits the risk exposure.

Estimate activity duration techniques include expert judgment, analogous estimate, parametric estimate, three-point estimate, and reserve analysis. These techniques will be described next.

Expert Judgment

Project management decisions are frequently based on the opinion of experts, such as team members, external consultants, and professional associates. During planning, expert judgment is used to estimate the activity durations based on prior experience. Estimating based on expert judgment has, however, some common drawbacks. These estimates are frequently biased by subjective factors, such as the attitude of the estimator toward the project, or its most recent experiences. Moreover, this type of estimate does not have a scientific and documented base, which does not allow the organization to improve throughout time. Hence, expert judgment should be used moderately. Ideally, expert judgment should be combined with other estimating methods and should be based on as many experts as possible to reduce bias.

Analogous Estimate

An analogous estimate assesses the duration or costs using historical information accumulated in the organization. Selecting which historical information to use and adapting it to the project context depend on the estimator's expert judgment. Although it's possible to estimate the duration of project activities by analogy, this method is usually used in a top-down approach. An analogy is used to estimate large work elements, such as a phase or a deliverable, and the estimate will be progressively broken down into smaller estimates. Later when more information becomes available and more precise estimates can be prepared, the project management team may use the analogous estimate as a reference value pertaining to historical information and management's expectations.

> An analogous estimate allows the project management team to understand management expectations.

The advantages of analogous estimates are that they:

- They can be obtained on early stages of the project.
- They require little time to develop.
- They can be used to set an acceptable range of a future detailed estimate.
- They can set expectations until a more precise estimate is defined.

The disadvantages of analogous estimates are that:

- They are not precise.
- There may not be a similar project in the organization's history.
- It is hard to justify an analogous estimate, due to its level of subjectivity.

Parametric Estimate

The parametric estimate uses a statistical relationship between historical data and project variables. For example, you can use a parametric model that estimates it takes 10 minutes to paint each square meter of wall. Preparing the estimation model for a parametric estimate requires a lot of time. However, once the model is developed, the estimate can be rapidly obtained.

A parametric estimate requires historical information to be precise.

The advantages of a parametric estimate are that it:

- It requires little time.
- It is very precise.
- It is easily justifiable, because it uses the organization historical information.
- It supports scenario analysis.

The disadvantage of a parametric estimate is that:

- A lot of time is required for developing the model.

Padding

Are you familiar with Parkinson's law? This project management law states that the work will grow to fill in the time available. Hence, if you estimate four days to paint a wall, the work will not last less than four days. Even if the wall could have been painted in three days, people tend to use the additional time available to improve the work or to respond to other professional or personal demands.

Padding is an estimating technique that attempts to manage risk by inflating the estimate. This technique is usually perceived as a poor project management practice. The reason is that according to Parkinson's law, the additional amount of time available will be spent inefficiently, instead of being used to manage risk.

Padding is not a contingency reserve (see Chapter 11).

One-Point Estimate

One-point estimate means that the estimator generates only one duration or cost value per each activity. You may be asking yourself the question: *Estimating one value per activity is not the typical approach?* Estimating one value per activity is undoubtedly frequent, but has some serious disadvantages:

- Estimating only one value per activity may inflate estimates, because the estimator tends to increase the estimate to account for risk.
- These inflated estimates may easily lose credibility, leading to trust and conflict issues with the customer and management.
- It is not possible to assess the uncertainty of each activity. If the activity duration was estimated as a one-point estimate, it is impossible to assess the probability of meeting or failing to meet the estimated value.
- Instead of using a one-point estimate, it is usually a better option to show estimates as a range of values, or as a three-point estimate.

> Although one-point estimates are not the best estimating approach, they are used throughout the book to make examples and exercises simpler.

Three-Point Estimate

A three-point estimate uses three points to determine the duration or the cost of an activity. The most common technique is the Program Evaluation and Review Technique (PERT) that uses an optimistic (O), a most likely (MP), and a pessimistic (P) value to estimate the duration of an activity.

The PERT method, created in the 1950s in a US Navy military program, was born from the observation of a pattern of behavior within project activities. When repeating an activity, it was observed that most of the time its actual duration is concentrated around a most likely value. However, it was also observed that the most likely value usually was closest to the minimum duration, rather than to the maximum. In other words, it is not likely that the activities can be significantly accelerated, but they can be significantly delayed. As a result, if all activities are estimated according to their most likely value, there is a tendency to underestimate the project's duration.

> Three-point estimates are usually more pessimistic than one-point estimates.

The **PERT method** estimates the activities' durations by considering their most likely value, but also their optimistic and pessimistic values. (See Figure 6.8.) In this method, the weighted average places more weight, with a factor of four, on the most likely value, while calculating the activities' duration.

$$\text{Activity duration estimate} = \frac{(O + P + 4 \, ML)}{6}$$

> The PERT method may be used to estimate the activities' durations or costs.

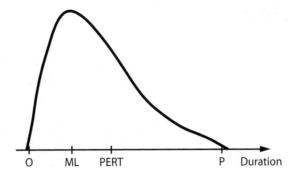

Figure 6.8 PERT probabilistic distribution

To calculate the expected range of variation, the PERT method uses the concept of **standard deviation**, or sigma, which measures the statistical dispersion from the average. The PERT method assumes that the standard deviation is calculated as:

$$\text{Activity standard deviation or sigma} = \frac{(P - O)}{6}$$

Once the standard deviation is known, the PERT method may calculate the expected range of variation considering:

$$\text{Minimum range of expected variation} = \text{activity duration estimate} - \text{activity standard deviation}$$

$$\text{Maximum range of expected variation} = \text{activity duration estimate} + \text{activity standard deviation}$$

The following example analyzes the minimum and maximum ranges of expected variation of the activities durations based on the PERT method:

	Three-Point Estimates			**Indicators**		**Range**	
Activity	**O**	**P**	**ML**	**PERT**	**Sigma**	**From**	**To**
X	2	4	12	5	1.66	3.33	6.66
Y	13	20	35	21.33	3.66	17.66	25
Z	5	10	19	10.66	2.33	8.33	13
				$\frac{(O+P+4ML)}{6}$	$\frac{(P-O)}{6}$	PERT − sigma	PERT + sigma

> PERT estimates obtained to estimate activity duration, may be used on simulation methods (such as Monte Carlo analysis) to analyze the project schedule risk.

The advantages of a PERT estimate are:

- The activity uncertainty can be assessed.
- The project uncertainty can be assessed.
- It fosters commitment, as the team is encouraged to understand the activities and share that information.
- Team members have less incentive to inflate estimates, because they are sharing information regarding the activities' risks.
- It is easier to identify the risks that are behind the uncertainty around the activities' durations.
- It minimizes the influence of human optimistic and pessimistic assessments.

Reserve Analysis

During the estimate activity durations process, the schedule contingency reserve should also be estimated. This reserve is a provision of time to deal with identified risks. The schedule contingency reserve is not incorporated into the activities' duration but is held as an independent element controlled by the project manager (see the section on reserve analysis in Chapter 7).

> This technique is shared with the estimate costs, determine budget, control costs, and control risks process.

Develop Schedule

Develop schedule is the process that calculates the start and finish dates of each activity, based on the activity duration estimates, network diagram, resource requirements, activity list, resource calendar, and scope statement. The main outcome of this process is the **project schedule**, which defines the start and finish dates for each activity. A project schedule may be developed within multiple contexts:

- At the beginning of the project, a **preliminary schedule** may be developed based on preliminary and inaccurate information. This plan will remain as preliminary until there is a confirmation of resource availability, planning iterations are performed, and the project management plan is ready.
- A **target schedule** may also be developed based on deadlines set by management or the customer.
- At more advanced planning stages, a **schedule baseline** is determined as a formally approved schedule objective.
- While controlling, the **actual schedule** includes information about the actual start and finish dates of the project activities.

The inputs to the **develop schedule** process are:

- Schedule management plan
- Activity list
- Activity attributes
- Sequences
- Durations
- Resource requirements
- Resource calendars
- Resource breakdown structure
- Scope statement
- Enterprise environmental factors
- Organizational process assets

The schedule may be developed in different formats and for different audiences:

- **Bar chart or Gantt chart**   Represents the activities schedule through horizontal bars, complemented with additional information such as durations and dates. (See Figure 6.9.) The bar charts may be represented based on detailed or high-level information. In its purest format, the bar chart does not include dependencies or resources. Its format is ideal for project monitoring, making it easier to assess variances between the baseline and actual performance. Because it's based on detailed information, it is an instrument best suitable for communicating with the team.

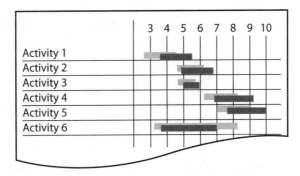

Figure 6.9 Gantt chart

- **Milestones chart** High-level schedule that identifies project milestones and their specific dates. (See Figure 6.10.) Because it's based on high-level information, it is an instrument best suitable for communicating with management or the customer.

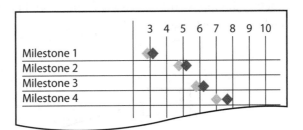

Figure 6.10 Milestones chart

- **Project schedule network diagram** When PDM is used, it may represent activities and their dependencies without a time scale. When a time scale is included, it is known as a time-scaled schedule network diagram or logic bar chart.

Supporting data used while developing the schedule should be documented for future reference. This **schedule data** can include activities, dependencies, resources, deadlines, schedule compression alternatives, risks, and reserves. **Schedule network analysis** is a very wide term that covers several analysis techniques such as the critical path method, the critical chain method, resource leveling, simulation, crashing, fast tracking, and scheduling tools.

Critical Path Method

The critical path method (CPM) plans the project duration, analyzing the longest project path, that is, the sequence of critical activities that cannot be delayed without delaying the project.

To calculate the critical path, this method uses the concept of early dates, latest dates, forward pass, backward pass, and floats. An **early date** represents the earliest date that an activity can start or finish, because all predecessor activities have been completed. Early start and early finish dates are calculated starting with the first activity and adding durations successively. This approach that moves from the project beginning to its end is known as **forward pass**. (See Figure 6.11.)

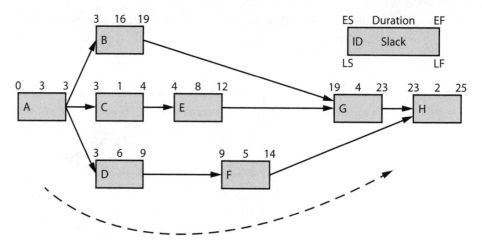

Figure 6.11 Forward pass in the critical path method

A common graphical convention used in the critical path method represents early dates at the top corners of the activities, latest dates at the bottom corners, duration on top, and the float in the center.

A **late date** represents the latest date that an activity may start or finish without delaying the project. Late start and late finish dates are calculated starting with the last project activity and subtracting durations. This approach, from the end of the project to its beginning, is known as **backward pass**. (See Figure 6.12.)

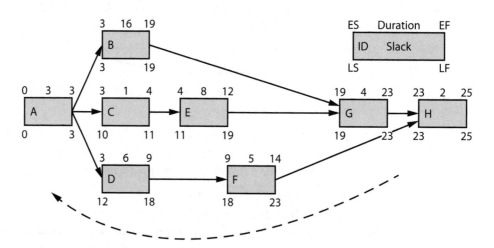

Figure 6.12 Backward pass in the critical path method

There are two types of float or slack:

- **Float (or total float)**   Time frame during which an activity may be delayed, from its early start, without delaying the project.
- **Free float (or local)**   Time frame during which an activity can be delayed without delaying the early start of a successor activity. In other words, it is the number of days that one activity can be delayed without removing total float from a successor activity.

A float (or total float) may be determined by subtracting the early start date from the late start date. A similar result could be achieved by subtracting the early finish date from the late finish date. If the last activity is scheduled to finish after a previously defined deadline or baseline, the project has a **negative float**. In such cases, the negative float of the project and activities shows how many days have to be recovered to meet the deadline or baseline. The **critical path** is the path where all activities are critical, that is, they have a zero float. (See Figure 6.13.) If the duration of a critical activity increases, the project duration will also increase.

> In a network diagram, the project critical path is the path with the longest duration.

The **near-critical path** is a sequence of activities with a low float.

> The schedule generated by the critical path method may not be feasible because the method does not consider resource availability while calculating the project dates.

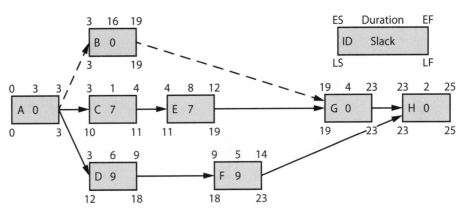

Figure 6.13 Floats and the critical path

REVIEW EXERCISE 2

Considering the information in the following table, answer the questions.

Activity	Predecessor	Duration
A		7
B		14
C	B, H	5
D	C	10
E	A	4
F	E	6
G	D, F	2
H		3

1. What is the project critical path? _____
2. What is the float of activity E? _____
3. What is the path with the largest float? _____
4. If the project deadline is set for 25, what is the float of activity A? _____
5. If the resource of activity D is replaced by another with twice the productivity, what is the new project duration? _____

> It is usually not necessary to calculate the early and late start and finish dates for each activity. You can save time by drawing only one network diagram with the activities, dependencies, and durations, recording the duration of each alternative path. For easier reading of the diagram, you can graphically represent the project's start and finish as an independent event.

REVIEW EXERCISE 3

Considering the information in Figure 6.14, answer the questions.

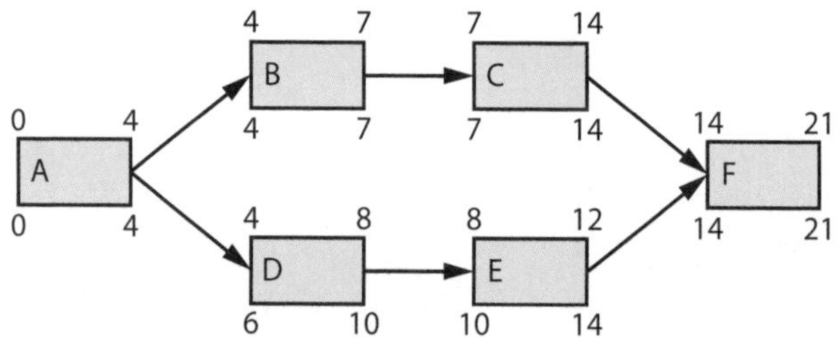

Figure 6.14 Network diagram

1. What is the project critical path? _____
2. What is the float of activity D? _____

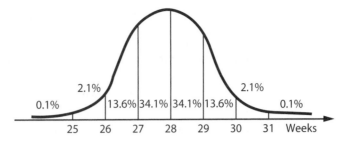

Figure 6.15 Monte Carlo probabilistic distribution example

Monte Carlo Analysis

A Monte Carlo analysis is a technique that assesses schedule risk based on the simulation of multiple project iterations. Each iteration generates a duration for all project activities, using as an input the PERT values (optimistic, most likely, and pessimistic) issued by the team. Each iteration will lead to an overall project duration, according to the dependencies of the network diagram. By completing multiple iterations, the Monte Carlo analysis can calculate the probabilistic distribution of the project duration. (See Figure 6.15.) Examples of questions that the Monte Carlo simulation may help to answer are:

- What is the probability of finishing the project within a specific project duration?
- What is the project duration that has a specific level of confidence?

Using the example in Figure 6.15, there is a 0.1 percent probability of completing the project within 25 weeks. To raise the level of confidence to 99.9 percent, you would need to estimate a total duration of 31 weeks.

> The Monte Carlo is a simulation technique because it can analyze multiple potential alternative scenarios. It uses PERT estimates as inputs.

Critical Chain Method

The critical chain analysis is a schedule network analysis technique that can be used as an alternative to the critical path method. This method is based on leveling resources and reducing multitasking. Other important elements in the critical chain analysis are buffers, used to protect the project from variances in activity durations or resource utilization.

Schedule Compression

A schedule compression is a reduction of the overall project duration, using a combination of changes in scope, time, costs, quality, human resources, and risks.
Examples of schedule compression methods are:

- **Fast tracking** The schedule is reduced by overlapping activities that would normally be done sequentially. Fast tracking usually leads to an increase in the risk of need to rework.
- **Crashing** The schedule is reduced through an increase in project resources. Crashing usually leads to higher costs caused by a decrease in resource productivity and an increase in communication costs. To minimize this cost increase, this technique includes an analysis of the available duration reduction alternatives.

The following tips may help to select the most suitable schedule compression technique on the exam:

- Do not use fast tracking if the network diagram cannot be changed or if the project risk is already too high.
- Do not use crashing if it is not possible to increase the costs.
- To compress the schedule, the project manager should concentrate on critical activities, because compressing noncritical activities has no impact on project duration.

Schedule Compression Options	Main Impact
Crashing	Increases costs
Scope reduction	Likely impact on satisfaction
Quality reduction	Likely impact on satisfaction
Fast tracking	Increases risk
Moving resources from noncritical activities to critical activities	Increases costs and may increase risk

REVIEW EXERCISE 4

The following table represents different schedule compression options, with the displayed periods representing weeks. If you need to compress the schedule in four weeks, what is the best option?

Activity	Original Duration	Crashed Duration	Crashing Cost	Critical?
C	10	2	4,000	Yes
E	8	1	3,000	Yes
H	12	2	3,000	Yes
L	9	1	1,000	Yes
X	7	3	3,000	No

Resource Optimization Techniques

The critical path method does not consider the available resources while planning the schedule. For example, even if there is just one resource to perform all the activities, the critical path method will still calculate that the project duration is eight days. As a result, the resource will be allocated above its availability. (See Figure 6.16.)

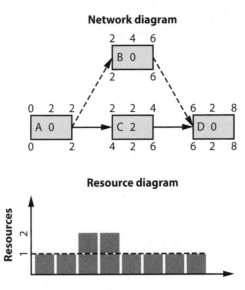

Figure 6.16 The critical path method and resource availability

Schedule development may use two techniques to optimize resource utilization:

- **Resource leveling** The priority of resource leveling is adapting resource utilization to avoid planning above capacity. In Figure 6.16, resource leveling would change resource assignment to activities B and C to avoid overallocation. Resource leveling can also be used to adapt utilization to temporary resource constraints (e.g., a resource that is available only in a specific time frame). The result of resource leveling is often delaying activities or increasing their duration.
- **Resource smoothing** The priority of resource smoothing is promoting constant resource utilization, using the flexibility provided by the activities' float. Resource smoothing outcome cannot change the project duration nor change the project critical path.

Control Schedule

Control schedule is the time management monitoring and controlling process. Through this process, people can monitor schedule performance and manage schedule changes. Controlling the schedule may include:

- Analyzing the actual schedule performance
- Comparing the actual performance with the plan
- Identifying corrective and preventive actions when there is a schedule variance
- Fast tracking or crashing the remaining work to correct a schedule delay
- Adjusting the leads and lags of future activities to prevent a schedule delay
- Forecasting schedule performance
- Identifying schedule changes
- Assessing the impact of changes
- Influencing seeking to minimize negative changes and maximize positive changes
- Ensuring that changes go through a change control system
- Maintaining a change log
- Protecting the baselines' integrity
- Communicating changes

MEMORIZATION EXERCISE

> The following exercise was designed to facilitate the memorization of the main concepts on this chapter. Assign the following definitions to a time management concept.

1. A zero duration project event with a significant meaning

   _____

2. Additional relevant information regarding activities, such as assumptions and constraints

   _____

3. Any activity on a critical path

   _____

4. Estimating method that uses the statistical relationship between historical data and project variables

   _____

5. Estimating technique that attempts to manage risk by inflating the estimate

   _____

6. Estimating the duration or costs using historical information accumulated in the organization

   _____

7. Graphical representation of the activities, events, and dependencies

   _____

8. How many days have to be recovered to meet a deadline or project baseline

   _____

9. Path where all activities are critical, that is, have a zero float

   _____

10. Main technique used to sequence activities, where boxes represent activities and arrows represent dependencies

    _____

11. Progressive elaboration planning technique that plans the short term in detail and prepares a high-level plan for the long run

    _____

12. Represents the activities schedule through horizontal bars, complemented with additional information such as durations and dates

    _____

13. Resources required to perform the project activities, including people, materials, services, and equipment

    _____

14. Schedule compression technique that reduces the project duration through an increase in project resources

    _____

15. Schedule compression that reduces the project duration by overlapping activities that would normally be done sequentially

    _____

16. Schedule network analysis technique based on resource leveling, reducing multitasking and using buffers to account for risk

    _____

17. Scheduling technique that plans the project duration, analyzing the longest project path, that is, the sequence of critical activities that may not be delayed without delaying the project

    _____

18. Technique that assesses schedule risk based on the simulation of multiple project iterations

    _____

19. Type of three-point estimate that uses optimistic, most likely, and pessimistic values to determine the duration or cost of an activity

    _____

20. Used when the schedule needs to be accelerated by overlapping activities

    _____

Process Exercises

The following exercises were designed so you could learn how to recognize the processes and understand their logical sequence. Time management processes are listed next, including their unique number in the *PMBOK Guide*:

- 6.1 Plan schedule management
- 6.2 Define activities
- 6.3 Sequence activities
- 6.4 Estimate activity resources
- 6.5 Estimate activity durations
- 6.6 Develop schedule
- 6.7 Control schedule

PROCESS EXERCISE 1

| Assign processes to the following activities. |

1. Analyze schedule variances. _____
2. Calculate probability of completing the project on a specific duration. _____
3. Compress the schedule. _____
4. Calculate the activities' start and finish dates. _____
5. Develop a resource breakdown structure. _____
6. Document activities and their characteristics. _____
7. Estimate activity durations. _____
8. Estimate the contingency reserve. _____
9. Estimate resource requirements. _____
10. Identify leads and lags. _____
11. Identify the project milestones. _____
12. Influence schedule changes. _____
13. Level the schedule. _____
14. Sequence activities according to their dependencies. _____

PROCESS EXERCISE 2

| Assign processes to the following inputs. |

Inputs   **Processes**

1. Project schedule   _____
2. Work performance data   _____
3. Activity duration estimates   _____
4. Scope baseline   _____
5. Activity list   _____
6. Project charter   _____

CHAPTER 6 EXAM

> The following questions were designed to test your knowledge on this chapter's topic. Read each question carefully, and choose the option that most accurately answers the question. Once you have completed the exam, compare your answers with the solution and read through the justification provided. Note the topics where you have the most difficulty, and make sure that you dedicate enough study time to them.

1. Which of the following is NOT part of a schedule management plan?
   A. Rules on how to estimate
   B. Performance metrics used to detect variances
   C. Activity attributes
   D. Formats used to report schedule performance

2. How would you describe the difference between a WBS and a list of activities?
   A. A WBS is focused on deliverables, while activities are focused on the work required to create those deliverables.
   B. A WBS is focused on project scope, while activities are focused on product scope.
   C. They are essentially the same.
   D. A WBS describes mandatory work, while activities are optional.

3. Which of the following sentences regarding milestones is NOT TRUE?
   A. Senior management may impose milestones.
   B. They can be used as checkpoints.
   C. They are defined during the sequence activities process.
   D. They are not work activities.

4. Which of the following statements regarding the decomposition technique is TRUE?
   A. It is used to identify the project deliverables and define activities.
   B. It is used to identify work packages and activities.
   C. It is used to describe the product and activities.
   D. It is used to identify work packages and dependencies.

5. In what plan can you document activities, events, and dependencies?
   A. WBS
   B. Activity list
   C. Network diagram
   D. Sequence activities

6. One week after starting the development of a new electronic component, you can begin technical documentation. Which of the following would you use to model such dependency?
   A. Use a start-to-start relationship with a one-week lag.
   B. Use a start-to-start relationship with a one-week lead.
   C. Use a finish-to-start relationship with a one-week slack.
   D. Use a start-to-start relationship with a one-week slack.

7. Which of the following is NOT part of the estimate activity resources process?
   A. Leveling resources
   B. Identifying potential resources
   C. Creating a resource breakdown structure
   D. Identifying resource requirements by activity

8. All of the following are advantages of using an analogous estimate EXCEPT:
   A. May be obtained on early project stages
   B. Can set expectations until a more precise estimate is defined
   C. May be used to set an acceptable range of a future detailed estimate
   D. Is a precise estimate

9. The team is struggling to estimate activity durations. Which of the following is the MOST likely cause?
   A. The project manager is not an expert in the application area.
   B. The scope is poorly defined.
   C. The team is preparing parametric estimates.
   D. A rough order of magnitude estimate was prepared during project initiation.

10. A project manager has estimated all the activities' durations and is about to move on to develop the project schedule. What has he forgotten to do?
    A. Sequence activities.
    B. Estimate resource requirements.
    C. Define communication requirements.
    D. Estimate a contingency reserve.

11. If your company has little information from previous projects, which technique should be used to estimate activity durations?
    A. Analogous estimating
    B. Bottom-up
    C. Expert judgment
    D. Parametric estimating

12. Which of the following techniques estimates durations considering the risk involved in the activities?
    A. Reserve analysis
    B. Parametric
    C. Monte Carlo
    D. Three-point estimating

13. How would you BEST describe the develop schedule process?
    A. Sequencing activities, identifying resources, estimating durations, and determining start and finish dates for each activity
    B. Determining the project duration
    C. Determining the path with the least amount of schedule flexibility
    D. Determining the start and finish dates for each activity

14. Which of the following is NOT part of the develop schedule process?
    A. Determining the scheduling methodology
    B. Crashing
    C. Having the team approve the schedule
    D. Leveling resources

15. In which of the following situations would you prefer to use a Gantt chart instead of a network diagram?
    A. Analyze multiple critical paths.
    B. Identify fast tracking opportunities.
    C. Identify the required work to complete a project milestone.
    D. Analyze schedule variances.

16. Which of the following is NOT an example of crashing the schedule?
    A. Reallocating resources from a noncritical to a critical activity
    B. Assigning additional resources to the project
    C. Reducing the duration estimates
    D. Increasing the productivity of project resources

17. You need to compress the schedule without changing the network diagram. What is the BEST thing to do?
    A. Crash the project.
    B. Use some of the project reserve.
    C. Perform a value analysis.
    D. Fast track the project.

18. You need to compress the schedule. If there are no additional resources available, how should you proceed?
    A. Crashing
    B. Resource leveling
    C. Performing a Monte Carlo analysis
    D. Fast tracking the project

19. After developing the schedule using the critical path method, some resources were planned above available capacity. Which of the following can help solve the problem?
    A. Monte Carlo
    B. Resource smoothing
    C. Resource leveling
    D. Critical chain method

20. Which scheduling technique determines project duration by analyzing activities with zero slack?
    A. Critical chain method
    B. Critical path method
    C. Sensitive analysis
    D. Resource smoothing

21. Which of the following CANNOT be used to calculate activity slack?
    A. Amount of time the activity can be delayed without delaying the project
    B. Amount of time the activity can be delayed without pushing the project behind the schedule deadline
    C. Difference between early start and late start
    D. Waiting time between activities performed in sequence

22. Which of the following options is a limitation of the critical path method during schedule development?
    A. It does not consider activity sequences.
    B. It does not consider resource availability.
    C. It does not consider a schedule contingency reserve.
    D. It is used only for cost estimating purposes.

23. You have a project with the following activities. Activity A takes 4 days and can start immediately. Activity B takes 5 days and can start immediately. Activity C must start after activity A and takes 7 days. Activity D must start after B and C and takes 8 days. Activity E must start after C and takes 10 days. Activity F must start after E and takes 2 days. Which activities are in the critical path?
    A. A, B, D
    B. A, C, E, F
    C. A, C, D, E, F
    D. A, D

24. You have a project with the following activities. Activity A takes 4 days and can start immediately. Activity B takes 5 days and can start immediately. Activity C must start after activity A and takes 7 days. Activity D must start after B and C and takes 8 days. Activity E must start after C and takes 10 days. Activity F must start after E and takes 2 days. What would be the critical activities if a less experienced resource were used for activity D so that it would actually take 12 days?
    A. A, B, D
    B. A, C, D, E, F
    C. A, C, D
    D. A, D

25. Monte Carlo is BEST used to:
    A. Estimate activity durations
    B. Assess overall schedule risk
    C. Estimate overall project costs
    D. Calculate the expected monetary value of individual risks

26. The project manager has just completed the initial project schedule. What should be done NEXT?
    A. Plan project costs.
    B. Identify assumptions and constraints.
    C. Create the WBS.
    D. Identify and describe the project deliverables.

27. Updating schedule performance information and forecast future schedule performance are part of which project management process?
    A. Plan schedule management
    B. Develop schedule
    C. Control schedule
    D. A project management information system

28. While preparing technical documentation in an engineering project, you realized that the construction effort was underestimated. After further analysis, you concluded that the approved scheduled cannot be met without redefining the project. As project manager, how should you proceed?
    A. Discuss the issue and alternative solutions with the sponsor.
    B. Eliminate scope components that were required by your organization but were not required by the customer.
    C. Request additional funding from the sponsor to compress the schedule.
    D. Review the project schedule, document the issue in a status report, and gather lessons learned regarding the schedule variance.

ANSWERS
Review Exercise 1

1. Schedule management plan
2. WBS
3. WBS dictionary
4. Deliverables, assumptions, and constraints documented on the scope statement
5. Activity templates, policies, and procedures documented on organizational process assets
6. Enterprise environmental factors

Review Exercise 2

Figure 6.17 represents the project network diagram.

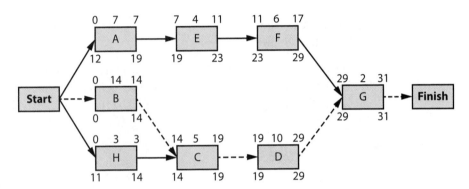

Figure 6.17 Solution

Alternative paths:

    Start-A-E-F-G-Finish: 19 days
    Start-B-C-D-G-Finish: 31 days
    Start-H-C-D-G-Finish: 20 days

1. The critical path is Start-B-C-D-G-Finish with 31 days.
2. The float of activity E is 12 days.
3. The path with the largest float is Start-A-E-F-G-Finish with 12 days.
4. If the project deadline is set for 25, activity A has a float of 6 days.
5. If the resource of activity D is substituted by another with twice the productivity, the new project duration is 26 days.

Review Exercise 3

Figure 6.18 represents the project network diagram.

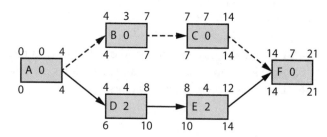

Figure 6.18 Solution

There are two alternative paths:

Start-A-B-C-F-Finish: 21 days
Start-A-D-E-F-Finish: 19 days

1. The project critical path is Start-A-B-C-F-Finish with duration of 21 days.
2. The float of activity D is 2, as the difference between the late start (6) and the early start (4), or the difference between the late finish (10) and the early finish (8).

Review Exercise 4

Crashing alternatives:

C + H, with a crashed duration of 4 weeks and a cost of 7,000
C + E + L with a crashed duration of 4 weeks and a cost of 8,000
E + H + L with a crashed duration of 4 weeks and a cost of 7,000

Therefore, options C + H or E + H + L are cheaper.

Memorization Exercise

1. Milestone
2. Activity attributes
3. Critical activity or zero float activity
4. Parametric estimate
5. Padding
6. Analogous estimate
7. Network diagram
8. Negative float
9. Critical path
10. Precedence diagramming method (PDM) or activity on node (AON)
11. Rolling wave planning
12. Gantt chart or bar chart
13. Activity resource requirements
14. Crashing
15. Fast tracking

16. Critical chain method
17. Critical path method
18. Monte Carlo
19. PERT estimate
20. Lead

Process Exercise 1

1. 6.7
2. 6.6
3. 6.6
4. 6.6
5. 6.4
6. 6.2
7. 6.5
8. 6.5
9. 6.4
10. 6.3
11. 6.2
12. 6.7
13. 6.6
14. 6.3

Process Exercise 2

1. 6.7
2. 6.7
3. 6.6
4. 6.2
5. 6.3, 6.4, 6.5, 6.6
6. 6.1

Chapter 6 Exam

1. **C** Activity attributes are identified during the define activities process. All other options may be part of a schedule management plan.

2. **A** The WBS is a deliverable-oriented treelike representation of project work. An activity list is a detailed work description, in which WBS elements are decomposed for estimating, scheduling, and monitoring purposes. Activities are not limited to product scope (answer B). A WBS is not an activity list (answer C). Activities are not optional (answer D).

3. **C** Milestones are defined during the define activities process. Therefore C is not a correct statement. All other statements are correct.

4. **B** The decomposition technique is used during the create WBS process (to identify work packages) and during the define activities process (to identify activities). All other options are not correct, because the decomposition technique is not used to identify or describe the deliverables, product, and dependencies.

5. **C** The network diagram represents the activities, events, and dependencies graphically. Answers A and B are not correct because the WBS and the activity list do not document events and dependencies. Answer D is a process, not a plan.

6. **A** There is a waiting time of one week from starting the development of the electronic component to starting the technical documentation. Therefore, there is start-to-start dependency with a one-week lag.

7. **A** Resource leveling is part of the develop project schedule process. All other options are part of the estimate activity resources process.

8. **D** The analogous estimate is usually not very precise. All other options are advantages of the analogous estimate.

9. **B** Poorly defined scope can lead to difficulties while estimating activity durations. The project manager is not necessarily an expert in the application area (answer A). Parametric (answer C) and rough order of magnitude estimates (answer D) will not lead to difficulties while estimating activity durations.

10. **D** The project manager is in the estimate activity durations process. The only available option that is part of this process is estimate a contingency reserve.

11. **C** With little information from previous projects, it's not possible to use an analogous estimate or a parametric estimate. Bottom-up estimates are used to estimates costs. Hence, expert judgment is the best option.

12. **D** Three-point estimating uses three points to determine the cost or the duration of an activity. The most commonly used three-point technique is PERT, which uses optimistic (O), most likely (ML), and pessimistic (P) estimates. The reserve analysis (answer A) and the Monte Carlo technique (answer C) are not used to estimate the durations of activities. The parametric estimate (answer B) is typically a top-down estimate used to estimate the project, phases, or major deliverables.

13. **D** The develop schedule process determines the start and finish dates for each activity based on the activities' durations, network diagram, resource requirements, activity list, resource calendar, and scope statement. Answer A refers to several time management processes. Answer B may be an indirect outcome of developing a schedule but is an incomplete definition. Answer C is describing the critical path method technique.

14. **A** Determining the schedule development methodology is part of the plan schedule management process. All other options are part of the develop project schedule process.

15. **D** The Gantt chart is primarily used to analyze schedule variances, comparing the actual schedule with the schedule baseline. You need to examine dependencies to analyze multiple critical paths (answer A), identify fast tracking opportunities (answer B), and identify the work required to complete a project milestone (answer C). The network diagram is the main tool used to examine project dependencies.

16. **C** Reducing the duration estimates, without changing other project management constraints, is not an alternative to compress the schedule. All other options are examples of crashing.

17. **A** Crashing can reduce the overall schedule duration without changing the network diagram. Using some of the project reserve (answer B) cannot reduce the project duration. Performing a value analysis (answer C) is used to reduce costs. Fast tracking (answer D) can reduce the project duration but will change the network diagram.

18. **D** Crashing (answer A) can reduce the schedule duration but would require additional resources. Resource leveling (answer B) and Monte Carlo (answer C) analysis do not compress the project schedule. Fast tracking is the only feasible option.

19. **C** Resource leveling adapts resource utilization to avoid planning above capacity. Monte Carlo is used to analyze schedule risk (answer A). Resource smoothing is used to promote constant resource utilization (answer B). The critical chain method could have avoided overallocation, but cannot be used to eliminate resource overallocations generated by the critical path method (answer D).

20. **B** The critical path method determines the project duration by identifying the longest project path, that is, the sequence of activities that cannot be delayed without delaying the project.

21. **D** A lag is a waiting time between two sequential activities. A lag is not an activity slack. All other options are alternative ways to calculate a slack.

22. **B** The critical path method does not consider the available resources while developing the project schedule. All other answers are not correct.

23. **B** Alternative paths are:

    A-C-E-F with a duration of 23 days

    A-C-D with a duration of 19 days

    B-D with a duration of 13 days

    Therefore, A-C-E-F is the critical path.

24. **B** Before the resource change, the alternative paths were:

    A-C-E-F with a duration of 23 days

    A-C-D with a duration of 19 days

    B-D with a duration of 13 days

    If the duration of activity D increases from 8 to 12 days, the new paths are:

    A-C-E-F with a duration of 23 days

    A-C-D with a duration of 23 days

    B-D with a duration of 17 days

    Therefore, two critical paths include the activities: A-C-D-E-F.

25. **B** Monte Carlo analysis assesses schedule risk based on the simulation of multiple project iterations. All other answers are not correct.

26. **A** Assumptions, constraints, WBS, and deliverables should already be established before starting schedule development. Plan project costs is the best option available.

27. **C** Updating schedule performance information and forecasting future schedule performance are part of the control schedule process. Answers A and B are not technically correct. Answer D is not a process.

28. **A** The project manager does not have the authority to eliminate scope (answer B), sacrifice the budget (answer C), or sacrifice the schedule (answer D). The project manager should analyze the options and discuss them with the sponsor.

7 Cost Management

The **cost management** area assesses the project resources in monetary values, determines the budget, and controls the costs. The following list reviews some typical examples of cost management activities:

- Planning the cost management process
- Estimating costs based on project resources
- Estimating the project cost contingency
- Determining the budget
- Reconciling the budget with the funds available
- Analyzing the project cost variances
- Forecasting the project estimate at completion
- Managing changes to the project budget

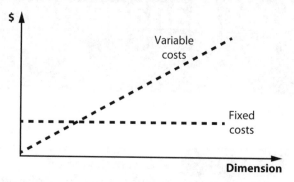

Figure 7.1 Fixed versus variable costs

Costs can be categorized in many different ways. Costs may be classified according to the project's capacity to influence them:

- **Direct costs**   Costs incurred by the project in order for it to exist. Examples of direct costs include equipment costs and team travel expenses.

- **Indirect costs**   Costs that are incurred for the benefit of more than one project and are therefore shared among different projects. Indirect costs are not controlled by the project manager, nor do they depend on project decisions. Examples of indirect costs are infrastructure, insurance, and taxes.

Costs may also be classified according to how they vary with the project's dimensions:

- **Fixed costs**   Costs that are not impacted by changes to the size of the activity or project. Examples of fixed costs are building costs and machines.

- **Variable costs**   Costs that depend on the size of the activity or project. Examples of variable costs are wages and cost of materials and electricity. (See Figure 7.1.)

Costs may also be classified according to their frequency:

- **Recurring costs**   Project costs that occur on a repetitive basis. Examples of recurring costs are wages and materials.

- **Nonrecurring costs**   Costs that occur once throughout the project and do not tend to repeat themselves. Examples of nonrecurring costs are advertising and personal computers costs.

The following table displays the cost management processes with their respective process group:

Cost Management Processes

Process	Process Group
Plan cost management	Planning
Estimate costs	Planning
Determine budget	Planning
Control costs	Monitoring and controlling

Plan Cost Management

As with all other project management areas, rules can be created to guide cost management. The cost management plan specifies the procedures, tools, and techniques used for managing costs, including:

- Cost management responsibilities
- Adopted estimating methods
- Budget changes procedures
- Methods used to measure actual costs
- Methods used to assess the status, progress, variances, and future project performance
- Acceptable range of cost variance
- The level of work breakdown structure (WBS) detail that the control and the reporting will be performed
- Reports used to control costs

Estimate Costs

Estimating costs is like taking a financial photograph of the project, giving everyone a glance at all direct and indirect costs, of all the resources required to complete the project. (See Figure 7.2.)

Resources may include work, materials, services, equipment, and financial costs. You should also consider the cost of risk, incorporating a cost contingency reserve into the overall project costs.

> Each estimated cost should be expressed in monetary values in order to be comparable with all types of resources.

While estimating costs you can document the **basis of estimates**, that is, additional details that support and justify your estimates.

A common challenge of people studying for the PMP certification exam is understanding the difference between the estimate costs process and the **determine budget** process. Planning decisions frequently involve choosing among different balances of scope, time, quality,

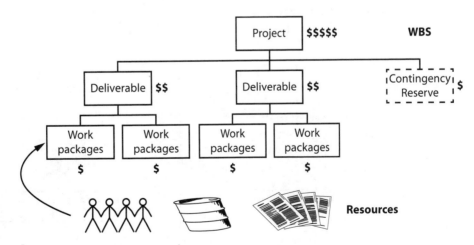

Figure 7.2 Estimate project costs

resources, communication, risks, procurement, and costs. For example, outsourcing work to an external entity may compress the schedule, but it can also have an impact on overall project costs. The purpose of the estimate costs process is to keep an updated photograph of the costs of the different planning alternatives. The purpose of the determine budget process, on the other hand, is to define one budget and a cost baseline.

The estimate costs process shares the tools and techniques used to estimate activity durations, such as expert judgment, analogous estimate, parametric estimate, reserve analysis, and three-point estimate. Additionally, it uses bottom-up estimates, cost of quality, and vendor bid analysis.

> Projects can only be estimated with 100 percent certainty once they are finished. A range of estimates is always better that a one-point estimate because it provides information about the estimate uncertainty.

Bottom-Up Estimate

A bottom-up estimate estimates the costs starting from the lowest levels of the WBS. These detailed estimates, frequently performed at the work package level, may then be summarized to obtain the cost of higher levels of the WBS. For example, to decide whether you should develop or procure a deliverable, you may need to estimate the cost of the deliverable based on the sum of the costs of its work packages. (See Figure 7.3.)

In more advanced stages of planning, when there is more and better information, this estimating method is an accurate option. At the start of the project, when the available information does not support an adequate WBS decomposition, this method tends to produce inaccurate estimates.

A bottom-up estimate can be compared with a top-down estimate to assess its quality. Top-down estimating perceives the project from a high-level perspective and comes up with a total cost (or duration) estimate. This method, typically used during project initiation, enables senior management to provide an estimate without requiring detailed project information. Top-down estimating may be based on analogous or parametric estimates (see the section on estimate activity durations in Chapter 6). Top-down estimates are not usually accurate, but they can be rapidly calculated.

The advantages of bottom-up estimates include:

- The estimate accuracy improves throughout the project, as more and better information becomes available.
- Producing bottom-up estimates helps build the team and gain project commitment.
- Estimates are easily justifiable because they are built on detailed information.
- It establishes a base that can facilitate controlling.

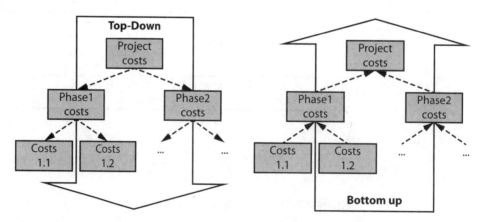

Figure 7.3 Top-down and bottom-up estimates

The disadvantages of bottom-up estimates include:

- Preparing bottom-up estimates is time consuming.
- In initial stages of the project, this estimate may not be accurate.

Vendor Bid Analysis

Project costs may be estimated based on estimates provided by vendors' proposals. Estimates received can be reviewed and detailed according to additional information available.

Heuristic

A heuristic is an accepted empirical rule. When estimating costs, you can use a heuristic as a form of expert judgment. For example, to estimate the costs of developing a software component, you can adopt a heuristic where 30 percent of the effort is assigned to analysis, 40 percent to development, and 30 percent to tests.

Reserve Analysis

Reserve analysis will be used when estimating costs and determining the budget to define the cost contingency reserve. By using the reserve analysis technique, you can identify:

- **Contingency reserve** Provision of time or costs, held by the project manager to deal with identified risks. The contingency reserve is not incorporated into the estimates of each deliverable or work package but is held as an independent element controlled by the project manager. Hence, the contingency reserve may not be used by the team without a prior authorization. The contingency reserve is created to manage the **known-unknowns**, that is, risks that were identified through the risk management processes.
- **Management reserve** Provision of time or costs, held by management, to compensate for unforeseen events. These unidentified risks, or **unknown-unknowns**, often include potential unforeseen work that is within agreed-upon project scope.

> Throughout the project, the **control costs** and **control risks** processes will verify if the available reserve is enough to account for the project's residual risks.

Estimates Precision

The estimates created at the project's start may not have the same accuracy as estimates created later. It is accepted as a good practice that the estimates are presented as a range of values, with the extent of the range being reduced as more information becomes available.

Rough order of magnitude estimates (ROM) are prepared during initiation, with large upper and lower ranges of variation. A typical order of magnitude estimate may apply a range of −25 percent to +75 percent relative to the most likely estimate. A ROM with an expected duration of 8 months corresponds to a range from 6 (−25 percent of 8) to 14 (+75 percent of 8) months.

A **budget estimate** is prepared during planning ranging from −10 percent to +25 percent from the most likely estimate. Later as better information becomes available, **definitive estimates** may be prepared ranging from −10 percent to +10 percent, or even −5 percent to +5 percent. The level of estimates precision adopted throughout the project, along with the supporting information that must be provided to support those estimates, may be defined by the project management office.

> The level of precision of the estimates may be defined on the cost management plan.

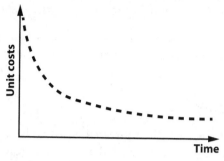

Figure 7.4 Learning curve

Learning Curve

The learning curve shows how work productivity increases as team members become familiarized with the work. (See Figure 7.4.) This means that the unit cost is reduced when the activity is repeated. The learning curve may be useful when you need to estimate work that is repeated throughout the project life cycle.

Life Cycle Costing

Planning based on the product life cycle lets you include within project decisions all the costs required to develop, operate, and discontinue the product. Project decisions may be improved by weighting all product life cycle costs, instead of only considering project costs. For example, saving on documentation costs may reduce project costs but lead to a significant increase in the product's maintenance costs.

Option	Project Cost	Maintenance Cost	Total Cost
Use better project documentation	300,000	400,000	700,000
Use worse project documentation	200,000	700,000	900,000

Sunk Costs

Sunk costs are all the costs that cannot be avoided even if the project was cancelled. These costs are relevant to assess the project performance but should not be relevant deciding whether the project should proceed or be cancelled. For example, you cannot recover the price of the ticket if you decide to leave the cinema during the presentation.

REVIEW EXERCISE 1

The type of costs considered in the estimate costs process may include:

1. _____

2. _____

3. _____

4. _____

5. _____

6. _____

7. _____

8. _____

Determine Budget

Determining the budget establishes a cost baseline that can be used to guide and assess the project. Additionally, this process determines the budget, as the financial amount required to perform the project and reconciles it with the funds available.

Cost Baseline

It has been previously discussed how project objectives can be defined in terms of scope and schedule baselines. You can also formalize a cost objective as a cost baseline, expressing the limit of funds that the project manager is authorized to use. Hence, a cost baseline is also known as authorized funds.

The cost baseline is calculated by a process of cost **aggregation** along the WBS. Work package costs are rolled up into a project estimate. Optionally, the project can establish control accounts to control performance at specific levels of the WBS (see the section on the WBS and the level of cost control in Chapter 5). Project costs are added to the contingency reserve to obtain the cost baseline (see the earlier section on reserve analysis). The management reserve, as funds held by management to account for nonidentified risks, are explicitly excluded from the cost baseline. Therefore, when you add the management reserve to the cost baseline, you obtain the project budget. (See Figure 7.5.)

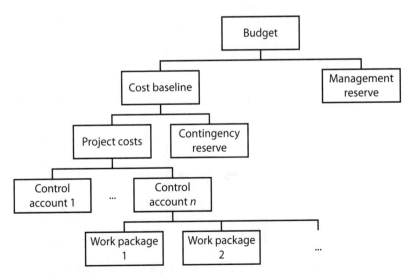

Figure 7.5 Budget composition

The cost baseline can be time-phased, according to the project schedule. This phasing allows people to compare the actual costs with the planned costs as of today, in order to detect variances and generate corrective or preventive actions. This authorized time-phased budget is also known as the **S curve**, because its graphical representation typically has the shape of an "S." (See Figure 7.6.) This "S" behavior reflects the costs being frequently less intense on early project phases, intensifying during the project intermediate phases, and slowing down at the very end.

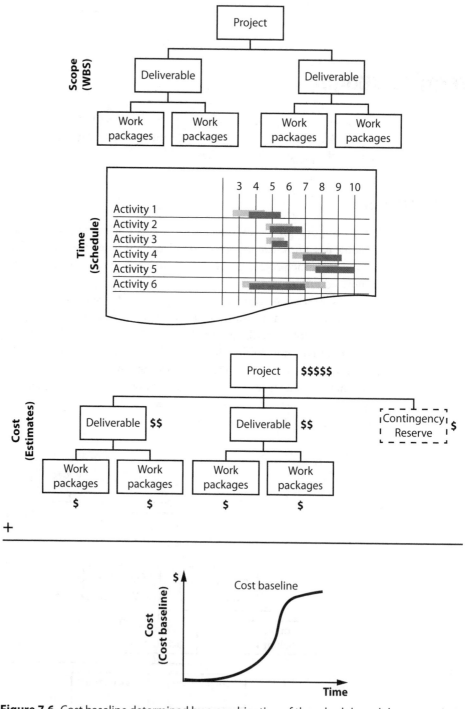

Figure 7.6 Cost baseline determined by a combination of the schedule and the cost estimates

REVIEW EXERCISE 2

Based on the following table, and assuming that all activities have a weekly cost of 5,000, prepare a time-phased budget filling in the second table.

Activity	Start	Duration in Weeks
A	0	2
B	0	4
C	3	3
D	4	2

Week	0	1	2	3	4	5
Activities performed						
Planned costs						
Accumulated costs						

Funding Limit Reconciliation

The cost baseline may also be used to compare the use of funds with the existing financial constraints. (See Figure 7.7.) This reconciliation allows you to determine if the project's planned pace adheres to imposed funding limits, or if it is necessary to slow down work, enforce date constraints, revise scope, or revise costs.

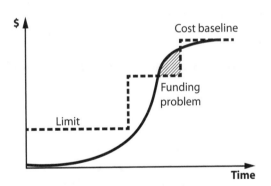

Figure 7.7 Funding limit reconciliation

Control Costs

Control costs is the cost management monitoring and controlling process that monitors cost performance and manages changes to the cost baseline.

Controlling costs activities may include:

- Determining the actual costs
- Comparing the work performed with the cost baseline
- Comparing the work performed with the actual costs
- Comparing the actual costs with the authorized funds
- Estimating future performance
- Identifying cost changes and their impact
- Encouraging positive cost changes and discouraging negative changes
- Ensuring that changes go through a change control system
- Maintaining a change log
- Protecting the baselines' integrity
- Communicating changes

Traditional Control Process Limitations

Let's use a project example to analyze how the traditional control process may lack sophistication in certain ways. This project example consists of five deliverables. Each is budgeted for 100 and should take a week. At the end of the third week, 100 was spent on deliverable A, 150 on B, and 150 on C. Deliverables A, B, and C were completed, and deliverables D and E have not been initiated. Analyzing the schedule, at the end of the third week, deliverable A has been completed as planned, deliverable B took one week and a half, and deliverable C was completed in half a week. The team now believes that the project schedule delay may be recovered by completing activities D and E in half a week each. (See Figure 7.8.)

What can you conclude about the project's performance? Is the project behind schedule, on target, or ahead of schedule? Is the project under budget, on budget, or over budget?

Starting the analysis in the context of schedule, which of the following statements is more accurate?

A. The project is on schedule because it will end on the date initially planned.
B. The project is late, but you believe that it will be possible to recover from that schedule delay.
C. The project is late because it performed less work than planned.

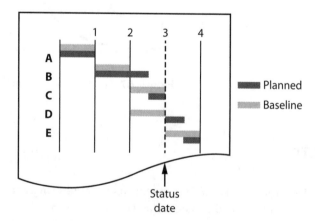

Figure 7.8 Traditional control process limitations

Maybe all these options appear justifiable, but only one of them is correct. Following a traditional control process, you can be tempted to choose option B. Just by observing the schedule, you have no basis to question the feasibility of the schedule recovery planned for the last week.

Analyzing the project in the context of cost performance, which of the following statements looks more accurate?

A. The project is over budget because it spent 400 in completing activities budgeted for 300.
B. The project is on budget, because at the end of week 3, it spent 400 as planned.

If you adopt a simple comparison between the accumulated budget at the end of the third week (400) and the accumulated actual cost in the same period (400), you can be tempted to conclude that the project is on budget. Next, you will analyze how the earned value management technique will answer these questions.

Earned Value Management

Earned value management (EVM) is a consistent cost control technique that analyzes project performance by combining and integrating scope, time, and costs assessment. EVM is based on three base metrics: planned value, actual cost, and earned value.

- **Planned value (PV)** assesses the progress planned up to a specific date. This value is calculated by analyzing the budgeted cost of the work scheduled to be accomplished up to that date. If activities A, B, C, and D should already have been completed according to the schedule baseline and were budgeted as 100 each, then the total planned value is 400.
- **Actual cost (AC)** assesses the costs actually incurred up to a specific date. If a total of 400 was spent on activities A, B, and C, then the total actual cost is 400.
- **Earned value (EV)** assesses the progress performed up to a specific date. This value is calculated by analyzing the budget cost of the work completed by that date. If activities A, B, and C are complete and were budgeted as 100 each, then the total earned value is 300.

REVIEW EXERCISE 3

> **Based on the following data, how would you interpret the project performance? What is the percentage of work completed?**
>
> Planned value (PV) = 400
> Actual cost (AC) = 400
> Earned value (EV) = 300

Using the base metrics, the EVM technique calculates variance metrics that represent positive or negative variances to the plan. The main variance metrics used by the EVM technique are (see Figure 7.9):

- **Cost variance (CV)** Difference between the earned value and the actual cost. A positive variance means savings. A negative variance means a cost overrun.

$$CV = EV - AC$$

Metrics		Time		
		SV > 0 & SPI > 1.0	SV = 0 & SPI = 1.0	SV < 0 & SPI < 1.0
Cost	CV > 0 & CPI > 1.0	Ahead of schedule Savings	On schedule Savings	Behind schedule Savings
	CV = 0 & CPI = 1.0	Ahead of schedule On budget	On schedule On budget	Behind schedule On budget
	CV < 0 & CPI < 1.0	Ahead of schedule Overrun	On schedule Overrun	Behind schedule Overrun

Figure 7.9 Earned value management (EVM) metrics

- **Schedule variance (SV)** Difference between the earned value and the planned value. A positive schedule variance means that the project is ahead of schedule. A negative schedule variance means the project is late.

$$SV = EV - PV$$

Assessing variances in monetary values may not be easily understood, particularly when addressing schedule variances. Furthermore, variances expressed in monetary values do not adequately translate the relative size of the variance. For example, a variance of 10 is very significant if the budget is 20, but is far less significant if the budget is 200. To translate the project performance to relative values, EVM uses two indexes:

- **Cost performance index (CPI)** Represents efficiency through the ratio of earned value to actual costs. A favorable value, greater than 1, shows that the costs are under budget. An unfavorable value, lower than 1, shows that the costs are over budget

$$CPI = \frac{EV}{AC}$$

- **Schedule performance index (SPI)** Represents speed through the ratio of earned value to planned value. A favorable value, greater than 1, shows that the project is ahead of schedule. An unfavorable value, lower than 1, shows that the project is late.

$$SPI = \frac{EV}{PV}$$

Any control process, whether or not it uses the EVM technique, compares the approved plan with the actual performance. When you analyze costs, this comparison uses:

- **Budget at completion (BAC)** Budgeted value for the project or activity total costs
- **Actual cost (AC)** All incurred costs, direct and indirect, up to a specific date
- **Estimate to complete (ETC)** Estimated cost to complete a project or activity

- **Estimate at completion (EAC)** The expected total cost of an activity or project when the work is completed. Note that this estimate is the sum of the actual cost and the estimate to complete

$$EAC = AC + ETC$$

- **Variance at completion (VAC)** Difference between the budget at completion and the estimate at completion. A positive variance means a favorable cost performance.

$$VAC = BAC - EAC$$

Budget at Completion (BAC) (1)	*Actual Cost (AC)(2)*	*Estimate at Completion (ETC)(3)*	*Estimate at Completion (EAC) (4) = (2) + (3)*	*Variance at Completion (VAC) (5) = (1) − (4)*
500	400	200	600	−100

Example of a Control Table

Forecasting future cost performance is part of the control system's role. A traditional control system determines the estimate at completion (EAC) based on the actual cost (AC) and an estimate to complete (ETC) obtained from the team. The EVM technique may add accuracy to this forecast by using information regarding the project performance to date to estimate the ETC and EAC. (See Figure 7.10.)

There are four possible approaches to estimate future performance:

- **New estimate** Future work will be estimated again, ignoring the performance to date.

$$EAC = AC + ETC$$

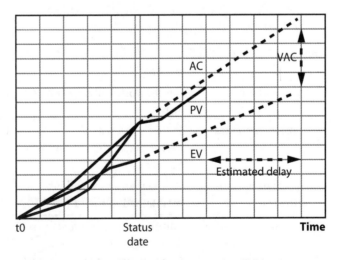

Figure 7.10 Forecasting performance using EVM

- **Work performed at the budgeted rate or atypical estimate**   This approach assumes that the past cannot be used as a reference to estimate future performance. Future work will be performed according to the budgeted rate. Hence, the estimate at completion is the sum of the actual cost and an estimate to complete determined by the budgeted rate.

$$ETC = BAC - EV$$

$$EAC = AC + ETC = AC + (BAC - EV)$$

- **Work performed at the present CPI, typical or optimistic estimate**   This approach assumes that past performance will be maintained in the future. Hence, the estimate at completion is the sum of the actual cost and an estimate to complete that takes into account the performance to date.

$$ETC = \frac{(BAC - EV)}{CPI}$$

$$EAC = AC + ETC = AC + \frac{(BAC - EV)}{CPI} = \frac{BAC}{CPI}$$

- **Estimate considering both CPI and SPI or pessimistic estimate**   This approach assumes that future performance will take into account the past cost and schedule performance. The idea is that the future cost performance may be worse than the present performance when the project is behind schedule.

$$ETC = \frac{(BAC - EV)}{(CPI \times SPI)}, \text{ when SPI} < 1$$

$$EAC = AC + ETC = AC + \frac{(BAC - EV)}{(CPI \times SPI)}, \text{ when SPI} < 1$$

> Unless specifically requested otherwise, on the exam use the typical estimate to estimate the EAC. The formula $EAC = \frac{BAC}{CPI}$ is easy to memorize. Even if the question on the exam asks you to calculate the ETC, you may calculate first the EAC and subtract the AC, that is, $ETC = EAC - AC$.

Method	Meaning	Formula
New estimate	Future work will be estimated again.	$EAC = AC + ETC$
Atypical estimates	Future work will be performed at the rate initially budgeted.	$EAC = AC + (BAC - EV)$
Typical or optimistic estimates	Past performance will be maintained in the future.	$EAC = AC + \frac{(BAC - EV)}{CPI} = \frac{BAC}{CPI}$
Pessimistic estimates	Future cost performance may be worse than the present performance when the project is behind schedule.	$EAC = AC + \frac{(BAC - EV)}{(CPI \times SPI)}$ and SPI < 1

The EVM technique may also use a to-complete performance index (TCPI) as the performance required in the future in order to achieve a previously defined objective. This desirable performance in the future may be calculated by using one of two alternative approaches:

- **TCPI based on BAC** Performance required of the remaining work in order to meet the cost baseline.

$$\text{TCPI} = \frac{(\text{BAC} - \text{EV})}{(\text{BAC} - \text{AC})}$$

- **TCPI based on EAC** The TCPI based on BAC is usually a theoretical concept, with little practical application. If the project accumulated unfavorable cost variances, it is not likely that those can be recovered in the future. The TCPI based on EAC is far more interesting. It demonstrates the performance required of the remaining work in order to meet a new objective that was previously reviewed and agreed upon by management.

$$\text{TCPI} = \frac{(\text{BAC} - \text{EV})}{(\text{EAC} - \text{AC})}$$

REVIEW EXERCISE 4

Based on the following table, how would you interpret the project performance? Fill in the second table, specifying the formula, result, and meaning.

	A	B	C	D
Budgeted	80,000	100,000	40,000	80,000
Planned	82%	70%	45%	35%
Performed	88%	50%	50%	5%
Actual costs	75,000	60,000	25,000	40,000

Metric	Formula	Result	Meaning
BAC			
EV			
PV			
AC			
CV			
SV			
CPI			
SPI			
EAC			
ETC			
VAC			

REVIEW EXERCISE 5

> Activity A was budgeted as 400, is 100 percent complete, should have been completed on day 1, and has an actual cost of 300. Activity B was budgeted as 50, is 50 percent completed, should have been completed on day 2, and has an actual cost of 50. Activity C was budgeted as 500, is 75 percent completed, should have been started and finished on day 3, and has an actual cost of 400. The total budget is 2,000.

1. What is the project planned value on day 2?
2. What is the project CPI?
3. What is the project cost variance?
4. What is a project variance at completion?
5. What is the project percent of completion?

Rules of Performance Measurement

EVM uses different approaches to assess the performance of accomplished work. The most common approaches are:

- **Fixed-formula** A percentage is assigned when the work package starts, and the rest is assigned when it finishes. An example of a fixed-formula is the 20–80 percent rule that assigns 20 percent progress when a work package starts and the remaining 80 percent when it finishes. This approach may be applied to small work packages that have durations of less than one or two performance measurement periods. Most projects have a weekly performance measurement period.
- **Percentage complete** The performance is assessed through a subjective assessment of the percentage of work completed.
- **Weighted milestones** Progress is assigned by meeting previously defined milestones. Work packages are broken down into specific milestones to reflect the way the work is organized. Each milestone is assigned to a percentage of work completion. For example, the project may define that producing a document is 20 percent complete when all the preparation work is done, 60 percent when the document is delivered, and 100 percent when the document is approved. This approach is appropriate for large work packages.
- **Percentage complete with milestone gates** The progress is measured through a subjective assessment of the percentage of work completion. However, this estimate is constrained to previously established milestones. This approach is appropriate for large work packages.
- **Level of effort (LOE)** The performance is measured indirectly by the performance of other work packages or proportionally to the elapsed time. For example, the progress of the documentation quality control may be proportional to the documentation progress.

REVIEW EXERCISE 6

> The progress of ongoing activities is frequently overestimated. What are the most important motives that lead to this problem?

1. _____

   _____

2. _____

   _____

3. _____

   _____

4. _____

   _____

5. _____

   _____

MEMORIZATION EXERCISE

> The following exercise was designed to facilitate the memorization of the main concepts on this chapter. Assign the following definitions to a cost management concept.

1. A project management technique that measures performance combining and integrating measurements of scope, schedule, and cost

   _____

2. Approved version of the authorized time-phased budget

   _____

3. Additional details that support and justify your estimates

   _____

4. Graphical representation of an authorized time-phased budget

   _____

5. Comparing the use of funds with the existing financial constraints

   _____

6. Costs actually incurred up to a specific date

   _____

7. Costs that are incurred for the benefit of more than one project and are therefore shared among different projects

_____

8. Costs that are not impacted by changes on the size of the activity or project

_____

9. Estimate prepared during planning ranging from −10 percent to +25 percent from the most likely estimate

_____

10. Estimates prepared during the initiating process group, with large upper and lower ranges of variation

_____

11. Estimates prepared during project execution with a precision ranging from −10 percent to +10 percent, or even −5 percent to +5 percent

_____

12. Estimates the costs starting from the lowest levels of the WBS

_____

13. Estimating technique that produce an overall estimate that later can be decomposed in to smaller components

_____

14. Include within project decisions all the costs required to develop, operate, and discontinue the product

_____

15. Project costs that occur on a repetitive basis

_____

16. Summing the cost estimates of the WBS work packages and the risk contingency reserve along the WBS

_____

17. Technique used to define the contingency reserve when estimating durations and costs. While controlling, it can be used to compare existing reserve with remaining risk.

_____

18. Assessing work performance by assigning a percentage of progress when the work package starts and the rest when it finishes

_____

19. Assessing work performance by assigning specific percentages when meeting previously defined milestones

_____

20. Work productivity increasing as the worker becomes familiarized with the work

_____

Process Exercises

The following exercises were designed so you could learn how to recognize the processes and understand their logical sequence. Cost management processes are listed next, including their unique number in the *PMBOK Guide*:

- 7.1 Plan cost management
- 7.2 Estimate costs
- 7.3 Determine budget
- 7.4 Control costs

PROCESS EXERCISE 1

Assign processes to the following activities.

1. Analyze project reserves. _____
2. Compare the performance with the cost baseline. _____
3. Delay work to reconcile resource utilization with existing constraints. _____
4. Determine the project actual costs. _____
5. Determine the rules to measure ongoing work performance. _____
6. Document the basis of estimates. _____
7. Establish the cost baseline. _____
8. Estimate costs. _____
9. Estimate future performance. _____
10. Identify changes to the cost baseline. _____

PROCESS EXERCISE 2

Assign processes to the following inputs.

1. Basis of estimates _____
2. Work performance data _____
3. Activity cost estimates _____
4. Project funding requirements _____
5. Project charter _____

CHAPTER 7 EXAM

The following questions were designed to test your knowledge on this chapter's topic. Read each question carefully, and choose the option that most accurately answers the question. Once you have completed the exam, compare your answers with the solution and read through the justification provided. Note the topics where you have the most difficulty, and make sure you dedicate enough study time to them.

1. During project execution, some team members are discussing how to measure work performance. One team member is arguing that milestones with weighted values should be used, and another wants to use a 50-50 rule. As project manager, what can you recommend to the team members?
   A. They should use the method required by the customer.
   B. They should follow the cost management plan.
   C. Team members should not worry about measuring work performance. That responsibility belongs to the project manager.
   D. They should use earned value management (EVM) instead of measuring work performance.

2. To address a cost overrun, you should focus on:
   A. Fixed and direct costs
   B. Variable and fixed costs
   C. Fixed and indirect costs
   D. Variable and direct costs

3. The project manager wants to estimate the cost of a deliverable based on the costs of the work packages required to complete it. Which estimating technique is being used?
   A. Top down
   B. Bottom up
   C. Aggregation
   D. Padding

4. You know that to paint a wall it takes an average of 5 centiliters of paint per square meter of surface painted. This is an example of what type of estimating technique?
   A. Learning curve
   B. Parametric
   C. Analogous
   D. Life cycle costing

5. On a recently initiated engineering project, management requested a project cost estimate. How should the project manager proceed if he does not have enough information to provide an accurate estimate?
   A. Include a contingency reserve in the project budget.
   B. Provide a rough order of magnitude estimate (ROM).
   C. Provide a budget estimate.
   D. Do not provide the estimate until the scope is defined.

6. Which of the following is NOT relevant when deciding whether to proceed with a troubled project?
   A. CPI
   B. Sunk costs
   C. The estimated project cash flows
   D. ETC

7. Cost estimates should:
   A. Be prepared only at work package level
   B. Be prepared as a range of values
   C. Be documented in the cost management plan
   D. Include a contingency reserve in each activity to account for risk

8. The organization project management office (PMO) is progressively introducing parametric models to support the planning effort. When should parametric estimating be adopted?
   A. When a significant part of the project has already been completed
   B. When it can be applied to every work package
   C. When there is sufficient historical data
   D. When it is used to calculate the cost contingency reserve

9. The purpose of life cycle costing is to include _____ within project decisions.
   A. Project life cycle costs
   B. Operational costs
   C. Project and operational costs
   D. Costs estimated with a rolling wave approach

10. Which of the following sentences regarding a contingency reserve is NOT correct?
    A. It should not be hidden from management.
    B. It is part of the budget.
    C. It is used to manage unknown-unknowns.
    D. It is managed by the project manager.

11. The project manager has just determined cost estimates and is about to move into the next planning process. What has she forgotten to do?
    A. Determine funding requirements.
    B. Provide a cost baseline.
    C. Provide the project CPI.
    D. Provide the basis of estimates.

12. After you submitted the project management plan for approval, management asks you for a 5 percent reduction on overall project costs. What is the BEST thing to do?
    A. Perform a value analysis.
    B. Reduce the estimates to meet the 5 percent reduction target, but document the associated risks.
    C. Provide the most accurate estimate.
    D. Do not reduce the activity cost estimates, but decrease the project contingency reserve to meet the 5 percent reduction target.

13. The cost baseline is an output of which project management process?
    A. Estimate costs
    B. S curve
    C. Determine budget
    D. Control costs

14. The cost baseline can be illustrated as:
    A. Influence curve
    B. S curve
    C. Cost aggregation curve
    D. Life cycle curve

15. When should the cost baseline be established?
    A. As soon as the cost estimates are complete
    B. Just before starting project execution
    C. When required by the sponsor
    D. After completing all the planning processes and performing the necessary planning iterations

16. In which process are funding requirements determined?
    A. Estimating costs
    B. Determining budget
    C. Controlling costs
    D. Funding limit reconciliation

17. Which of the following should NOT be included in the cost baseline?
    A. Indirect costs
    B. Financial costs
    C. Management reserve
    D. Labor costs

18. The project manager is using earned value analysis to determine project performance. Which project management process is she performing?
    A. Determine budget
    B. Monitoring and controlling
    C. Control costs
    D. Cost management

19. You want to know what was originally budgeted for each month of the project. What performance metric should you use?
    A. AC
    B. EV
    C. PV
    D. Budget

20. If EV = 1,000, AC = 1,000, PV = 1,200, how is the project performance?
    A. On budget and behind schedule
    B. On budget and ahead of schedule
    C. Over budget and behind schedule
    D. There is not enough information.

21. The project performance report is showing that the actual costs are 180,000 and the planned value is 120,000. How would you describe the project performance?
    A. There is a cost overrun.
    B. It is ahead of schedule.
    C. It is behind schedule.
    D. There is not enough information to assess performance.

22. If the project CPI is 0.8 and the SPI is 1.1, how is the project performance?
    A. The project is behind schedule.
    B. The project has a positive cost variance.
    C. The project has a TCPI greater than 1.
    D. The project has an unfavorable rate of return.

23. When the BAC equals the EV:
    A. The project has no more funding.
    B. The project should have been completed.
    C. The project is complete.
    D. The project has a cost overrun.

24. What does a CPI of 1.1 represent?
    A. The SV is positive.
    B. The CV is negative.
    C. The EAC is under the BAC.
    D. The EAC is over the BAC.

25. The project manager determined that a problem with electricity during hardware installation was the cause of an unfavorable CPI. The electricity problem can no longer occur. Which of the following should the project manager use to calculate the project EAC?
    A. Typical EAC
    B. Atypical EAC
    C. Other projects as a reference
    D. Pessimistic EAC

26. A TCPI of 1.2 means:
    A. There is a cost overrun.
    B. The project is saving money.
    C. The project is behind schedule.
    D. The project's benefits exceed its costs.

27. Which of the following options would you use to assess the performance of a work package with a duration of less than one control period?
    A. Weighted milestones
    B. Percentage complete with milestone gates
    C. Fixed formula
    D. Level of effort

ANSWERS

Review Exercise 1

1. Work performed in the project
2. Materials used
3. Costs with subcontracting
4. Other direct costs such as travelling and accommodations
5. Indirect costs such as management oversight costs, electricity, and building rents
6. Cost of risk
7. Profit
8. Financial costs

Review Exercise 2

Week	0	1	2	3	4	5
Activities performed	A, B	A, B	B	B, C	C, D	C, D
Planned costs	10,000	10,000	5,000	10,000	10,000	10,000
Accumulated costs	10,000	20,000	25,000	35,000	45,000	55,000

Review Exercise 3

The project is late, because the value of the work completed (EV) is lower than the value of the work planned (PV). The project is over budget, because the value of the work completed (EV) is lower than the actual cost (AC). The project percentage of work completed is 60%, calculated as:

$$\text{Progress} = \frac{\text{EV}}{\text{Budget}} = \frac{300}{500} = 60\%$$

Review Exercise 4

Metric	Formula	Result	Meaning
BAC	Nonapplicable	300,000	Budgeted cost
EV	% performed × budget	144,400	Budgeted cost of the work completed
PV	% planned × budget	181,600	Budgeted cost of the work scheduled
AC	Nonapplicable	200,000	All incurred costs
CV	EV – AC	–55,600	Difference between the earned value and the actual cost
SV	EV – PV	–37,200	Difference between the earned value and the planned value
CPI	$\frac{\text{EV}}{\text{AC}}$	0.72	Represents efficiency, through the ratio of earned value to actual costs
SPI	$\frac{\text{EV}}{\text{PV}}$	0.80	Represents speed, through the ratio of earned value to planned value
EAC	$\frac{\text{BAC}}{\text{CPI}}$	415,512	Expected total cost when the project is completed.
ETC	EAC – AC	215,512	Estimated cost to complete the project.
VAC	BAC – EAC	–115,512	Difference between the budget at completion and the estimate at completion

Review Exercise 5

	BAC	%	AC	PV	EV	CPI	EAC	ETC	VAC
A	400	100	300	400	400	1.3	300	0	100
B	50	50	50	50	25	0.5	100	50	−50
C	500	75	400	0	375	0.94	533.3	133.3	−33.3
. . .									
Total	2,000	40%	750	450	800	1.07	1,875	1,125	125

1. 450 as the sum of the planned values on day 2
2. 1.06 as $\dfrac{800}{750}$ $\left(\text{CPI} = \dfrac{\text{EV}}{\text{AC}}\right)$
3. 50 as 800 − 750 (CV = EV − AC)
4. 125 as 2,000 − 1,875 (BAC − EAC)
5. 40% as $\dfrac{800}{2,000}$ $\left(\dfrac{\text{EV}}{\text{BAC}}\right)$

Review Exercise 6

1. Without other reference information, the progress is measured according to elapsed time. The team perceives that the progress is overvalued only when it approaches the planned finish date.
2. People may want to deny that there are performance problems, wishing that the reality were different.
3. Human nature may anchor the team to an initial estimate, denying the problem until almost the very end.
4. The team may not reveal an unfavorable variance, in order to avoid conflict.
5. Complex problems usually accumulate in the final stages of the work packages.

Memorization Exercise

1. Earned value management (EVM)
2. Cost baseline
3. Basis of estimate
4. S curve
5. Funding limit reconciliation
6. Actual cost (AC)
7. Indirect cost
8. Fixed cost
9. Budget estimate
10. Rough order of magnitude estimate (ROM)
11. Definitive estimates
12. Bottom-up estimates
13. Top-down estimate
14. Life cycle costing
15. Recurring cost
16. Cost aggregation
17. Reserve analysis
18. Fixed-formula rule
19. Weighted milestones rule
20. Learning curve

Process Exercise 1

1. 7.2
2. 7.4
3. 7.3
4. 7.4
5. 7.1
6. 7.2
7. 7.3
8. 7.2
9. 7.4
10. 7.4

Process Exercise 2

1. 7.3
2. 7.4
3. 7.3
4. 7.4
5. 7.1

Chapter 7 Exam

1. **B** The team should follow the procedures adopted in the cost management plan, including the rules used to measure work performance. Adopted procedures are not necessarily those that were required by the customer (answer A). The team can be involved in measuring accomplished work (answer C). EVM is not a substitute for measuring work performance (answer D).

2. **D** The project manager can only reduce direct and variable costs. Therefore, D is the only valid option.

3. **B** A bottom-up estimate estimates the costs starting from the lowest levels of the WBS. These detailed estimates, frequently performed at the work package level, may then be summarized to obtain the cost of higher levels of the WBS. Aggregation is used in the determine budget process (answer C). Top-down estimates (answer A) and padding (answer D) cannot be used to roll-up costs throughout the WBS.

4. **B** A parametric estimate uses a statistical relationship between historical information and project variables to build a mathematical model. In this case, the model relates centiliters of paint with the surface area painted.

5. **B** A ROM is prepared during initiation, when there is not enough information to produce a more precise estimate. This ROM can be used to set initial expectations. Answers A and C are not correct because the project manager does not have enough information to prepare a detailed and accurate estimate. Answer D is not realistic.

6. **B** Sunk costs are all the costs that cannot be recovered. All other options can be relevant to the decision.

7. **B** Preparing estimates as a range of values provides information regarding the most likely estimate and the existing uncertainty around the estimate. All other statements are not correct.

8. **C** The parametric estimate requires historical information to be precise. Answer A is not correct, because a parametric estimate can be used in the beginning of the project. Answers B and D are not correct, because the parametric estimate is not usually used to estimate work packages and contingency reserves.

9. **C** Life cycle costing includes development, operational, and disposal costs on project decisions. Hence, project decisions should improve by taking into account the costs of the complete product life cycle, instead of just considering the project life cycle. Answers A and B are incomplete, because they are only concerned with either the project or the operation costs.

10. **C** Unknown-unknowns are not managed by the contingency reserve. They are managed by the management reserve. All other statements are correct.

11. **D** The project manager is in the estimate costs process. The only available option that is part of this process is to provide the basis of estimates. Answers A and B are part of the determine budget process. Answer C is part of the control costs process.

12. **C** A value analysis (answer A) could reduce costs, but the project manager should already have done everything possible to reduce costs before submitting the estimates for approval. Reducing the estimates (answer B) and decreasing the contingency reserve (answer D) would not be an acceptable option from the project manager. Providing the most accurate estimate is the best option.

13. **C** The cost baseline is an output of the determine budget process.

14. **B** The S curve shape is the natural consequence of the typical resource consumption rate. Costs are frequently less intense on early project phases, intensify during the project intermediate phases, and slow down at the very end.

15. **D** Project baselines can only be established after planning all knowledge areas and performing the planning iterations required to ensure project integration. Therefore, answers A and C are not correct. Answer B is not correct, because project execution is started before the baselines are defined.

16. **B** Project funding requirements are identified during the determine budget process. Answers A and C are not technically correct. Answer D is not a process.

17. **C** Management reserve is a provision of costs held by management to compensate for unforeseen events. This provision of costs is part of the budget but is not part of the cost baseline. Indirect costs, financials costs, and labor costs can be part of the cost baseline.

18. **C** EVM is part of the control costs process. Answer A is not technically correct. Answer B is a process group, and answer D is a knowledge area.

19. **C** Planned value (PV) is the budgeted cost of the work scheduled to be completed. Answers A and B are technically incorrect. Answer D is not the best answer because the budget is not a performance measurement baseline. The budget is the cost baseline plus the management reserve.

20. **A** The project is on budget because the earned value (EV) equals the actual cost (AC). The project is behind schedule because the earned value (EV) is less than the planned value (PV).

21. **D** Without earned value information, it is not possible to assess schedule and cost performance.

22. **C** TCPI is the performance required of the remaining work in order to meet the cost baseline. An unfavorable cost performance (CPI < 1) means that the TCPI is greater than 1. Answers A and B are not correct, because the project is ahead of schedule (SPI > 1) and has a negative cost variance (CPI < 1). Answer D is not correct, because there is not enough information about the project internal rate of return.

23. **C** When all the work is completed, the earned value (EV) equals the budget at completion (BAC). Answers A and D are not correct because there is no information regarding actual costs. Answer B is not correct because the project may have finished ahead of schedule.

24. **C** If the cost performance index (CPI) is greater than 1, there is a favorable cost performance. When the cost performance is favorable, the cost variance (CV) is positive and the estimate at completion (EAC) is less than the budget at completion (BAC). Hence,

C is the only valid answer. You could have reached the same conclusion by following the formula EAC = BAC / CPI. If CPI > 1, then EAC < BAC.

25. **B** If the electricity problem can no longer occur, you can assume that the past cannot be used as a reference to estimate future performance. Therefore, the project manager should use an atypical estimate at completion (EAC).

26. **A** The to complete performance index (TCPI) is the performance required in the future in order to meet the cost baseline. A TCPI greater than 1 means that the project had an unfavorable cost performance in the past.

27. **C** A fixed formula may be applied to small work packages that have durations of less than one or two performance measurement periods. Weighted milestones (answer A) and percentage complete with milestone gates (answer B) are typically used in larger work packages. Level of effort (answer D) is used when you want to measure performance indirectly by the performance of another work package or proportionally to the elapsed time.

8 Quality Management

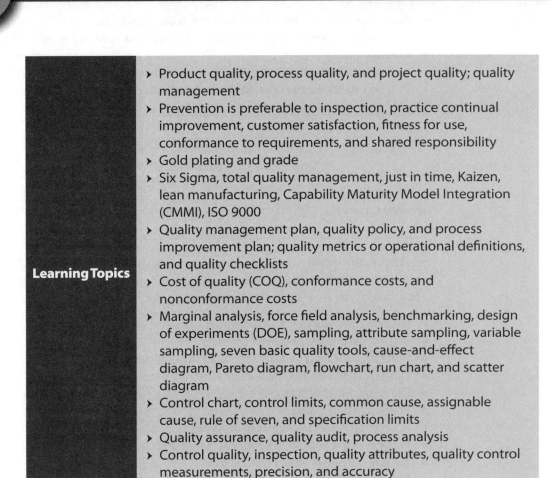

Learning Topics

> Product quality, process quality, and project quality; quality management
> Prevention is preferable to inspection, practice continual improvement, customer satisfaction, fitness for use, conformance to requirements, and shared responsibility
> Gold plating and grade
> Six Sigma, total quality management, just in time, Kaizen, lean manufacturing, Capability Maturity Model Integration (CMMI), ISO 9000
> Quality management plan, quality policy, and process improvement plan; quality metrics or operational definitions, and quality checklists
> Cost of quality (COQ), conformance costs, and nonconformance costs
> Marginal analysis, force field analysis, benchmarking, design of experiments (DOE), sampling, attribute sampling, variable sampling, seven basic quality tools, cause-and-effect diagram, Pareto diagram, flowchart, run chart, and scatter diagram
> Control chart, control limits, common cause, assignable cause, rule of seven, and specification limits
> Quality assurance, quality audit, process analysis
> Control quality, inspection, quality attributes, quality control measurements, precision, and accuracy

If you are familiar with some of the following questions, then you are ready to explore project quality management: *Are we delivering the right product? What is the right product? Are we delivering the product the customer needs? Are we doing the work properly? Can we improve? Is project performance aligned with the objectives?*

Quality

Quality assesses how well the requirements are being met, and it can be decomposed into the following:

- **Project quality** assesses if the project is meeting its schedule, costs, and scope objectives. It can also assess if the project is meeting the business need that justified the project.
- **Product quality** assesses if the project's product is meeting its requirements. Some of the terms used to assess the product quality are *performance, grade, durability, defects,* and *errors.*
- **Process quality** assesses the efficiency and effectiveness of the adopted processes.

Type	Example
Project quality	We want to keep the cost and schedule performance index inside an acceptable range of variation.
Product quality	We want to establish a minimum width for the building's walls.
Process quality	We want to define a maximum number of days to validate change requests.

Hence, the **quality management** area includes the activities required to ensure that the project, the product, and the adopted processes meet requirements. Is this still somewhat confusing? The following are some examples of quality management activities:

- Develop the quality management plan.
- Prepare the process improvement plan.
- Determine the level of quality that best suits the project.
- Define quality standards and quality metrics.
- Define quality checklists.
- Perform quality audits.
- Analyze processes to suggest improvements.
- Perform inspections to determine if there are product defects.
- Identify the causes of identified defects.
- Perform quality audits to ensure that the processes are being followed.
- Use checklists.
- Validate deliverables.

Like all other management disciplines, quality management was developed based on theoretical principles. There are several quality management principles:

- **Prevention is preferable to inspection** The cost of preventing defects is usually lower than the cost of inspecting and correcting them. This principle was introduced by Philip Crosby as a basis for eliminating defects.
- **Practice continual improvement** The product and process should be improved through a continuous effort to introduce small enhancements. This principle is based on the plan-do-check-act cycle developed by W. Eduard Demings and Walter A. Shewhart and is the basis for quality management models such as Kaizen and total quality management (TCM).
- **Satisfy the customer by meeting his or her expectations** Customer expectations are met by a combination of:
  - **Quality is fitness for use** During planning, the team should translate customer needs into requirements, to ensure that the product meets the customer's purpose.

- **Quality is conformance to requirements** The project should provide all the specified requirements and only the specified requirements. This principle is established to avoid offering extras to the customer. Hence, a project that goes beyond specified requirements can be classified as a failure. Offering extras is often referred to as **gold plating**.
- **Shared responsibility over quality** The responsibility for quality is shared among management, project manager, and team:
  - Management should provide resources.
  - The project manager is accountable for the overall project quality.
  - Each team member is responsible for his or her own work.

Grade

Quality and grade are different concepts. The grade is used to distinguish elements with the same utility but different technical attributes. Sophisticated products will have a high-quality grade but may have low quality if they do not meet the needs for which they were developed. At the same time, other products may have a high level of quality even with an unsophisticated set of functionalities.

Quality Management Models

There are multiple quality management models including:
- **Six Sigma** Quality management approach that tries to eliminate defects by improving processes. In Six Sigma, less than 3.4 defects may occur for every one million tests. Six Sigma finds its application in large organizations and specific application areas, such as pharmaceutical and aerospace.
- **Total quality management (TQM)** Management system that guides the team throughout a continuous effort of improving product and process quality. This quality management philosophy was developed by authors like Demings and Crosby.
- **Just in time (JIT)** Management approach that reduces stocks to zero or nearly zero by requesting suppliers to deliver materials only when they are required. This approach requires high-quality manufacturing and logistic processes.
- **Kaizen** *Kaizen* is the Japanese word for "improvement" or "change to better," and it refers to the Japanese continuous improvement philosophy, born in the industrial sector after World War II. This philosophy is based on small but constant changes to obtain large results. Just like in the plan-do-check-act cycle, changes are planned, implemented, assessed, and repeated.
- **Lean manufacturing** Lean manufacturing is a management approach developed by Toyota, focused on eliminating work that does not add value. Waste is reduced, while overall customer value is preserved.
- **Capability Maturity Model Integration (CMMI®)** Model that assesses quality processes maturity, as well as establishes objectives and improvement guidelines.

ISO 9000

ISO 9000 is a set of standards from the International Organization for Standardization (ISO) that assesses the capacity of the organization to follow its own quality procedures.

The following table displays the quality management processes with their respective process group:

Quality Management Processes

Process	Process Group
Plan quality management	Planning
Perform quality assurance	Executing
Control quality	Monitoring and controlling

Plan Quality Management

Plan quality management translates needs and expectations into quality requirements and standards, while determining how these will be achieved. The results of this planning effort are the quality management plan, the process improvement plan, quality metrics, and checklists.

Quality planning includes tools such as cost-benefit analysis, benchmarking, design of experiments, sampling, brainstorming, force field analysis, nominal group techniques, and cost of quality. It can also include the **seven basic quality tools**: cause-and-effect diagram, flowchart, checklist, Pareto diagram, histogram, control chart, and scatter diagram.

Quality Management Plan

The quality management plan is a subsidiary plan of the project management plan. It identifies the quality requirements and describes how the organization or program quality policy will be implemented on the project.

> All projects should have a quality management plan and be able to demonstrate that the plan is being followed.

The **quality policy** establishes a set of rules and guidelines that should be adopted by the organization's, or program's, quality management approach. When developing the project quality management plan, the project management team should make sure that it is aligned with the quality policy.

Process Improvement Plan

Process improvement optimizes existing processes to improve their efficiency. This process improvement effort can be standardized and built into the project management approach. The process improvement plan is another subsidiary plan of the project management plan that describes how the processes can be progressively improved.

Quality Metrics or Operational Definitions

Quality metrics describe the specific product or project requirements that should be achieved. An example of a quality metric is the time needed to execute a software program, measured in seconds.

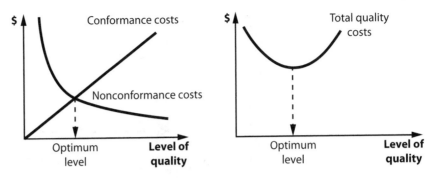

Figure 8.1 Cost of quality (COQ)

Checklists

A quality checklist or check sheet is a list of the elements that need to be checked to ensure that the deliverable, or process, was performed according to specifications.

Checklists are prepared during planning to be used as part of the control quality process.

> Within project management, checklists are also used to identify risks.

Cost of Quality (COQ)

Planning quality management includes determining the level of quality that minimizes costs. The cost of quality (COQ) technique (see Figure 8.1) identifies all the quality costs, classifying them as:

- **Conformance costs**   Costs of preventing and assessing defects. Examples of conformance costs are developing procedures, organizing trainings, studying, and performing product verifications.
- **Nonconformance costs**   Costs of solving internal and external failures. Examples of nonconformance costs are rework, stock costs, claims administration, crisis management, legal costs, and penalties for contract breaches.

> A low level of quality leads to an increase of nonconformance costs. Common consequences of reducing the quality level are cost and risk increases, poor morale, low customer satisfaction, and constant rework.

Marginal Analysis

Imagine that on a hot summer day, you are very thirsty and you drink a nice glass of cold water. The water tastes so good that you decide to have another glass. This time, you drink the water a little slower. Once you have drunk the second glass, you are still thirsty enough to drink a third glass, but this time you do not drink all the water. Adopting an economical perspective on thirst, you can conclude that the utility of drinking water diminishes with each additional glass of water. An economist would say that the utility of drinking water decreases marginally.

In quality management, **marginal analysis** can be used to define the optimum level of quality costs, analyzing the savings generated by a one-unit increase in quality spending. When you increase the conformance costs, the nonconformance costs will be reduced but the savings generated usually decrease marginally. The optimum level is achieved when the additional savings generated by the quality improvement equal the additional costs.

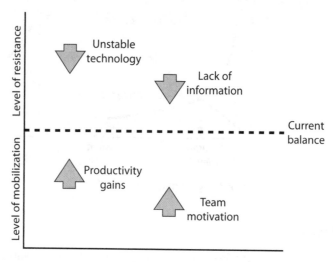

Figure 8.2 Force field analysis

Force Field Analysis

A force field analysis is a quality planning tool that helps highlight the favorable and unfavorable factors, or forces, that drive the quality improvement decision. (See Figure 8.2.)

Benchmarking

Most companies aspire to improving their processes and products. The benchmarking technique analyzes other projects, internal or external to the organization, in order to establish references, generate improvement ideas, and create a basis for comparison.

Design of Experiments (DOE)

Often a large number of variables can impact the quality of a specific product or process. Each variable can interact with others, minimizing or potentiating their impact. It is therefore difficult to isolate the quality impact of specific variables.

The design of experiments (DOE) is a quality planning tool that statistically analyzes the influence of different variables on the product, project, or process quality. It is operated by producing changes to one variable, while all other identified variables remain constant, and observing the impact on overall quality. For example, to analyze the resistance of an automobile piece, you can assess the different combinations of material types, thickness, and dimensions.

> The design of experiments technique may also be used to statically analyze the influence that changes in quality level have on project costs.

Sampling

The sampling technique selects part of the population in order to infer the characteristics of the entire population. There can be two types of sampling:

- **Attribute sampling**   Each measurement is classified as either conforming or nonconforming to requirements, according to the existence of predefined attributes (e.g., minimum weight).

- **Variable sampling**   A measurement is classified on a continuous numerical scale that rates the degree of conformance or nonconformance.

The confidence level applied to the sample may vary according to the level of exigency adopted in the organization:

1 Sigma = 68.26%
2 Sigma = 95.46%
3 Sigma = 99.73%
6 Sigma = 99.99%

The most frequently adopted level of confidence is 3 Sigma.

Cause-and-Effect Diagram, Ishikawa, or Fishbone

A cause-and-effect diagram, also known as Ishikawa or fishbone due to its shape, high-lights how specific causes may lead to actual or potential problems. (See Figure 8.3.) When applied to quality management, this diagram allows us to identify the root causes of nonconformities.

The cause-and-effect diagram may also help us understand why a project failed, highlighting the causes that led to project failure.

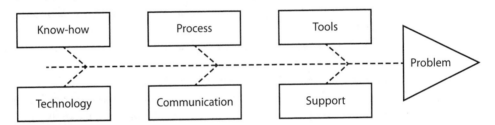

Figure 8.3 Cause-and-effect diagram

Pareto Diagram

The Pareto diagram is based on the famous Pareto law that states that 80 percent of problems are based on 20 percent of the causes. In quality management, this diagram is used to graphi-cally display the most common causes of defects, the most frequent type of defects, or the most frequent customer complaints, ordered by the number of times they occur. This sorted display enables people to prioritize the work of preventing, inspecting, and correcting defects and thus achieve better and faster results.

Flowchart

A flowchart is a graphical representation of the steps required to achieve an objective or the steps associated with a process. (See Figure 8.4.) A flowchart may be used in any of the quality man-agement processes:

- In planning quality management it can be used to determine where to establish quality standards.

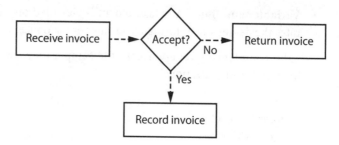

Figure 8.4 Flowchart

- In performing quality assurance it can be used to identify process improvement opportunities.
- While controlling quality it can be used to identify the causes that led to defects.

Control Chart

A control chart represents data over time to determine if the product, process, or project performance is under control or needs intervention. For example, the number of stakeholders' open issues may be monitored over time to analyze the project's ability to manage issues.

This diagram has upper and lower **control limits** that define the range of acceptable variation in the process. A variation inside that range is known as random or **common cause**. A variation outside that range is known as an assignable cause, or special cause. An **assignable cause** means that the process is out of control and that an effort should be made to identify the causes that led to the nonconformity. The **rule of seven** is also an indicator that the process is out of control. This rule is applied when there are seven measurements in a row that are on one side of the mean, even if they are within the control limits.

A control chart can also include **specification limits** that define the customer specification or contract requirements. (See Figure 8.5.) Control limits are typically more demanding than specification limits, to minimize the risk of failing to meet contract requirements. Remember that it is usually cheaper to deal with internal failures (defects identified by the team) than external failures (defects identified by the customer).

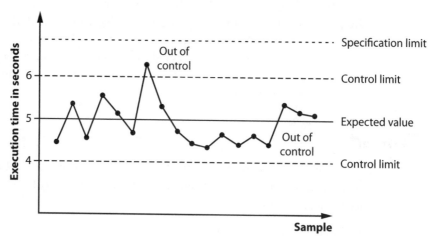

Figure 8.5 Control chart

Figure 8.6 Run chart

Run Chart

A run chart displays time-phased data to detect a trend and forecast future performance. (See Figure 8.6.) For example, a run chart may be used to represent the number of product defects over time.

Scatter Diagram

A scatter diagram is a graphical representation of the measurements of two variables along two axes to verify if they are statistically correlated. (See Figure 8.7.) That is, it analyzes if variations in an input variable influence an output variable. For example, a scatter diagram may relate the number of traffic accidents to the number of cars on the road.

> Statistical correlation is graphically visible when measurements tend to be organized around a diagonal line.

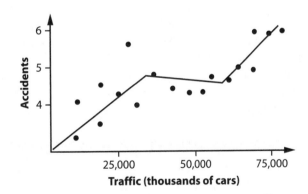

Figure 8.7 Scatter diagram

The following table matches potential situations to quality management tools:

Situations	Tools
Graphically represent meeting delays measured in minutes, to verify if the process of managing meetings is under control.	Control chart
Identify the reason why traffic on Mondays is more congested than on other days of the week.	Cause-and-effect diagram
Graphically represent the customer support process to identify potential improvement opportunities.	Flowchart
Group and order errors according to their cause.	Pareto diagram
Graphically represent the number of product defects to analyze its trend.	Run chart
Graphically represent the relationship between the number of traffic accidents and the number of cars on the road.	Scatter diagram
Analyze 20 percent of the team meetings to verify if the agenda is being met.	Sampling
Analyze other projects looking for relevant quality metrics.	Benchmarking
Statically analyze the relationship between the number of customer complaints and the day of the week, keeping all other relevant variables constant.	Design of experiments

Perform Quality Assurance

The **perform quality assurance** process provides confidence to stakeholders that the project is meeting quality requirements, that these requirements are appropriate, and that the project is following the adopted quality management approach. Perform quality assurance is an execution process and is performed through quality audits and process analysis.

Quality Audits

What should be done when there are doubts regarding whether the project is meeting the required policies, processes, and procedures? A **quality audit** is an independent evaluation of project quality compliance led by internal or external auditors. It can effectively raise stakeholders' confidence regarding the project's quality. Audits may also list all nonconformities and suggest improvements based on industry best practices and the organization's historical information.

> The quality audit's main input are quality control measurements.

Process Analysis

How many times have you identified processes that are too bureaucratic or inadequate? Wouldn't it be interesting to include a regular effort of rethinking the processes in the project? One of the roles of quality assurance is to execute the process improvement plan, looking for obstacles and non-value-added activities. Often, the implementation of a process improvement leads to a change request.

REVIEW EXERCISE

> The inputs to the perform quality assurance process are:

1. _____

2. _____

3. _____

4. _____

5. _____

Control Quality

Control quality is probably the most easily understood quality management process. As with any typical control process, it compares actual performance against the plan. While controlling quality, it measures project deliverables, processes, and project management performance to assess if they meet the established quality standards and to determine corrective actions when required.

Quality control occurs throughout the project and is essentially performed through inspections. It can also use the following tools and techniques: sampling, control chart, flowchart, cause-and-effect diagram, Pareto diagram, scatter diagram, checklist, and histogram.

Inspection

An inspection is a verification to determine if a deliverable meets the specified quality requirements. This verification may be performed by observation or by a more sophisticated measurement process.

> There is a difference between inspecting and preventing. The inspection effort identifies process or product defects to keep these defects from being handed over to the customer. The prevention effort attempts to avoid defects altogether.

Quality Attributes

Quality attributes define specific and measurable properties of the product or process, and are used to verify compliance. You can think of quality attributes as units of measure. Examples of quality attributes are minutes or number of complaints.

Quality Control Measurements

Quality control measurements are the actual values obtained by the quality control inspections.

> It is not possible to draw conclusions about the overall project quality without quality control measurements.

The quality management plan should determine the right level of quality control measurements' precision and accuracy. **Precision** assesses if the values measured during quality control are close to the actual values. **Accuracy** assesses if repeated quality control measurements show the same results.

> You have seen how a process variation may be classified as common cause or assignable cause. Quality control intervenes on assignable causes to correct processes that are out of control. By contrast, process improvements intervenes on common causes.

The following table can help you identify which quality management process you are in.

Situation	Process
The project is determining what quality standards will be used or how quality will be managed.	Plan quality management
There is a specific problem on the product, process, or project performance.	Control quality
There is a general concern about the quality of the product, process, or project performance.	Perform quality assurance
You need to provide confidence regarding the project quality to stakeholders.	Perform quality assurance

MEMORIZATION EXERCISE

> The following exercise was designed to facilitate the memorization of the main concepts in this chapter. Assign each of the following definitions to a quality management concept.

1. Ability to meet the customer's need while developing a product or service

_____

2. Actual values obtained by the quality control inspections

_____

3. Assesses how well the requirements are being met

_____

4. Chart that represents data over time, to determine if the product, process, or project performance is under control or needs intervention

5. Graphical representation of the steps required to achieve an objective or the steps associated with a process

6. Highlights how specific causes may lead to actual or potential problems

7. Can be used in quality management to define the optimum level of quality costs, analyzing the savings generated by a one-unit increase in quality spending

8. A diagram used in quality management to graphically display the most common causes of defects, the most frequent type of defects, or the most frequent customer complaints, ordered by the number of times they occur

9. Independent evaluation of project quality compliance, led by internal or external auditors

10. Limits within a control chart that define the acceptable range of process variation

11. Limits within a control chart that define the customer specification or contract requirements

12. List of the elements that you have to check to ensure that the deliverable, or process, was performed according to specifications

13. Providing all the specified requirements and only the specified requirements

14. Quality management principle that encourages product and process improvements through a continuous effort to introduce small enhancements

15. Quality management principle that suggests that the cost of preventing is usually lower than the cost of correcting

16. Quality planning tool that statically analyzes the influence of different variables on the product, project, or process quality

_____

17. Rule applied on a control chart to determine that a process is out of control; applied when there are seven measurements in a row that are on one side of the mean, even if they are within the control limits

_____

18. Subsidiary plan of the project management plan that describes how the organization's or program's quality policy will be implemented on the project

_____

19. Technique that identifies all quality conformance and nonconformance costs

_____

20. Verification to determine if a deliverable meets the specified quality requirements

_____

Process Exercises

The following exercises were designed so you could learn how to recognize the processes and understand their logical sequence. Quality management processes are listed next, including their unique number in the *PMBOK Guide*:

- 8.1 Plan quality management
- 8.2 Perform quality assurance
- 8.3 Control quality

PROCESS EXERCISE 1

> **Assign processes to the following activities.**

1. Analyze processes to identify improvement opportunities. _____
2. Collect project performance measurements. _____
3. Determine quality standards. _____
4. Determine the level of quality suitable for the project. _____
5. Develop checklists. _____
6. Generate a change request to eliminate a quality management activity. _____
7. Identify the causes of occurred defects. _____
8. Perform quality audits to ensure that processes are being followed. _____

9. Prepare the process improvement plan. _____

10. Prepare the quality management plan. _____

11. Use checklists. _____

12. Validate deliverables. _____

PROCESS EXERCISE 2

> **Assign processes to the following inputs.**

1. Deliverables _____

2. Quality checklists _____

3. Quality control measurements _____

4. Quality metrics _____

5. Stakeholders' register _____

CHAPTER 8 EXAM

> The following questions were designed to test your knowledge on this chapter's topic. Read each question carefully, and choose the option that most accurately answers the question. Once you have completed the exam, compare your answers with the solution and read through the justification provided. Note the topics where you have the most difficulty, and make sure that you dedicate enough study time to them.

1. You are managing a customer support services implementation project. While preparing the project management plan, which of the following options should you focus on to maximize the impact on customer satisfaction?
   A. Manage project changes.
   B. Deliver the product on schedule.
   C. Determine fitness for use and conformance to requirements.
   D. Deliver above expectations.

2. "Prevention is preferable to inspection" means:
   A. Quality should be continuously improved.
   B. Quality should be as high as possible.
   C. Costs are lower when quality is decreased.
   D. Costs are higher when quality is decreased.

3. Poor morale, low customer satisfaction, and constant rework are symptoms of:
   A. Lack of human resource management planning
   B. High risk project
   C. Low quality
   D. High conformance costs

4. During a research and development project, the product is not performing according to its planned quality. Who is accountable for the performance problems?
   A. Project manager
   B. Sponsor
   C. Product manager
   D. Team

5. All of the following are part of the plan quality management process EXCEPT:
   A. Describe how quality assurance and quality control will implement the existing quality policies.
   B. Identify the project quality standards.
   C. Develop checklists to assist in quality measurements.
   D. Identify process improvements.

6. Which of the following is an example of a conformance cost?
   A. Developing quality procedures
   B. Rework
   C. Claims administration
   D. Inventory costs

7. After submitting your project management plan for approval, management wants to reduce the time spent in quality management. Which of the following concepts would BEST support the argument in favor of your current project management plan?
   A. Practice of continual improvement
   B. Cost of quality
   C. Sampling
   D. Conformance to requirements

8. As a project manager in a large pharmaceutical project, you are determining how the project may meet the customer's quality standards. In which process are you working?
   A. Develop project management plan
   B. Plan quality management
   C. Perform quality assurance
   D. Control quality

9. Halfway through a construction project, a major scope change occurred. The team is determining which quality standards will be impacted by the change. In which process is the team working?
   A. Perform quality assurance
   B. Plan quality management
   C. Control quality
   D. Scope definition

10. The team is analyzing the savings generated by a one-unit increase in quality spending. What technique is the team using?
    A. Plan quality
    B. Cost of quality
    C. Sensitivity analysis
    D. Marginal analysis

11. Examining non-value-added activities is part of:
    A. Process analysis
    B. Plan quality management
    C. Quality inspections
    D. Quality audits

12. Process improvement addresses:
    A. Assignable causes of variation
    B. Specification limits
    C. Common causes of variation
    D. Quality checklists

13. How does plan quality management differ from perform quality assurance?
    A. Quality assurance is the monitoring of specific project results to determine whether they comply with relevant quality standards, as well as identifying ways to eliminate the causes of unsatisfactory performance. Plan quality management is planning quality standards.
    B. Plan quality management is performed only at early stages of the project.
    C. Quality assurance is performed only by people who do not belong to the project, while plan quality management is performed by team members.
    D. Plan quality management determines which quality standards to use, while quality assurance assesses project performance to provide confidence that the project will satisfy the quality standards.

14. While managing a telecommunication project, management informs you that they are worried the project will not meet the quality standards. What should you do?
    A. Perform a quality inspection.
    B. Prepare a presentation to management explaining the adopted quality management plan.
    C. Perform a quality audit.
    D. Create a quality management plan.

15. Before initiating a quality audit, you absolutely need to have:
    A. Quality benchmarks
    B. Checklists
    C. Nonconformance costs
    D. Quality control measurements

16. The quality audit team recommended the implementation of a best practice. The NEXT step should be to complete a:
    A. Checklist
    B. Quality inspection
    C. Cost-benefit analysis
    D. Change request

17. The team is analyzing why a particular software module was not developed according to the adopted quality standards. In which process is the team working?
    A. Identify risks
    B. Perform quality assurance
    C. Control quality
    D. Lessons learned

18. Which of the following is NOT a quality management tool?
    A. Cause-and-effect-diagrams
    B. Value analysis
    C. Run charts
    D. Flow charts

19. A control chart is used to:
    A. Determine quality metrics
    B. Verify if a process has an acceptable variation
    C. Identify the root causes of nonconformities
    D. Forecast future results

20. What should be done if a control chart shows six results in a row outside the control limit?
    A. Identify an assignable cause for such variation.
    B. Ignore the variation as long as the results are within customer specification limits.
    C. Adjust the control limits to accurately represent the process variance.
    D. Ignore the variation provided that a rule of seven has not occurred.

21. Two weeks before the scheduled finish date, your project still has a significant number of open product defects. You want to focus the defect repair effort on the more frequent defects. Which tool should you use?
    A. Pareto diagram
    B. Cause-and-effect diagrams
    C. Cost of quality
    D. Sampling

22. A project has been completed with a history of product quality problems. Which of the following tools would be of MOST help?
    A. Control chart
    B. Ishikawa diagram
    C. Scatter diagram
    D. Pareto diagram

ANSWERS

Review Exercise

1. Quality control measurements
2. Quality management plan
3. Process improvement plan
4. Quality metrics
5. Quality documents

Memorization Exercise

1. Fitness for use
2. Quality control measurements
3. Quality
4. Control chart
5. Flowchart
6. Cause-and-effect diagram, Ishikawa, or fishbone

7. Marginal analysis
8. Pareto diagram
9. Quality audit
10. Control limits
11. Specification limits or tolerance limits
12. Quality checklists
13. Conformance to requirements
14. Practice continual improvement
15. Prevention is preferable to inspection
16. Design of experiments
17. Rule of seven
18. Quality management plan
19. Cost of quality (COQ)
20. Quality inspections

Process Exercise 1

1. 8.2
2. 8.3
3. 8.1
4. 8.1
5. 8.1
6. 8.2
7. 8.3
8. 8.2
9. 8.1
10. 8.1
11. 8.3
12. 8.3

Process Exercise 2

1. 8.3
2. 8.3
3. 8.2
4. 8.2, 8.3
5. 8.1

Chapter 8 Exam

1. **C** Project management pursues customer satisfaction through a combination of fitness for use and conformance to requirements. Fitness for use is the product's ability to meet the customer's purpose. Conformance to requirements means providing all the specified requirements and only the specified requirements. Answers A and B are not enough to meet customer satisfaction. Answer D is not aligned with the conformance to requirements principle.

2. **D** "Prevention is preferable to inspection" is a quality management principle that suggests that the cost of preventing is usually lower than the cost of inspecting and correcting them. This means that reducing the quality level may in fact increase overall costs because

the increase in nonconformance costs is greater than the decrease in conformance costs. Answer A does not represent the "prevention is preferable to inspection" principle. Answers B and C are technically incorrect.

3. **C** Cost and risk increases, poor morale, low customer satisfaction, and constant rework are common symptoms of low quality.

4. **A** The project manager is accountable for the overall project quality. The sponsor should provide resources (answer B). The product manager may, once the project is completed, be responsible for the product quality. However, he is not responsible for the project quality (answer C). Each team member is responsible for his or her own work (answer D).

5. **D** Identify process improvements is part of the perform quality assurance process. All other answers are part of the plan quality management process.

6. **A** Developing quality procedures is an example of a conformance cost. All other answers are examples of nonconformance costs.

7. **B** Analyzing the costs of quality could help demonstrate to management that by reducing conformance costs, the nonconformance costs would increase.

8. **B** The question is referring to quality standards that will be implemented in the future. Therefore, the project manager is planning quality management.

9. **B** Scope changes frequently lead to changes to other components of the project management plan. In this example, the team is analyzing the impact of a change on quality standards. Therefore, the team is planning quality management.

10. **D** In quality management, the marginal analysis concept refers to the process of analyzing the incremental savings generated by a one-unit increase in quality spending. Optimal level of quality is achieved when the benefits generated by the quality increase equal the required costs to secure it. Answer A is a process and not a technique.

11. **A** Process analysis executes the process improvement plan, examining problems and activities that do not add value. It is part of the perform quality assurance process. Thus answer B is not correct. Process analysis is not an inspection (answer C) and is not an audit (answer D).

12. **C** Process improvement is about optimizing processes and not correcting defects. Therefore, answers A, B, and D, associated with quality control, are not correct. Answer C is correct because process improvement acts on processes that are under control, trying to reduce their variation.

13. **D** Plan quality management determines which standards should be used, while quality assurance assesses performance to provide confidence that the project will meet those standards. Quality assurance is not about monitoring specific project results (answer A). Plan quality management may be performed throughout the project (answer B). Quality assurance may be performed by project team members (answer C).

14. **C** The quality audit is an independent assessment that can effectively raise stakeholders' confidence regarding the project's quality. If management is worried with the project quality, an audit is the best option.

15. **D** It is not possible to assess project quality without quality control measurements. Checklists are used during quality control (answer B). Quality benchmarks (answer A) and nonconformance costs (answer C) are analyzed during quality planning.

16. **D** The perform quality assurance process may generate a change request to implement a best practice. The other answers would not be the next step after the quality audit recommendation.

17. **C** Analyzing the causes of nonconformance is part of quality control.

18. **B** Value analysis is a product analysis technique focused on reducing product development costs without changing the scope. All other options may be used as quality management tools.

19. **B** A control chart represents data over time, to verify if the product, process, or project performance is under control or needs intervention.

20. **A** One point outside the control limit is enough to determine that the process is not under control and that an assignable cause should be identified.

21. **A** A Pareto diagram can be used to prioritize quality defects by their frequency of occurrence. All other options would not support such analysis.

22. **B** If the project has a history of product quality problems, the team should find the causes of such problems. The Ishikawa diagram can reveal the problems' root causes and is therefore a good option. None of the other options can be used to analyze the problems' causes.

Human Resource Management

Learning Topics	⟩ Human resource management ⟩ Human resource management plan, staffing management plan, role, responsibility, hierarchy, project organization chart, resource breakdown structure (RBS), organizational breakdown structure (OBS), responsibility assignment matrix (RAM), RACI chart, text format description, resource calendars, histograms, recognition and rewards system, fringe benefits, and perquisites ⟩ Resource negotiation, pre-assignment, acquisition, and virtual teams ⟩ Team performance assessment, team-building activities, ground rules, colocation, and Tuckman team development model ⟩ Conflict management: problem solve, force, compromise, smooth, and withdraw ⟩ Project performance appraisal ⟩ Motivation: Maslow's hierarchy of needs, Herzberg's theory, McGregor's Theory X and Theory Y, Ouchi's Theory Z, expectancy theory, David McClelland's theory of needs ⟩ Issue log ⟩ Basis of power: legitimate, expert, reward, coercive, referent, and informational

The previous chapters discussed the importance of adopting procedures and techniques while planning and controlling the project. Regardless of the importance of an adequate project management approach, it is essential not to forget that the procedures and techniques will only be effective if the team is able to implement them appropriately. Project success will depend on having the right people who have the right knowledge and skills, know what to do, feel motivated and engaged, and are able to work as a team.

The human resource management area includes the processes required to manage the team. Some examples of human resource management activities are:

- Planning roles and responsibilities
- Planning where and how team members will be acquired
- Planning the recognition and rewards system
- Negotiating resources with the functional manager
- Contracting resources
- Organizing trainings for the team
- Organizing team-building activities
- Solving problems and disputes
- Assessing the team's performance

The following table displays the human resource management processes with their respective process group:

Human Resource Management Processes

Process	Process Group
Plan human resource management	Planning
Acquire project team	Executing
Develop project team	Executing
Manage project team	Executing

Plan Human Resource Management

The **plan human resource management** process determines how team members will be acquired and managed, establishes their roles and responsibilities, and defines the project hierarchy. The final output is a **human resource management plan** that may include a staffing management plan, a definition of the roles and responsibilities, resource calendars, and a recognition and rewards system.

Staffing Management Plan

Have you ever experienced watching resources being taken out of your project without being able to review the schedule or budget? Have you thought about the advantages of having an approved plan specifying resource utilization?

A staffing management plan determines how the resource requirements, identified while planning the time management knowledge area, will be acquired by the project. The staffing management plan may also specify:

- Where and how the team members will be acquired
- The procedures used to recruit people
- The resources calendars and histograms
- Security authorizations required for the resources
- The team members' training plan
- Recognition and rewards criteria
- Procedures used to release team members from the project

The staffing management plan should be reviewed and approved by the functional managers. Additionally, any change to the approved plan should be managed through the change control mechanism.

Roles, Responsibilities, and Hierarchies

The human resource management plan may specify the following for each team member:

- **Role**   The role specifies the function assigned to the team member. Examples of project roles are project manager, programmer, and maintenance technician. Each role may require a specific set of skills. An example of a project manager skill is being able to use the earned value management (EVM) technique.
- **Responsibility**   The responsibility determines the activities required to perform the work properly. Examples of the responsibilities of an analyst are collecting requirements from the customer, documenting those requirements, and verifying documents.
- **Hierarchy**   The hierarchy determines to whom each team members reports during the project. For example, one electrician may report to the intervention team leader. Each hierarchy level may also have a predefined level of decision-making autonomy. For example, one electrician on an equipment installation project may have enough authority to adopt the best technical solution for the customer requirement.

There are several tools to establish the roles, responsibilities, and hierarchies:

- **Project organization chart**   Diagram that displays the reporting hierarchy between team members. (See Figure 9.1.)
- **Resource breakdown structure (RBS)**   Hierarchical diagram that displays the relationship between the work and the resource types. (See Figure 9.2.) The work is decomposed according to the resource types involved. This type of diagram is frequently used to control and report the project costs.
- **Organizational breakdown structure (OBS)**   Hierarchical diagram that displays the relationship between the work and the organizational units. (See Figure 9.3.) The work is decomposed by departments or business functions to more easily control the resources.
- **Responsibility assignment matrix (RAM)**   Another typical element of a human resource management plan is a RAM. This matrix is a relationship between the work breakdown structure (WBS) and the team members. (See Figure 9.4.) It ensures that the responsibilities over each work package are assigned. A **RACI chart** is a type of RAM that categorizes responsibilities as Responsible, Accountable, Consulted, and Informed.
- **Text format description**   Roles and responsibilities described in a text format.

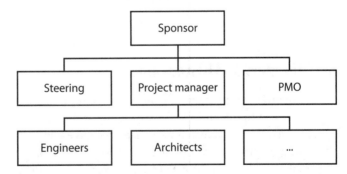

Figure 9.1 Project organization chart

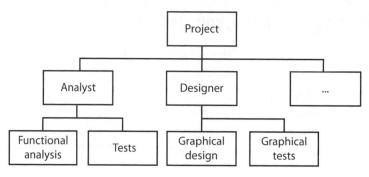

Figure 9.2 Resource breakdown structure (RBS)

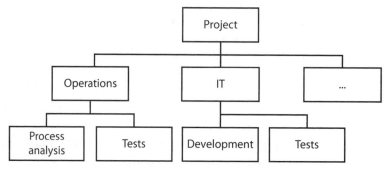

Figure 9.3 Organizational breakdown structure (OBS)

	Claire	Peter	Bruce	Sarah	Rita	Martha
Analysis		X	X		X	X
Design		X		X	X	
Development		X		X		X
Tests	X	X				
Integration	X		X			
Transition	X		X	X		
Production	X				X	

Figure 9.4 Responsibility assignment matrix (RAM)

Resource Calendars and Histograms

An important part of planning human resource management is determining when resources will be allocated to the project. The histogram is the most common tool used to represent resource calendars. It represents a time-phased resource allocation, usually through vertical bars. Additionally, the histogram may include information about the resource's available capacity in order to detect potential problems of lack or excess of resources.

Recognition and Rewards System

The purpose of a recognition and rewards system is to establish a clear relationship between individual performance and reward, and thereby increase motivation and improve individual and team performance.

> When the team displays lack of project support, it may be a symptom of an inadequate recognition and rewards system.

The project manager may prepare one set of rules, formal or informal, defining how team members will be recognized and compensated. These rules should be applied consistently and in accordance with the individual levels of responsibility and authority. The decisions to recognize and reward should be based on team performance assessments. A recognition and rewards system is particularly relevant within matrix organizations, where individual performance may be impacted by conflicts of loyalty and priority.

> In a functional and weak matrix organization this system is controlled by functional managers.

A recognition and rewards system may include fringe benefits and perquisites. **Fringe benefits** are standard compensation, added to direct wages, formally given to all employees. Company cars and health insurance can be examples of fringe benefits. **Perquisites**, or **perks**, are special compensation given to some employees for their outstanding performance. Examples of perquisites are parking spaces or traveling vouchers.

REVIEW EXERCISE 1

> What human resource management tool would you use in each of the following situations?

1. Describe the procedures used to acquire and release team members, describe resource calendars, and establish recognition and rewards.

   _____

2. Assign the WBS work packages to team members.

   _____

3. Display the relationship between work and organizational units.

   _____

4. Display the hierarchies among team members.

   _____

5. Display the relationship between the work and the resource types.

   _____

6. Describe the roles and responsibilities in a text format.

   _____

7. Graphically represent the time-phased resource allocation.

   _____

Acquire Project Team

The **acquire project team** process means obtaining the people required to work on the project. The project team members may be acquired through a negotiation between the project manager and the functional managers, pre-assignments, external acquisition, or virtual teams.

The project manager may not be the main person accountable for selecting the resources that will be acquired for the project. In many organizations, this responsibility belongs to functional managers, a human resources department, or senior management. Other times, resources are acquired externally based on previously established agreements. Whatever the case, the project manager has some responsibility over project team acquisition. He should try to influence resource selection and avoid changes to resources that can negatively impact the plan.

Because resource changes are frequent, particularly within matrix organizations, there is a strong relationship between resource acquisition, change management, and risk management. In other words, changes to the staffing management plan should be reflected in the other planning dimensions.

Resource Negotiation

Resources are acquired for the project through a negotiation between the project manager and other entities. When resources are acquired within the organization, the project manager negotiates with the functional managers, or in some organizations, with other project managers. When resources are acquired outside the organization, the project manager negotiates with external suppliers.

Pre-Assignment

In **pre-assignment**, resources are assigned to the project without any type of negotiation with the project manager. This pre-assignment may occur due to many reasons, including:

- There are no more resources available.
- Management has imposed specific resources.
- Part of the team was already working on the project when the human resource management plan was developed.
- There was a previous agreement with the customer regarding using specific resources.

Acquisition

The organization may not be able, or willing, to fulfill resources requirements from internal staff. Resources may be fully or partially acquired from outside sources. A typical example is to contract an external consultant for a period of time. Alternatively, part of the work may be transferred to a subcontractor.

Virtual Teams

The availability of communication technologies such as e-mail, instant messaging, and virtual meetings facilitates the existence of virtual teams, where team members cooperate remotely. Virtual teams can strongly reduce communication costs and also allow geographically scattered team members to be involved in project decisions.

Develop Project Team

The **develop project team** process is the human resource management process that improves the team's overall performance, acting at both individual and group levels on:

- Knowledge
- Skills
- Behaviors
- Ability to establish interpersonal relationships
- Ability to overcome cultural differences
- Trust
- Motivation
- Alignment with project objectives

To improve knowledge, skills, and behaviors, the project may include training, coaching, and mentoring.

To influence trust, motivation and interpersonal relationships, the project may adopt team-building activities, ground rules, mascots, and logos. It can also colocate team members in a single physical space.

To improve the team's alignment with the project, the project manager may establish recognition and rewards mechanisms and involve the team in project management decisions. It can also use consensus development techniques, such as the Delphi or nominal group technique.

The outcome of the develop project team process is not particularly tangible. It may be observed in formal or informal evaluations of the team's performance, known as **team performance assessment**.

REVIEW EXERCISE 2

> The main challenges of developing a project team in a weak matrix organization are:

1. _____

2. _____

3. _____

4. _____

5. _____

Team-Building Activities

Team-building activities are developed to increase the team's overall performance, focusing on improving collaboration and levels of trust. These activities may include milestone parties, involving the team in the planning effort, project status meetings, offsite activities, tours, kickoff meetings, logos, and mascots.

> These activities should start early in the project and be performed throughout the project.

Ground Rules

Ground rules are unwritten rules that define what behaviors are accepted and what behaviors are not accepted during the project. When communicated clearly, ground rules help reduce conflict and increase productivity. An example of a ground rule is establishing that the work performed by each team member should always be available to other team members.

Colocation

On many projects, particularly in matrix organizations, team members often work in physically separated places and are organized around their area of expertise. On such projects, communicating, coordinating resources, integrating the work, and developing a sense of teamwork will always be a challenge.

The colocation technique concentrates team members in a single physical space to facilitate communication, focus the team on the project objectives, and develop a sense of teamwork.

Involving Team Members on Project Management

Involving the team on estimating or planning risk responses will undoubtedly improve the quality of the plans. Furthermore, involving the team improves commitment. No plan will ever be perfect. It is critical that the team has enough energy to overcome the obstacles that inevitably occur during all projects and continue to pursue the project objectives.

> The team's involvement on the project management effort is critical.

Stages of Team Development

The team development model, proposed by Bruce Tuckman, establishes several development phases:

- **Forming**   As team members start to work together, they tend to act as independent individuals and adopt an expectant attitude toward changes. While in the forming phase, team members strongly depend on the leader for guidance.
- **Storming**   When iterations between team members begin, the first conflicts occur, usually concerning roles, approaches, problems, and expected behaviors. The leader should adopt a coaching style, helping the team deal with conflict and focus on the objectives.
- **Norming**   When the team already has some collaboration experience, work relationships start to normalize, leading to common understandings over previous points of conflict. Roles and responsibilities are now understood and accepted. The leader acts as a facilitator.
- **Performing**   When the team already has a lot of practice working together, it may achieve an advanced level of development with high levels of performance. At this performance level, there is no excessive level of conflict and no significant need for the team leader's intervention.
- **Adjourning**   Team members are released.

While observing behaviors, the project manager may recognize the development phase the team is in and adapt his or her management style accordingly.

Manage Project Team

The project manager may influence the team's performance, making sure that there is no loss of productivity due to existing obstacles, lack of information, or insufficient resources.

Managing the team involves accompanying the team to observe, assess, and influence performance. **Manage project team** activities may include:

- Constant and proactive communicating with the team, listening, and providing feedback
- Dealing with performance issues
- Removing obstacles
- Managing conflicts
- Influencing team motivation
- Managing team changes
- Performing project performance appraisals

Manage Performance Problems

The project manager cannot ignore performance problems. If a team member is not performing as expected, the project manager should speak with that member informally, and together they should understand the reasons behind the performance and identify a solution.

When a team member has constant performance problems, or has a severe and visible behavior problem, the problem can no longer be managed between the project manager and the team member. Discussing the problem exclusively with the team member not only would fail to solve the problem, since it is a constant and visible situation, but could also damage the credibility of the project manager. In these situations, the project manager should speak with the team member and with the team member's manager simultaneously to find a sustainable solution.

Manage Conflict

You know from your project experience that it is not possible to completely avoid conflict. Some levels of conflict may even be positive, allowing people to reach better decisions and reinforcing their ability to work as a team. However, conflict should be managed. It is important to prevent the conflict from growing and establishing itself firmly in the project, impacting productivity, and destroying the ability to work as a team. The following principles can be applied to conflict management within a project environment:

- When the conflict occurs, the project manager should act quickly, preferably in private and informally.
- The project manager should avoid the temptation of trying to solve all conflicts alone. Often, conflict can only be sustainably dealt with by the people directly involved in the situation. The role of the project manager is to facilitate the resolution, helping people isolate the conflict's cause and solution.
- When there is a situation of constant and inadequate conflict, the project manager can use formal conflict resolution channels.
- Constant communication, clear responsibilities, well-defined processes, and individual behavior ground rules may help avoid unnecessary conflict.

Unrealistic schedules, scarce resources, technical issues, and personal styles are among the most common sources of conflict.

There are five different conflict resolution techniques: problem solve, force, compromise, smooth, and withdraw.

Problem Solve, Collaborate, or Confront

In the problem solve technique, also known as collaborate or confront, the conflict situation is managed as a problem. The solution for the conflict is determined through structured and disciplined steps, which should not be initiated until all the previous steps have been successfully completed. Throughout the process, team members should maintain an open atmosphere where different opinions can be discussed and combined. This technique is based on the George Pólya approach to mathematical problems and includes the following steps:

- **Understand the problem** The first step is to understand the root causes of the problem that are beyond the visible symptoms. Understanding the problem often means communicating with the impacted stakeholders. An important part of this step is avoiding the temptation of discussing solutions with the team until there is comprehensive understanding of the problem.
- **Prepare a solution** Analyze alternatives, often through team discussions, to determine the solution that best suits the project's interests.
- **Implement a solution** When the solution requires some form of acceptance, this validation should first be obtained internally. Only when the sponsor or management has accepted the solution should a customer acceptance be requested.
- **Review** Once the solution is implemented, the outcome should be analyzed to understand what worked and what didn't.

> This technique is usually considered to be the best solution, promoting long-lasting resolutions in which all stakeholders win.

Force or Direct

In the force conflict resolution technique, also known as direct, someone's perspective is imposed on others.

> This solution is not usually a good option because it tends to generate antagonism and cause additional conflicts.

Compromise, Reconcile, or Negotiate

This solution to the conflict is reached when both parties give in and reject their initial perspectives. This technique is considered a "lose-lose" solution and tends to generate temporary solutions.

Smooth or Accommodate

Sometimes, people address conflict by dealing with its emotions instead of dealing with its root cause. The smooth conflict resolution seeks a conflict resolution by maintaining a comfortable environment. Often smoothing means accommodating the other's concerns ceding on one's own interests or opinions.

Withdraw or Avoid

Sometimes people choose to avoid or delay the conflict resolution. Maybe there are more urgent issues to deal with or maybe the stakeholder is not ready to deal with the conflict. Other times, delaying the conflict might be recommended if the parties are not emotionally ready to deal with the conflict.

Examples of Conflict Solutions

Situation	Conflict Resolution
"Let's perform some investigation until we have enough information to make a decision."	Problem solve
"The decision is made. We choose the new technology."	Force
"The defect is not that serious. Other projects have similar problems."	Smooth
"Why don't you swap seats periodically? That way you can all benefit from a window seat."	Compromise
"Why don't we discuss the issue at the next meeting?"	Withdraw

Project Performance Appraisal

A project performance assessment is a formal or informal evaluation of the team member's performance, providing feedback, clarifying responsibilities, identifying areas that require improvement, planning training needs, and removing existing obstacles. In a matrix organization, a formal performance assessment may later be incorporated into the employee's final performance assessment typically performed by the functional manager.

Motivation

There are multiple theories on how to motivate people, including Maslow's hierarchy of needs, Herzberg's theory, McGregor's Theory X and Theory Y, Ouchi's Theory Z, expectancy theory, and David McClelland's theory of needs.

Maslow's Hierarchy of Needs

Maslow's motivational theory states that there is a hierarchy, or pyramid, of human needs. (See Figure 9.5.) The most basic level of human needs should be fulfilled before the individual's attention is directed to a more sophisticated level of need. To motivate people, the manager should define rewards that meet the typical needs of the level at which the individual currently is. The steps of Maslow's pyramid are:

- Physiological needs related to physical survival, such as food and water
- Safety needs related to physical, job, financial, or health safety
- Love and belonging needs related to maintaining family relationships, friendships, and affections
- Esteem needs related to self-respect, trust, and other people's respect
- Finally, self-actualization needs related to achievement, creativity, and spontaneity

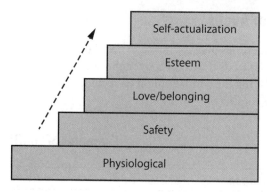

Figure 9.5 Maslow's hierarchy of needs

Herzberg's Theory or Hygiene Theory

Herzberg's theory states that motivation may be influenced by hygiene factors and motivating agents. Hygiene factors may destroy motivation if they are not met, but cannot increase motivation. Examples of hygiene factors are working conditions, base salary, fringe benefits, number of vacation days, and the office space.

In contrast, motivating agents may lead to additional motivation. Examples of motivating agents are performance recognition, perquisites, and personal fulfillment.

McGregor's Theory X and Theory Y

McGregor's Theory X and Theory Y are motivational theories that state there are two types of managers:

- Managers X assume that people can't be trusted and should be permanently micromanaged.
- Managers Y assume that people are ambitious, are self-motivated, and exercise self-control; therefore, they should be involved in decisions and have some autonomy.

Ouchi's Theory Z

Ouchi's Theory Z, made popular during the 1980s' Japanese economic boom, argues that employees are motivated by a spirit of trust, commitment, and development. The organization can influence employees' motivation by creating strong and long-term bonds with them. Bonds can derive from job security, empowerment, finding balances between work and family life, or maintaining strong and consistent ethical behaviors.

Expectancy Theory

Expectancy theory states that people are motivated if they believe that there is an expected relationship between effort, performance, and rewards. (See Figure 9.6.) To positively influence a team's performance, the manager should define objectives that are credible and linked to valuable rewards.

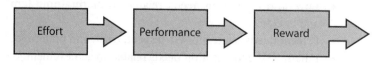

Figure 9.6 Expectancy theory

Issue	Description	Date	Author	Responsible	Actions	Status

Figure 9.7 Issue log

David McClelland's Theory of Needs

David McClelland's theory of needs suggested that there are people motivated by power, people motivated by affiliation, and people motivated by results. The manager should recognize what motivates each team member in order to manage them.

Issue Log

The issue log is a tool used to manage the team and other stakeholders' engagement by documenting and tracing problems, obstacles, and expectations, from identification to resolution. (See Figure 9.7.)

The issue log has an impact on both the technical and the human side of project management. From a technical perspective, it allows the project manager to keep track of open issues and resolutions. This control avoids problems that can negatively influence the team's performance and stakeholders' behavior.

An absent management style, which does not deal with existing problems and obstacles, may lead to performance problems, conflict, and low morale.

From a human perspective, the issue log provides evidence to stakeholders and the team that their worries and expectations were heard, allowing the project manager to maintain relationships of trust and commitment.

The use of an issue log is shared with the **manage stakeholder engagement** process.

Basis of Power

According to the social psychologists John French and Bertram Raven, there are different bases for power: legitimate, expert, reward, coercive, and referent. Later, French introduced the informational basis of power. When applying this theory to project management, the project manager's different bases of authority are:

- **Legitimate** Based on the hierarchical position of the project manager in the organization. Legitimate power does not usually lead to team commitment
- **Expert** Based on knowledge, skills, and experience
- **Reward** Based on the ability to reward
- **Coercive** Based on the ability to punish; considered the worst form of authority
- **Referent** Based on an authority not formally assigned, but that exists indirectly due to other factors such as personality
- **Informational** Based on the ability to access and use information to his or her own advantage

The legitimate, reward, and coercive forms of power derive from the position in the organization. The expert and referent forms of power are more related to the characteristics of the individual.

The expert and reward types of power are usually the preferred authorities because by being more aligned with the team's expectations and interests, they tend to have more sustainable impact. In the beginning of the project or when the project manager is only assigned at advanced project stages, legitimate power is particularly important because the project manager needs immediate authority and there is no time to develop and consolidate other types of power.

MEMORIZATION EXERCISE

The following exercise was designed to facilitate the memorization of the main concepts on this chapter. Assign the following definitions to a human resource management concept.

1. Concentrates team members in a single physical space to facilitate communication, focus the team on the project objectives, and develop a sense of teamwork

2. Conflict management technique that attempts to maintain a comfortable environment, instead of seeking a conflict resolution

3. Conflict management technique where someone's perspective is imposed on others

4. Conflict resolution technique that avoids the conflict or delays its resolution

5. Conflict resolution technique that manages each conflict situation as a problem that requires a solution

6. Determines how team members will be acquired and managed, establishes their roles and responsibilities, and defines the project hierarchy

7. Component of the human resource management plan that determines how the resource requirements will be acquired by the project and how they will be managed

8. Graphical representation of a time-phased resource allocation, usually through vertical bars

9. Hierarchical diagram that displays the relationship between the work and the organizational units

_____

10. Hierarchical diagram that displays the relationship between the work and the resource types

_____

11. Motivational theory that states that motivation may be influenced by hygiene factors and motivating agents

_____

12. Motivational theories that state there are two types of managers: managers X assume that people need to be micromanaged permanently; managers Y assume that people should have some autonomy

_____

13. Motivational theory that states there is a pyramid of human needs: each individual is particularly motivated to satisfy the needs of a particular pyramid step. When those needs are met, the individual will be motivated to meet the needs of the next step.

_____

14. Relationship between the WBS and the team members to ensure that the responsibility over each work package is assigned

_____

15. Resources are selected for the project without any type of negotiation with the project manager

_____

16. Set of rules that define how team members will be recognized and compensated

_____

17. Special compensation given to some employees for their outstanding performance

_____

18. Team members cooperating remotely using communication technology

_____

19. Tool used to manage the team's and other stakeholders' engagement by documenting and tracing problems, obstacles, and expectations, from identification to resolution

_____

20. Unwritten rules that define what behaviors are accepted and what behaviors are not accepted during the project

_____

Process Exercises

The following exercises were designed so you could learn how to recognize the processes and understand their logical sequence. Human resource management processes are listed next, including their unique number in the *PMBOK Guide*:

- 9.1 Plan human resource management
- 9.2 Acquire project team
- 9.3 Develop project team
- 9.4 Manage project team

PROCESS EXERCISE 1

Assign processes to the following activities.

1. Assess the project's performance. _____
2. Assess the team's performance. _____
3. Contract resources. _____
4. Deal with conflicts. _____
5. Define resource calendars and histograms. _____
6. Establish ground rules. _____
7. Group people in a single physical space. _____
8. Negotiate resources with the functional manager. _____
9. Organize team-building activities. _____
10. Organize trainings for the team. _____
11. Plan roles and responsibilities. _____
12. Plan the recognition and rewards system. _____
13. Plan where and how the team will be acquired. _____
14. Update the issue log. _____

PROCESS EXERCISE 2

Assign processes to the following inputs.

1. Project staff assignments _____
2. Human resource management plan _____
3. Issue log _____
4. Activity resource requirements _____

CHAPTER 9 EXAM

> The following questions were designed to test your knowledge on this chapter's topic. Read each question carefully, and choose the option that most accurately answers the question. Once you have completed the exam, compare your answers with the solution and read through the justification provided. Note the topics where you have the most difficulty, and make sure that you dedicate enough study time to them.

1. The project manager has completed a preliminary project schedule. What should be done NEXT?
   A. Acquire project resources.
   B. Approve the schedule.
   C. Prepare a work breakdown structure (WBS).
   D. Determine how the organization will fulfill resource requirements.

2. Which of the following is NOT an output of planning human resource management?
   A. Responsibility assignment matrix (RAM)
   B. Timetable for acquiring the project team
   C. Resource requirements
   D. Staffing management plan

3. A resource histogram defines:
   A. Role and responsibility assignments
   B. A resource pool description
   C. How staff will be managed throughout the project
   D. Resource utilization over time

4. You need to know the exact responsibility of a team member in the project. What should you do NEXT?
   A. Ask the functional manager.
   B. Check the resource breakdown structure (RBS).
   C. Check the RAM.
   D. Check the staffing management plan.

5. During the last two months, several team members chose to leave the project. You are also concerned about symptoms of low motivation and low team performance. As project manager, what is your BEST approach for the problem?
   A. Negotiate additional resources with functional managers and perform team review meetings more often.
   B. Implement a recognition and rewards system.
   C. Improve team performance by placing more pressure on each team member.
   D. Review the communications management plan.

6. Which of the following is NOT a tool or technique of the acquire project team process?
   A. Colocation
   B. Negotiation
   C. Pre-assignment
   D. Virtual teams

7. When the project manager was allocated to a new process reengineering project, several project members had already been selected. This in an example of:
   A. Project management office
   B. Functional organizational
   C. Pre-assignment
   D. Virtual members

8. Which of the following statements regarding team development is NOT TRUE?
   A. Team development should start early in the project.
   B. Colocating the project team facilitates team development.
   C. Virtual teams are used as a team development tool.
   D. Ground rules are used as a team development tool.

9. Which of the following is NOT an outcome of the develop project team process?
   A. Increase individual knowledge and skills
   B. Increase team buy-in
   C. Negotiate the best resources for the project
   D. Prepare a team performance assessment

10. Which of the following statements regarding involving team members in planning activities is NOT correct?
    A. Involving team members in planning increases commitment.
    B. Team members' estimates should be reviewed by their functional manager.
    C. Involving team members in planning increases its accuracy and consistency.
    D. During early planning stages, part of the team may not be assigned to the project yet.

11. Which of the following is NOT a technique used to develop a project team?
    A. Use Delphi to generate consensus
    B. Training
    C. Develop a project logo
    D. Manage conflict

12. How does a weak matrix organization constrain the project team development?
    A. Team development is constrained by conflicting authorities.
    B. Team development is easy because the project manager can use the recognition and rewards system.
    C. Team development is complex because the project management office has control over the team.
    D. Team development is easy because resources are shared.

13. What are the stages of team development according to Tuckman?
    A. Smooth, force, compromise
    B. Plan, develop, manage
    C. Forming, storming, norming, performing, adjourning
    D. Build, develop, delegate, and perform

14. One team member complained that her activity is running late because she is facing problems with her project allocation. What is the FIRST thing to do?
    A. Review the communications management plan to be informed about schedule performance problems sooner.
    B. Review the staffing management plan.
    C. Update the issue log.
    D. Discuss the issue with the functional manager.

15. You are concerned that the level of project conflict can distract team members and disrupt their work rhythm. What is the BEST course of action?
    A. Smooth the conflict when it surfaces.
    B. Address conflict early, preferably in private, with a direct, collaborative approach.
    C. Discuss the conflict in project meetings to engage everyone in finding a solution.
    D. Use coercive authority to quickly resolve conflicts and refocus on the work.

16. Which conflict resolution technique addresses conflict as a problem that requires a solution?
    A. Collaborate
    B. Compromise
    C. Withdraw
    D. Force

17. In a scope control meeting, the customer is insisting that a new feature should be added to the product without reviewing the project schedule and budget. Under pressure from the customer, the project manager decided to postpone the meeting. Which technique is the project manager using?
    A. Withdraw
    B. Accommodation
    C. Compromise
    D. Problem solve

18. Which of the following is NOT part of the manage project team process?
    A. Conducting a project performance appraisal
    B. Providing feedback to a team member
    C. Managing an unexpected change to project staffing
    D. Providing recognition to a team member

19. While reviewing a deliverable provided by a team member, you notice that it has a number of mistakes. What is the BEST thing to do?
    A. Discuss the issue with the team member and his manager.
    B. Correct the deliverable, and perform a quality audit on the team member's work.
    C. Discuss the issue with the team member.
    D. Ask the team member to correct the deliverable.

20. A team member missed an important project meeting without giving prior notice. How should the project manager proceed?
    A. Reprimand the team member in private.
    B. Discuss the issue with the team member and his functional manager.
    C. Discuss the issue with the team member.
    D. Formally document and report the situation.

21. A team member has consciously and constantly missed project commitments. As the project manager, you should meet with the:
    A. Team member
    B. Human resources manager
    C. Sponsor
    D. Team member and his manager

22. Due to problems with the air conditioning system, the team has been forced to work in poor conditions. Team members have repeatedly complained, and their dissatisfaction is now visible in their performance. This is an example of:
    A. Conflict management
    B. Hygiene factors
    C. Maslow's theory of motivation
    D. McGregor's theory of motivation

23. One manager often asks for the team's opinion and stresses the importance of their involvement in project decisions. The manager is following which motivational theory?
    A. Maslow's theory
    B. McGregor's Theory Y
    C. Expectancy theory
    D. McGregor's Theory X

24. Which of the following types of power would BEST suit a project manager in a matrix organization?
    A. Legitimate
    B. Coercive
    C. Reward
    D. Referent

ANSWERS

Review Exercise 1

1. Staffing management plan
2. RAM
3. OBS
4. Project organization chart
5. RBS
6. Text format roles and responsibilities description
7. Histogram

Review Exercise 2

1. Team members may work on different physical locations.
2. Team members may face a conflict between their loyalty to the project and their loyalty to other projects or operations.
3. Resource allocation may be unstable, leading to constant team changes.
4. The project manager may not have enough authority.
5. Team members may have different cultures, have different behaviors, or speak different languages.

Memorization Exercise

1. Colocation
2. Smooth or accommodate
3. Force
4. Withdraw or avoid

5. Problem solve, collaborate, or confront
6. Human resource management plan
7. Staffing management plan
8. Histogram
9. Organizational breakdown structure (OBS)
10. Resource breakdown structure (RBS)
11. Herzberg's theory
12. McGregor's theories
13. Maslow's hierarchy of needs
14. Responsibility assignment matrix (RAM)
15. Pre-assignment
16. Recognition and rewards system
17. Perquisites
18. Virtual teams
19. Issue log
20. Ground rules

Process Exercise 1

1. 9.4
2. 9.3
3. 9.2
4. 9.4
5. 9.1
6. 9.3
7. 9.3
8. 9.2
9. 9.3
10. 9.3
11. 9.1
12. 9.1
13. 9.1
14. 9.4

Process Exercise 2

1. 9.3, 9.4
2. 9.2, 9.3, 9.4
3. 9.4
4. 9.1

Chapter 9 Exam

1. **D** In the early stages of planning, a preliminary schedule is prepared based on limited information about resource availability. Later, a staffing management plan is used to determine if and how the organization can fulfill resource requirements. Answer C should already have been completed. Answers A and B would always be performed after Answer D.

2. **C** Resource requirements are identified by the estimate activity resources process. These requirements are then used as an input into the human resource management plan to assess

if they can be covered by the staffing management plan. All other answer options are an output of the human resource management plan.

3. **D** A resource histogram is a time-phased graphical representation of resource allocation, usually through vertical bars. The other options are describing a responsibility assignment matrix (answer A), an element of a human resource management plan (answer B), and a staffing management plan (answer C).

4. **C** The RAM relates specific WBS elements to specific team members.

5. **B** A recognition and rewards system can establish a clear relationship between individual performance and reward, and thereby increase motivation and improve individual and team performance. The other options would not be able to deal with a generalized motivation and performance problem.

6. **A** Colocation is a tool of the develop project team process. All other options are tools and techniques of the acquire project team process.

7. **C** On pre-assignments, resources are assigned to the project without any type of negotiation between the project manager and the functional manager.

8. **C** Virtual teams are an acquire project team tool. All other statements are correct.

9. **C** Negotiate the best available resources is part of the acquire project team process. All other options are part of the develop project team process.

10. **B** Team members' estimates are not necessarily reviewed by their functional manager. All other options are correct statements.

11. **D** Conflict management is part of the manage project team process. All other options may be techniques of the develop project team process.

12. **A** In a matrix organization, team members may face a conflict between their loyalty to the project and their loyalty to other projects or operations. This conflict can constrain the project team development. The project manager does not have control over the recognition and rewards system in a weak matrix organization (answer B). The project management office does not have control over the team (answer C). Team development is not easier when resources are shared (answer D).

13. **C** The stages of team development according to Tuckman are forming, storming, norming, performing, and adjourning.

14. **C** Updating the issue log is the best option. The project manager would be able to keep track of the problem and its resolution as well as provide evidence to the team member that her concern was heard. Reviewing the staffing management plan (answer B) and discussing the issue with the functional manager (answer D) can be potential solutions. However, they should not occur once the problem is clearly identified.

15. **B** The project manager should manage the conflict in a proactive and collaborative way, engaging the team members directly concerned. Smoothing the conflict (answer A) or using coercive authority (answer D) does not usually lead to a sustainable conflict resolution. Handling the conflict in project meetings would involve team members that were not directly related to the conflict (answer C).

16. **A** The collaborate technique, or problem solve, approaches a conflict as a problem. The solution is determined through structured and disciplined steps, not advancing on the problem solution until each step is completed.

17. **A** The project manager chose to remove himself from the conflict situation. He adopted a withdraw conflict resolution technique.

18. **D** Providing recognition to a team member is part of the develop project team process. All other options are part of the manage project team process.

19. **C** Discussing the issue with the team member might clarify if there are mistakes in the report and define the most appropriate solution. The existence of mistakes is not enough reason to involve management (answer A). The deliverable should be corrected by the team member (answer B). The project manager must understand the problem before defining a solution (answer D).

20. **C** The first step should be to understand the problem. Therefore, he should discuss the issue with the team member. A solution can only be defined after the issue is understood.

21. **D** When a team member consciously and constantly misses a commitment, the problem can no longer be managed between the project manager and the team member. The project manager should speak with the team member and with the team member's manager simultaneously, in order to find a sustainable solution.

22. **B** Hygiene factors, such as problems with the air conditioning system, may destroy motivation if they are not dealt with.

23. **B** According to McGregor's theories, managers Y assume that people are ambitious, are self-motivated, and exercise self-control and therefore should be involved on decisions and have some autonomy.

24. **C** The reward type of power is usually preferred to other types of authority, because it is more aligned with the team's interests and it tends to have more sustainable impact.

10 Communications Management

The **communications management** area includes the activities required to identify, collect, process, and distribute project information. Some examples of communications management activities are:

- Identify the information requirements.
- Determine who, when, and how to provide the information.
- Determine the communication technology.
- Distribute information according to the communications management plan.
- Respond to unplanned information requests.
- Archive documentation according to the communications management plan.
- Collect information and work performance measurements.
- Prepare performance reports.
- Manage changes to the communications management plan.

The Project Manager and Communication

As discussed earlier, the project manager's main responsibility is protecting the project's integrity. This integration requires that the project manager maintain constant communication with all stakeholders. Some of the project manager's responsibilities concerning communication are:

- Establishing and maintaining formal and informal communication channels with project stakeholders, including management, other project managers, functional managers, customers, suppliers, and the team
- Facilitating and streamlining communication within the project

- Knowing what, when, and how to communicate
- Managing stakeholders proactively
- Addressing conflicts
- Providing guidance and assistance when needed

> Most of the project manager's time is spent communicating.

To ensure effective communication during the project, some rules should be considered:

- Encoding a message properly and requesting feedback
- Confirming that the message was understood, requesting clarifications, and providing feedback
- Selecting the communication technology, according to the urgency, type, frequency, size, and complexity of the information
- Avoiding communication barriers, such as noise, poor listening, incorrect encoding or decoding, and differences in language, education, and culture
- Grouping the team at a single physical location
- Using a war room to conduct the project management activities
- Organizing effective meetings with clear objectives, agendas, and minutes
- Resorting to face-to-face meetings whenever possible

The following table displays the communications management processes with their respective process group:

Communications Management Processes

Process	Process Group
Plan communications management	Planning
Manage communications	Executing
Control communications	Monitoring and controlling

Plan Communications Management

It is easy to recognize the importance of properly addressing communications on any project. You can also distinguish different communications requirements and environments on different projects. Therefore, it is only natural to acknowledge the role of communications management planning. From all the advantages of planning communications management the following can be highlighted:

- By systematizing communication you can obtain high-productivity gains through repetition and learning
- Planning communication minimizes the risk of running into expectation-related problems
- Planning communication facilitates the stakeholders' involvement in the project

Communications Management Plan

With a **communications management plan**, the communication requirements are identified and documented. (See Figure 10.1.) These communication requirements may include:

Description	From	To	Support	Medium	When	Content	...

Figure 10.1 Communications management plan

- What information
- Who needs the information
- Who will provide it
- When and how it will be provided
- What is the support and the medium for providing the information
- What is the level of detail
- How problems will be managed
- What technology should be used
- How the meetings will be managed
- Project glossary

There is a concern not only about sending the right information using the right method, but also with sending only the required information. Communicating inadequate information regarding content or format, communicating at the wrong time, or sending useless information are all symptoms of lack of communication planning.

Communication cannot be fully planned. There will always be information needs that could not have been foreseen.

REVIEW EXERCISE 1

Provide three examples of communication requirements, identifying the receiver, the support, and the moment when the information should be provided.

Description	Receiver	Support	When
1.			
2.			
3.			

REVIEW EXERCISE 2

Some symptoms of lack of communication planning on the project are:

---

1. _____

   _____

2. _____

   _____

3. _____

   _____

4. _____

   _____

5. _____

   _____

6. _____

   _____

Communication Channels

Communication channels are the existing one-to-one communication relationships within the project. The more channels there are, the more complex and expensive the project communication is. The number of existing channels is calculated by the formula:

$$\text{Channels} = \frac{(n^2 - n)}{2} = \frac{n(n-1)}{2}, \; n = \text{number of team members}$$

For example, if the number of team members increases from 4 to 5, the number of channels increases from 6 to 10. (See Figure 10.2.)

The importance of communication channels in project management is mostly related to how the number of channels grows geometrically as the number of people involved in communication increases. For example, increasing the number of resources may help you recover from a schedule delay, but it will also increase the communication costs exponentially.

The number of channels is also important when preparing the communications management plan, in which you have to identify all the channels that information is flowing through.

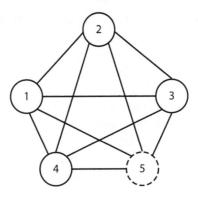

Figure 10.2 Communication channels
with five team members

War Room

A **war room** is a location used as the project command center. In a project context, a war room will be used to centralize planning and controlling, hold meetings, display performance charts, and coordinate work. This communication technique usually improves overall project communication.

Manage Communications

The role of the **manage communications** process is ensuring that project information is flowing from the source to whoever needs it. Managing this information flow requires collecting, processing, distributing, and archiving information according to the communications management plan. Because communication cannot be fully controlled, managing communications also means responding to unplanned requests for information.

The project manager should pay particular attention to structuring project communication, as well as adapting the communication model and technology to each specific situation. While formally communicating project performance, the project manager should also select the type of performance report that best fits each situation.

Structuring Communication

There are many ways to send a message, depending on its context, urgency, importance, impact, complexity, and size. A choice must be made regarding whether to communicate formally or informally, through writing or verbally, internally or externally, officially or unofficially, and actively, passively, or interactively.

Special care should be given to whether the message should be **formal** or **informal.** Formality in communication deals with conformance to established professional rules, standards, and processes.

> Some knowledge areas are by nature more formal than others. Procurement management is typically the most formal knowledge area because it involves contracts. Another particularly formal knowledge area is integration management.

When modeling communication, the sender must also choose between **written** and **oral communication** and **verbal** and **nonverbal communication.** Nonverbal communication, based on physical gesture such as facial expressions and body language can be particularly relevant when communicating face-to-face. **Paralingual** communication, such as the voice pitch, tone, and inflections, will also play an important role when transmitting a message. Verbal communication, based on words, can have a surprisingly low weight on the overall message. Albert Mehrabian, a professor from UCLA, analyzed the message's impact while communicating emotions face-to-face. According to his studies, nonverbal (55 percent) and paralingual (38 percent) communication will account for most of the message's impact, while verbal (7 percent) communication does not have a significant impact when communicating emotions. Mehrabian's findings are not applicable in many project situations. Still, a project manager should be aware of the potential impact of his or her body language, voice pitch, and tone.

Examples of Types of Communication

Situation	*Type of Communication*
Procurement documents (statement of work, contract . . .), integration documents (project management plan, change requests . . .), quality control measurements, issue logs, documents that require approval, recurring problems with a team member's performance	Formal written
E-mails exchanged within the team	Informal written
Presentations	Formal oral
Conversations	Informal oral

Concerning interactivity, communication may be:

- **Active** The sender unilaterally sends the message without requesting a response.
- **Passive** Information is placed in a repository that can be accessed by receivers.
- **Interactive** Two or more persons communicate interactively. This method is best used when communication requires a response or when interaction is required to ensure that the message was properly transmitted.

Communication may also be **vertical** or **horizontal**, **internal** or **external** to the project, and **official** or **unofficial**.

Communication Models

The communication model is a two-way process of reaching mutual understanding that includes the following components:

- **Sender and encoding** The sender encodes a message, adding nonverbal and paralingual communication.
- **Message and medium** The message is transmitted through a medium.
- **Receiver, decoding, and feedback** The receiver decodes the message and sends a response back acknowledging receipt of the message.
- **Noise** The message transmission may be negatively impacted by communication blockers that interfere with its comprehension. This noise in communication often results from differences in language, experience, knowledge, attitude, and culture between the sender and the receiver.

Both sender and receiver are responsible for making sure that the message is effectively transmitted and understood. The sender is responsible for choosing the communication medium, encoding the message, and avoiding communication blockers. The receiver is responsible for listening, confirming that the message was understood, and providing feedback.

> The most likely outcome of communication blockers is conflict.

REVIEW EXERCISE 3

> The message is not always effectively transmitted. Provide examples of communication blockers.

1. _____

2. _____

3. _____

4. _____

5. _____

Performance Reports

Performance reports are used to inform stakeholders about the project's health. There are different types of reports including:

- **Status report** Summarizes the project situation at a certain time (Think of a status report as a photograph of the current performance.)
- **Progress report** Describes what was completed during the reporting period
- **Trend report** Analyzes time-phased results and identifies trends
- **Forecast report** Predicts future performance
- **Earned value report** Integrates scope, time, and costs to assess performance
- **Variance report** Compares actual values with the baseline
- **Lessons learned report** Assesses what went well and what could have been improved
- **Dashboard** A control panel that provides an at-a-glance understanding regarding project performance. Dashboards typically include key performance indicators, trends, variance analysis, and items that require attention. A dashboard should be simple, be useful, and have clear graphics.

Project Records

The project records organize relevant information about the project, including e-mails, meeting minutes, and contract administration documents.

For project records to be effectively used, they should have a logical organization, be easily accessible, and reflect the actual project status.

Control Communications

Although an effort should be made to identify communication requirements, there will always be new information needs that were not planned and that often could not have been foreseen. This fact distinguishes communication control from controlling other knowledge areas, such as scope, schedule, or costs. Otherwise, control communications is a typical control process, trying to ensure that the stakeholders' need for information is met and that changes are managed when necessary.

To properly convey information, communications management processes need a supporting system. The **information management system** is a set of tools used to support project information, including e-mail, video conferencing, telephone, printed reports, and project management software.

MEMORIZATION EXERCISE

> The following exercise was designed to facilitate the memorization of the main concepts in this chapter. Assign the following definitions to a communications management concept.

1. A control panel that provides an at-a-glance understanding regarding project performance

   _____

2. Communication based on physical gestures such as facial expressions and body language

   _____

3. Communication based on pitch, tone, and inflections in the voice

   _____

4. Existing one-to-one communication relationships within the project

   _____

5. Location used as project command center to improve communication

   _____

6. Report that analyzes time-phased results and identifies trends

   _____

7. Report that compares actual values with the baseline

   _____

8. Report that describes what was accomplished in the reporting period

   _____

9. Statement that identifies communication requirements and determines how they will be managed throughout the project

_____

10. Two-way process of reaching mutual understanding that includes a sender, a message, a medium, a receiver, feedback, and noise

_____

Process Exercises

The following exercises were designed so you could learn how to recognize the processes and understand their logical sequence. Communications management processes are listed next, including their unique number in the *PMBOK Guide*:

- 10.1 Plan communications management
- 10.2 Manage communications
- 10.3 Control communications

PROCESS EXERCISE 1

> **Assign processes to the following activities.**

1. Archive documentation according to the communications management plan.

_____

2. Collect information and work performance measurements.

_____

3. Determine communication requirements.

_____

4. Determine the communication technology.

_____

5. Distribute information according to the communications management plan.

_____

6. Manage changes to the communications management plan.

_____

7. Respond to unplanned information requests.

_____

PROCESS EXERCISE 2

Assign processes to the following inputs.

1. Project communications _____

2. Work performance data _____

3. Stakeholder register _____

4. Issue log _____

CHAPTER 10 EXAM

The following questions were designed to test your knowledge on this chapter's topic. Read each question carefully, and choose the option that most accurately answers the question. Once you have completed the exam, compare your answers with the solution and read through the justification provided. Note the topics where you have the most difficulty, and make sure you dedicate enough study time to them.

1. Which of the following statements regarding communication is NOT TRUE?
   A. Project managers should spend most of their time communicating.
   B. Integration is performed through communication.
   C. All communication should be thoroughly planned.
   D. Communication channels grow exponentially.

2. During the lunch break, two team members are having a disagreement over a quality requirement. Which of the following will have the most impact on how each team member perceives the other's message?
   A. The words chosen
   B. Physical gestures such as facial expressions and body language
   C. Noise
   D. Formal and written documentation

3. Which of the following would be LEAST important to communicate important messages over e-mail?
   A. Ask for clarification.
   B. Pay attention to paralingual communication.
   C. Acknowledge that you understood the message.
   D. Ask for feedback.

4. What is the MOST likely outcome of noise in the communication?
   A. Conflict
   B. Defects
   C. Motivation
   D. Scope changes

5. Which of the following would be MORE appropriate for communicating complex technical issues to a team physically located in another country?
   A. Informal and written
   B. Push
   C. Formal and written
   D. Formal and verbal

6. In the communication model, who is responsible for ensuring that the message is clearly understood?
   A. Sender
   B. Receiver
   C. Sender and receiver
   D. None

7. In which of the following situations is formal written communication MOST required?
   A. An identified risk requires a response plan.
   B. The customer requires information regarding project performance.
   C. There is a change to the contracted scope.
   D. A deliverable is verified and validated.

8. A communications management plan includes descriptions of:
   A. Responsibility assignments
   B. Project performance
   C. Stakeholder communication requirements
   D. Decisions made on previous project management meetings

9. An important stakeholder complained that he is receiving too much technical documentation and no performance reports. Which process could have avoided this problem?
   A. Identify stakeholders
   B. Identify risks
   C. Report performance
   D. Plan communications management

10. All of the following options are part of a communications management plan EXCEPT:
    A. Communication technology
    B. Status meetings time and locations
    C. Stakeholders' names, power, and expectations
    D. Project glossary

11. Which of the following is NOT an input to the development of a communications management plan?
    A. Existing communication infrastructure
    B. An issue log
    C. Stakeholders' identification
    D. Historical information

12. Which of the following options is LEAST relevant for improving project communications?
    A. Use a project war room.
    B. Perform a kickoff meeting.
    C. Colocate the team.
    D. Prepare a resource breakdown structure (RBS).

13. Which of the following options BEST describes the importance of communication channels in project management?
    A. They determine communication technology.
    B. They are used to prepare a resource breakdown structure (RBS).
    C. They are used to identify stakeholders.
    D. Increasing the number of communication channels increases the project's complexity and costs.

14. A project has six team members. How many communication channels exist within the team?
    A. 6
    B. 10
    C. 15
    D. 30

15. The project manager has determined communication requirements, established reporting templates, determined the communication technology, and documented the project glossary. He is about to move on to the next project management process. What has the project manager forgotten to do?
    A. Identify communication risks
    B. Involve team members
    C. Identify stakeholders
    D. Establish a resource breakdown structure (RBS)

16. Which of the following reports would you use to compare what was completed with what should have been completed?
    A. Progress
    B. Variance
    C. Forecast
    D. Status

17. A project dashboard may be MOST useful to:
    A. Understand the project risks
    B. Describe what was completed during the reporting period
    C. Understand project variances
    D. Provide an at-a-glance understanding regarding project performance

18. Which of the following is NOT a tool or technique of the manage communications process?
    A. Publish information on the project website.
    B. Distribute project lessons learned.
    C. Use a videoconference to deliver a project presentation.
    D. Meet with the customer to understand his or her concerns.

ANSWERS

Review Exercise 1

1. Progress information   Project manager   Project plan file   Weekly (Friday)
2. Performance report   Sponsor, customer, and team   Attached to e-mail   Weekly (Monday)
3. Performance meeting minute   Sponsor, customer   Weekly meeting   Weekly (Tuesday)

Review Exercise 2

1. Stakeholders are receiving information that they don't understand and are not receiving information they need.
2. The functional manager removed team members from the project because he or she did not know the actual project status.
3. There are frequent changes because stakeholders' expectations are not being managed.
4. There is widespread dissatisfaction due to lack of knowledge about project performance.
5. Project procedures are not being adopted because they are not known.
6. The team completed unplanned work because it was not familiar with the change control system.

Review Exercise 3

1. Not mastering a language or a specific terminology
2. Sender and receiver not using the same terminology
3. Prejudice
4. Hostility
5. Use of an inadequate medium or support

Memorization Exercise

1. Dashboard
2. Nonverbal communication
3. Paralingual communication
4. Communication channels
5. War room
6. Trend report
7. Variance report
8. Progress report
9. Communications management plan
10. Communication models

Process Exercise 1

1. 10.2
2. 10.2
3. 10.1
4. 10.1

5. 10.2
6. 10.3
7. 10.2

Process Exercise 2

1. 10.3
2. 10.3
3. 10.1
4. 10.3

Chapter 10 Exam

1. **C** Communication cannot be fully planned. There will always be information needs that could not have been foreseen. All other statements are true.
2. **B** Most of the message's impact is based on nonverbal communication. Therefore, physical gestures such as facial expressions and body language are the best option.
3. **B** In a conversation through e-mail, paralingual communication is not received by the receiver. All other options can be relevant in an e-mail conversation.
4. **A** The message transmission may be negatively impacted by communication blockers that interfere with its comprehension. This noise in communication often results from differences in language, attitude, and culture between the sender and the receiver. If the message is not effectively transmitted, it will not be possible to share views and overcome differences. Therefore, the most likely outcome of communication noise is conflict.
5. **C** If the message is technically complex, formal and written communication will provide structure and traceability to the message.
6. **C** In the communication model, both sender and receiver are responsible for making sure that the message is effectively transmitted and understood.
7. **C** Because it involves contracts, procurement management is typically the most formal knowledge area.
8. **C** The communications management plan describes the stakeholders' information requirements. All other options are not part of a communications management plan.
9. **D** The project has a communication planning problem because stakeholders are not receiving the right information. The plan communications management process would identify and document communications requirements for specific stakeholders. Answers A and B are not correct because the problem is specific to communications management. Answer C is not correct because report performance is not a process.
10. **C** Stakeholders' names, power, and expectations are documented in the stakeholders' register during project initiation. All other options may be part of a communications management plan.
11. **B** An issue log is the tool used to manage the team and the project stakeholders. It is not typically used as an input to the development of a communications management plan. All other options are typically inputs of the communications management plan.
12. **D** An RBS is part of the human resource management plan. The war room (answer A), the kickoff meeting (answer B), and the team colocation (answer C) in the same physical space are tools and techniques used in communications management.
13. **D** Communication channels are the number of one-to-one communications that may exist. Communication channels grow exponentially with an increase in project size, triggering project complexity and costs.

14. **C** The number of communication channels is calculated by $n(n-1)/2$. A team with six team members has 15 communication channels.

15. **B** The project manager should always involve the team in the planning effort, including communication planning. The remaining options are not part of the communications management plan.

16. **B** A variance report is a type of performance report that compares actual values with a baseline. All other options are not focused on showing project variances.

17. **D** A dashboard is a control panel that provides an at-a-glance understanding regarding project performance. Dashboards typically include key performance indicators, trends, variance analysis, and items requiring attention.

18. **D** Meeting with the customer to understand his or her concerns is part of the manage stakeholder engagement process. Publishing information on the project website (answer A), distributing project lessons learned (answer B), and using a videoconference (answer C) can be tools and techniques of the manage communications process.

11 Risk Management

Do you recall what the project concept is? A project is a temporary initiative carried out with the aim of producing a unique product. This uniqueness is enough to ensure that all projects are subject to uncertainty. The supplier may deliver the materials late, the expected human resources may not be available, or the technology may not have the expected stability.

Although projects are uncertain, you have the capacity to understand and influence your exposure to risk. You know there are many risks that you have the ability to influence. You also know that each application area has its own risks that tend to occur more frequently. An analysis of the organization's history can provide hints on how to manage those risks. You know you can avoid chaos if you have a plan to implement should the risk occur. Finally, if you understand the project risks, you have greater ability to define feasible objectives and inspire trust among stakeholders.

The **risk management** area includes all the activities required to understand and influence the project risk factors, maximizing favorable risks and minimizing unfavorable risks. But how exactly do people understand and influence risk factors? The main activities of a structured risk management approach are:

- Plan risk management to adapt it to the project's dimension, criticality, and uncertainty
- Identify risks
- Analyze the risk's probability and impact so the team can concentrate on the most critical risks
- Analyze risks quantitatively
- Prepare the most adequate risk response
- Define the project reserve
- Monitor risks to understand if there are changes based on their probability and impact
- Verify if new risks arise during the project
- Implement risk responses
- Verify if the risk responses were effective
- Verify if the planned risk processes are being followed

Risk may be minimized by proactively managing risk events.

Two different, and complementary, perspectives on risk management can be adopted:

- **Micromanagement**   Micromanagement is the most commonly adopted approach to risk management. Micromanaging risk may include identifying, analyzing, prioritizing, quantifying, responding, and monitoring individual risks.
- **Macromanagement**   Macromanagement is concerned with the overall project risk. Risk macromanagement can include activities such as calculating a project risk score during qualitative risk analysis, completing a simulation during quantitative risk analysis, or performing an audit during risk monitoring.

Significant or widespread variances in project objectives are usually the result of inadequate or insufficient risk management.

REVIEW EXERCISE 1

> **Managing risk is important to:**

1. _____

2. _____

3. _____

4. _____

5. _____

6. _____

7. _____

8. _____

9. _____

10. _____

11. _____

12. _____

13. _____

Risk

Within a project context, a risk is an uncertain event that can have a positive or negative impact on project objectives. A risk with a negative impact is known as a threat, while a risk with a positive impact is known as an opportunity.

To understand a risk, you need to identify the uncertain **event**. Only by analyzing the event can you understand the risk probability. Let's observe the following examples of events, associated respectively to a threat and an opportunity:

- Resource requirements assumptions may not match the actual resource availability.
- Developed modules may be reused on the project.

Another risk dimension is its **cause** or causes. When planning a risk response, it is important to actually address causes instead of addressing events or impacts. Identifying the cause may also help us detect if there are causes shared among multiple risks. In the previous threat example, the cause may be that the functional manager is not sufficiently involved in the project. In the previous opportunity example, the cause may be that modules share a common structure.

Finally, it is important to understand the risk **impact** or impacts to assess its severity. In the previous examples, the impact of an incorrect resource requirements assumption can be a schedule delay and the impact of reusing modules can be compressing the schedule and saving costs. (See Figure 11.1.)

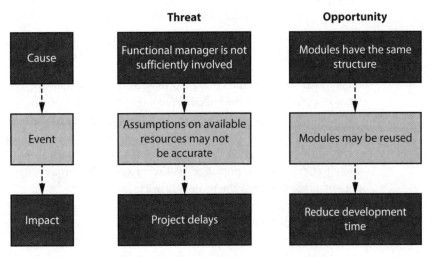

Figure 11.1 Risk anatomy

Factors That Can Influence Risk Priority

Many elements can influence your perception of the risk's importance. Some of these factors are:

- The event that may or may not happen
- The probability of occurrence
- The impact of the risk
- The moment on the project life cycle where the risk can occur
- The frequency that it may occur
- The risk trend
- The information available about the risk
- The organization's risk tolerance
- Your capacity to interfere with the risk
- The knowledge that others have of the risk occurrence

Risk Classification

There are different ways to classify risks. Risks can be organized according to their nature:

- **Pure or static risk**   There is a possibility of loss, but no possibility of gain. Examples of pure risks are a fire or flood.
- **Business, speculative, or dynamic risk**   There is a possibility of loss and a possibility of gain. These risks are directly related to the organization's business activity.

  Risks can also be organized according to their identification:

- **Known-unknown**   Risks that were identified, but due to the very definition of risk it is not known if they will occur. To protect the project from known-unknowns, the project managers should plan risk responses and include a contingency reserve for the residual risks.
- **Unknown-unknown**   Risks that were not or could not be identified on the project. To protect the project from unknown-unknowns, the project budget should include a management reserve based on the experience accumulated from previous projects.

You can also observe risks from an **individual** perspective and manage specific project risks, or form an overall project risk perspective. The **overall project risk** depends not only on the aggregation of individual risks, but also on risks that may have an impact at the project level. Examples of project-level risks are unrealistic schedule constraints, inadequate project management, lack of change management, lack of management support, and lack of methodology.

Attitude Toward Risk

How much risk should be accepted in each specific situation? What risks may be accepted, and what risks should be minimized? When do you know it is time to implement a risk response?

The attitude toward risks describes the stakeholders' willingness to accept risks or require immediate response actions. Such attitude can reflect the nature of the specific risks (e.g., a risk with an impact on the organization's public image might lead to strong reactions from stakeholders), the importance of the project, the organization's culture, the stakeholders' personalities, and even the project history.

The attitude toward risk may be analyzed in terms of risk appetite, risk tolerance, and risk limits. **Risk appetite** is a broad classification of the level of uncertainty that the organization is willing to accept. For example, project stakeholders might be averse to budget risks, but willing to consider all potential options while dealing with schedule risks. There are many alternative ways to describe the stakeholders' risk appetite, including:

- **Risk averse**   Stakeholders' satisfaction decreases with an increase of risk exposure. Hence, the less risk the better.
- **Risk neutral**   Stakeholders will consider available options taking into account both risk exposure and potential reward.
- **Risk seeking**   Stakeholders are eager to accept high risks in order to pursue high rewards.

Risk tolerances define how much risk the organization is willing to accept. Tolerances can be defined in terms of project constraints (e.g., tolerated variances in the schedule, costs, or planned resources) or can be defined in terms of specific project variables (e.g., tolerated number of system errors or tolerated number of days that a supplier can be late on a delivery).

Risk threshold is the limit beyond which stakeholders are not willing to accept the risk and additional risk responses are required. For example, the project may define that 15 days before the hardware delivery due date, the supplier will have to confirm the delivery in writing.

Risk thresholds have more than one use in risk management. They help the team select the most appropriate risk response, by setting a limit beyond which the risk should not be accepted. They can also be used to assess the effectiveness of risk responses by observing whether the risk recedes to an acceptable level.

The following table displays the risk management processes with their respective process group:

Risk Management Processes

Process	Process Group
Plan risk management	Planning
Identify risks	Planning
Perform qualitative risk analysis	Planning
Perform quantitative risk analysis	Planning
Plan risk responses	Planning
Control risks	Monitoring and controlling

Plan Risk Management

Plan risk management prepares the **risk management plan**, establishing one common understanding of the management approach that best suits the project's criticality and uncertainty. Another role of planning risk management is to ensure there are enough resources and time to perform the risk management activities.

Some of the elements defined in the risk management plan are:

- Procedures, metrics, tools, and templates used to plan, monitor, and report risks
- Risk management resources and responsibilities
- Risk management budget
- Categories used to classify the risks and risk breakdown structure
- Criteria used to classify probability, impact, trend, urgency, and data quality
- Attitude toward risk adopted by stakeholders
- Adopted probability and impact matrix
- Risk monitoring frequency
- Risk visibility

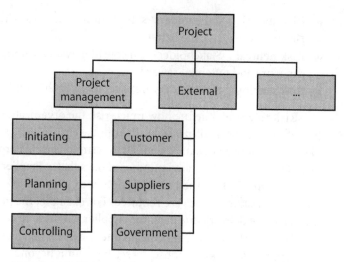

Figure 11.2 Risk breakdown structure (RBS)

Risk Categorization

As an organization begins to accumulate risks and responses information, their challenge is being able to effectively use that historical information. Risk categories are a logical way to group risks, facilitating and accelerating the reuse of accumulated historical information. For example, the team may identify project risks by browsing historical information regarding risks of specific categories.

Categories also adapt the risk management approach to the project's specific risks. For example, you can use a contract category to prepare a report to inform management about contract-related risks.

Finally, categories may help the team focus on sources of project risk, by identifying causes shared among multiple risks. Once this sharing of causes is identified, these risks may be prioritized on the scale of attention of the project management team.

Risk categorization may be done in a list or in a hierarchical format through a **risk breakdown structure (RBS)**. (See Figure 11.2.)

Do not confuse a risk breakdown structure with a resource breakdown structure.

REVIEW EXERCISE 2

Typical symptoms of ineffective risk management are:

1. _____

2. _____

3. _____

4. _____

5. _____

6. _____

7. _____

8. _____

9. _____

10. _____

Identify Risks

If you could be absolutely sure you would meet project objectives, you wouldn't have to worry about risk management. However, you know there are always events that threaten the project objectives and there are always opportunities to explore. If you do not identify and understand these events, how can you influence project risk? This uncertainty about the project's future justifies all the effort required to identify and understand the project risks.

Identify risks is the process that identifies, understands, and documents the uncertain events that may influence project objectives. This understanding should include:

- Identify risk events
- Identify the risk root causes and the risk impacts
- Identify potential risk responses

Risk identification can involve the project manager, team members, customers, risk management experts, and other relevant stakeholders, both inside and outside the organization. Engaging stakeholders in risk identification will also expedite planning risk responses and commit stakeholders to planned responses.

During the initial stages of planning, risk identification is a particularly iterative process. Planning decisions within all knowledge areas frequently have some degree of uncertainty that can lead to a revision of the identified risks.

Although most of the risk identification effort occurs in the early stages of planning, it may not be possible to fully understand the project risks at the beginning. As with other project knowledge areas, risks should be progressively identified throughout the whole project, as more and better information becomes available.

> The project manager has an ethical responsibility to communicate the risks identified.

The results of the risks identification should be documented in the **risk register**. This document will also be used to analyze, respond to, and control the risks. (See Figure 11.3.)

Risk	Cause	Event	Impact	Category	Potential response	...

Figure 11.3 Risk register

Risks may be collected through many tools and techniques, including:

- **Assumptions analysis**   Managing projects will always require establishing assumptions. These assumptions have, by definition, some level of uncertainty. The project team can identify risks by reviewing the consistency and information quality of the documented assumptions. The team can also perform multiple tests to validate the available assumptions.

- **Strengths, weaknesses, opportunities, and threats (SWOT) analysis**   The SWOT technique identifies risks by analyzing the strengths, weaknesses, opportunities, and threats associated with a specific topic. One of the advantages of this technique is that it covers both threats and opportunities.

- **Root cause analysis**   The root cause analysis technique attempts to better understand risks by analyzing prior problems, searching for their underlying causes.

- **Documentation reviews**   Analyzing project documents and plans is the main source of risk identification. For example, a scope statement analysis may reveal an option for an unstable technology and a network diagram may show multiple critical paths.

- **Delphi technique**   The Delphi technique obtains a consensus on project risks by repeatedly consulting experts, usually through an anonymous process (see the collect requirements process).

- **Cause-and-effect, Ishikawa, or fishbone diagrams**   This technique is based on the principle that in dealing with a risk, it is best to deal with its causes rather than its symptoms. Additionally, because many risks share the same cause, this technique can also lead to more effective risk responses. The cause-and-effect diagram graphically represents the risk and the causes that may lead to it (see the plan quality management process).

- **Flowcharts**   With a flowchart, you can graphically represent the steps required to complete a process and therefore better identify the risks involved (see the plan quality management process).

- **Checklists**   Think about most of the risks that occurred on your projects: they have already occurred on previous projects within the same organization. In other words, although risks are uncertain, there is often accumulated risk information in the organization. Checklists provide structure for this historical information, guiding the team while identifying potential risks.

- **Influence diagrams**   An influence diagram is a graphical representation of a decision process, highlighting the factors that may influence its outcome.

- **Brainstorming**   Brainstorming identifies risks based on an unconstrained exchange of ideas between different project stakeholders. The consistency of the risks is only assessed when all the ideas have been collected and documented.

- **Interviews**   Interviews collect risks by asking direct questions to project stakeholders.

- **Expert judgment**   Accumulated experience enables expert groups to identify project risks. Because an expert's judgment may be easily biased by interests or subjective factors, this technique should be used in conjunction with others.

> Throughout the project, it is the control risks process that verifies whether there are new risks.

REVIEW EXERCISE 3

> Identify examples of risks from the following knowledge areas.

Scope

1. _____

2. _____

3. _____

Time

1. _____

2. _____

3. _____

Resources

1. _____

2. _____

3. _____

Perform Qualitative Risk Analysis

Less important risks should not require the same time, attention, and response type as critical risks. A qualitative risk analysis aims to quickly prioritize risks according to their severity so that the project management team can concentrate on the most important risks. This severity, or importance, will depend mostly on the probability and impact, but also on other factors such as the quality of the information available, and the trend and urgency of the risks.

But how do you perform a qualitative risk analysis? A qualitative risk analysis may include the following activities:

- Evaluating the probability and impact of the identified risks
- Assessing the quality of the data available for each risk
- Using the probability and impact matrix to assign a score to each risk
- Ranking risks according to risk factors
- Preparing a risk watch list
- Identifying critical risks that should be closely managed
- Selecting risks for further analysis and response
- Highlighting risks that require a short-term response
- Obtaining a qualitative assessment of the overall project risk

To prioritize risks, the team starts to assign a rate to the risk probability and impact. Rating is considerably easier when the team has a common understanding of how to assess probability and impact. This understanding of probability and impact definitions should have been previously established on the risk management plan. The following table shows one example of a scale used to classify probability.

Probability	Condition to Classify the Risk
Low	Never occurred in the organization
Medium	Occurred once or twice in the organization
High	Occurred three times or more in the organization

To rate the probability and impact, the team may use expert judgment, interviews, measurements, the Delphi technique, and the nominal group technique (see Chapter 5).

Qualitative risk analysis is performed based on a subjective assessment.

Using the probability and impact ratings, the **probability and impact matrix** can assign a score to each risk (see Figure 11.4). The **risk score** is an assessment of the risk severity that enables the team to prioritize risks, as well as assess if the risk responses were effective in reducing risk exposure. The probability and impact matrix can also adopt a scheme of colors for a faster interpretation of the risks scores.

The probability and impact matrix, also known as look-up table, is often standardized as part of the organization's risk management policies and templates. However, during the plan risk management process, it can be customized to reflect the project stakeholders' risk appetite and tolerance. For example, if the project's stakeholders have a lower risk tolerance, risks will be more easily classified as critical.

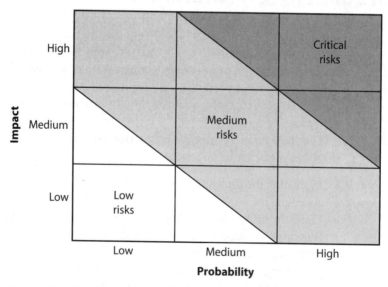

Figure 11.4 Example of a probability and impact matrix

Although qualitative risk assessment is usually performed based on probability and impact, other factors may be relevant. These factors that may help assess the risk severity are:

- **Data quality**   Assessing the quality of the data available can complement the risk assessment. A low probability and impact threat can be prioritized if you do not have access to significant information about the risk.
- **Trend**   Assessing the risk trend enables the team to determine if the risk evolution has been favorable or unfavorable, and to forecast future risk behavior.
- **Urgency**   Assessing the risk urgency enables the team to identify risks that require immediate attention.

Data quality assesses how much you know about the risk.

At the end of the qualitative analysis, the risk register is updated with qualitative information regarding probability, impact, and other risk factors, such as data quality and urgency.

Risk Ranking

Risks should be ranked based on their probability and impact, as well as other risk factors. The goal is to focus the team on managing critical risks. Risk ranking may also be used to sort the risks by considering only their impact on a specific objective, such as schedule or costs.

Risk Watch List

What should you do with noncritical risks? Risks with low severity should be monitored on a risk watch list. These risks should not be forgotten, because there is still some possibility of occurrence. The team should periodically review this list.

Risks Requiring Further Analysis

The project should identify the risks that require moving further on the risk management process, to quantitative analysis or response planning.

Risks Requiring Short-Term Responses

The team should also identify risks that require immediate attention. A risk might require a near-term response if there is a limited timeframe to implement the response. For example, an opportunity might only be available in the immediate future, or a response to a threat might require a long time to be implemented. A risk might also be deemed as urgent if the risk warning signs do not provide enough time to implement a reactive response if the risk occurs.

Overall Project Risk Qualitative Assessment

Instead of assessing each risk individually, the overall project risk assessment is focused on the whole project. The main role of this assessment is to take a photograph of the overall project risk that can be compared with the risk thresholds. For example, if the project has an overall risk score of 60 and an overall risk threshold of 50, it will definitely need to plan and implement risk responses. Additionally, this assessment allows the team to verify if the risk responses were effective in decreasing the overall project risk. Finally, this assessment enables the organization to compare the project risk exposure with other projects in the organization.

REVIEW EXERCISE 4

| Factors relevant to determine the importance of a risk to an individual or organization are: |

1. _____

2. _____

3. _____

4. _____

5. _____

6. _____

7. _____

8. _____

Perform Quantitative Risk Analysis

The risks considered as priorities by the qualitative analysis may be subject to a numerical analysis of probability and impact. This quantitative analysis can deepen the level of understanding of these risks and can also quantitatively assess the impact of the risks on the overall project.

The quantitative analysis of project risks may include the following activities:

- Estimating the probability of individual risks in percentage
- Assessing the impact of risks on project objectives
- Reviewing the risk ranking once priority risks have been quantitatively analyzed
- Using probabilistic models to calculate the schedule or budget so as to provide an acceptable level of confidence
- Using probabilistic models to determine the likelihood of meeting specific schedule or cost objectives
- Making informed project decisions under uncertainty
- Analyzing the trend of quantified risks, verifying if planned responses were effective

The quantitative analysis updates the risk register, specifying information about the percentage probability, the impact, the expected value, and the risk priority.

Techniques used in the quantitative analysis include:

- Interviews
- Expected monetary value
- Decision trees
- Probabilistic distribution
- Sensitivity analysis
- Simulation techniques such as Monte Carlo and sensitivity analysis
- Expert judgment

Quantitative risk analysis only adds value if the analyzed data have quality. When no data are available or the data have no quality, this analysis may not be possible.

Expected Monetary Value (EMV)

The expected monetary value (EMV) technique quantifies the risk using a combination of probability and impact. This quantification supports response planning by enabling a comparison between the expected value of the risk and the cost of the response. Another use of the EMV is allowing the team to make decisions within an uncertain context.

> A risk may have impact on both schedule and costs. The severity of this risk will depend on whether the organization priority is schedule or costs.

REVIEW EXERCISE 5

> Considering the information on the following table, answer the following questions:

Risk	Probability	Impact on Costs	Impact on Schedule
A	50%	6,000	6 weeks
B	20%	4,000	20 weeks

1. What risk is more critical if costs are a priority for the organization?
2. What risk is more critical if the schedule is a priority for the organization?

Decision Tree

Project decisions are often made in an uncertain context. The **decision tree** is a graphical treelike representation of alternative decisions with uncertain results. (See Figure 11.5.) Each alternative is represented on a tree branch, with the corresponding potential consequences and probabilities. A decision tree enables the team to calculate the EMV of each tree branch, in order to select the most favorable option. The decision tree is handled from right to left, calculating the expected cost of each alternative decision.

> On the exam, you have to perform only relatively easy calculations related to EVM, decision trees, and PERT estimates. You may use the existing calculator on the exam software to perform these calculations.

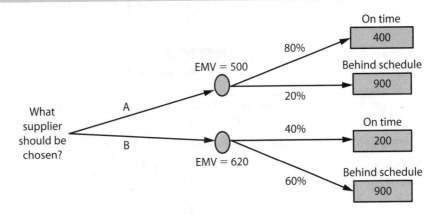

Figure 11.5 Example of a decision tree

REVIEW EXERCISE 6

To perform a project activity, the team is considering contracting a specialized company with an additional cost of 5,000. On either scenario, with or without the company, there is some uncertainty about the activity costs. The following table summarizes the activity expected cost with and without the company. What is the best decision?

| Speed | Without the Company | | With the Company | |
	Probability	Cost	Probability	Cost
Slow	0.6	2,600	0.9	0
Fast	0.4	9,200	0.1	1,500

Sensitivity Analysis

The **sensitivity analysis** technique determines which variables have the most impact on a specific final result. To do that, it generates small changes to one variable, maintaining all others at a constant and observing the impact on the final result. While dealing with risks, sensitivity analysis is used to determine which risks have the most potential impact on project objectives. Sensitivity analysis is frequently represented graphically through a tornado chart. (See Figure 11.6.)

On a quantitative risk analysis, sensitivity analysis is used to identify which risks have a greater impact on the project schedule or budget.

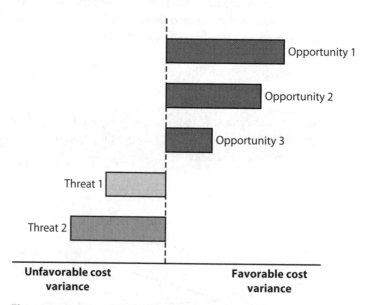

Figure 11.6 Example of a risk tornado chart

Probability Distribution

A probability distribution graphically represents the probability of a range of values (e.g., project costs). For example, a **Beta distribution** ranges between a minimum and a maximum value, concentrating around a most likely value, that is often skewed to one of the sides of the distribution (see the section on the three-point estimate in Chapter 6).

Simulation

The **simulation** technique uses a model to represent how uncertain elements may influence the project objectives. To analyze the schedule risk, the simulation randomly selects activity durations and calculates the corresponding overall duration. By repeating multiple calculation iterations, usually with the help of software, it can calculate a probabilistic distribution of the project duration. The most widely known project management simulation technique is the Monte Carlo simulation, analyzed in Chapter 6.

Plan Risk Responses

Plan risk responses is the risk management process that determines how to respond to risks, maximizing existing opportunities and minimizing threats. How can you methodically respond to risks? Risk response planning activities can include:

- Developing risk responses
- Defining who is accountable for implementing the risk responses
- Specifying the triggers that warn that the risks are imminent
- Establishing contingency plans to implement if the risk does occur, and specifying the triggers that activate those plans
- Preparing fallback plans to implement if the main responses are not effective
- Identifying residual risks that remain after response planning
- Describing secondary risks that resulted from the planned responses
- Determining the schedule and cost contingency reserves
- Updating the project management plan to transpose the adopted responses to the WBS, schedule, budget, and subsidiary plans
- Transferring risks to external entities and defining the contract terms that best respond to project risks
- Updating the assumptions log and technical documentation according to the adopted responses

The outcome of this planning is to update the risk register with information concerning adopted responses, owners, and implementation conditions. Additionally, the adopted responses may imply an update of the project management plan and project documents.

> A part of planning risk responses is identifying the risk owner, who is responsible for detailing the risk response, monitoring the risk, and implementing the response.

Response Strategies

A risk may require a response or a combination of different responses to be eliminated or minimized to an acceptable level.

> Risk response planning usually entails an update of one or more elements of the project management plan (e.g., scope statement, WBS, schedule).

Threat response strategies are:

- **Avoid**   Change the project management plan to completely avoid the risk. This strategy may require eliminating the risk cause, changing project objectives, or even cancelling the project.
- **Transfer**   Change the project management plan by transferring the ownership and impact of the risk to another entity. This response does not eliminate the risk. It only transfers it. The transfer may be complete or partial and is usually associated with risks that have an impact on costs.
- **Mitigate**   Change the project management plan, developing actions to reduce the risk probability and impact.
- **Accept**   A risk is accepted when the project management plan is not changed. Risk acceptance is typically adopted when other risk response strategies are not available or are economically unfeasible. Risk acceptance may be active or passive. A risk's active acceptance is adopted when the team establishes a contingency plan, which will be activated if the risk occurs, or holds a contingency reserve to account for the risk. A risk's passive acceptance is adopted when no immediate or conditional action is taken. Passive acceptance requires only that the risk is documented and that stakeholders accept its potential impact.

> The contract terms and conditions are responses to previously identified risks that were incorporated in the contract.

Opportunities response strategies are:

- **Exploit**   Updates the project management plan to completely remove the opportunity uncertainty, ensuring that the risk will occur.
- **Share**   Updates the project management plan by sharing the opportunity with another entity in order to increase its probability and impact.
- **Enhance**   Updates the project management plan by making decisions that increase the probability and impact of the opportunity.
- **Accept**   Does not change the project management plan.

> The accept strategy is the only one that is shared by both threats and opportunities.

Conditional Responses

Another way to address risk is through conditional responses, which are only activated if a specific condition occurs. The **contingency plan** is a conditional risk response, only activated if a risk trigger is hit. The **fallback plan** is an alternative risk response, or plan B, activated if the main risk response is ineffective. A fallback plan can also be activated if an accepted risk occurs.

Triggers, Symptoms, or Risk Warning Signs

Triggers are symptoms, or warning signs, that the risk is about to occur. They can also be used to indicate that it is time to implement the conditional response. If you know that it takes two days for the vendor to transport the equipment to your warehouse, you may define that the trigger of the risk of late delivery is not having a confirmation that the equipment has left the vendor warehouse two days before the delivery date.

Residual Risks and Secondary Risks

The adopted risk responses do not completely eliminate project uncertainty. The risks that remain after response planning are known as **residual risks**. For example, even after organizing team training, there is a residual risk that the project will be delayed due to technical problems. Moreover, there are **secondary risks** that result from the planned risk responses. For example, an additional supplier was brought in to reduce schedule risk due to poor design, but now there is a new risk of integration problems between the two teams.

Reserve

A reserve is a provision of time and costs to account for schedule and cost risk. A reserve may be a contingency reserve or a management reserve.

A **contingency reserve** is a provision of time or costs held by the project manager to deal with known-unknowns. The contingency reserve is not incorporated into the estimates of work packages and activities, but is held as a separate element managed by the project manager. A contingency reserve may not be used by the team without previous authorization.

A **management reserve** is a provision of time or costs held by management to compensate for unforeseen events. These unidentified risks, or unknown-unknowns, often include potential unforeseen work that is within agreed-upon project scope. If those risks do occur, the project manager may request funds from the management reserve.

REVIEW EXERCISE 7

Identify the adopted risk response strategy:

1. Cancel the project.

   _____

2. Change the technological solution in order to reuse historical information available.

   _____

3. Anticipate the procurement activities in order to have more time to attempt to negotiate better equipment prices.

   _____

4. Subcontract part of the project to a supplier, trying to reduce the project duration and benefit from the existing contract incentives.

   _____

5. Document the risk on the progress report.

   _____

6. Work remotely for fear of strike on transports.

   _____

7. Organize additional test cycles before delivering the product to the customer.

   _____

REVIEW EXERCISE 8

> **Identify the criteria that may be important to decide if a response should be implemented.**

1. _____

2. _____

3. _____

4. _____

5. _____

Control Risks

As the project moves forward, you will discover additional information about the existing risks. You can adjust your perspective on the identified risks or realize that the risks have changed. You can identify new risks or disregard others that can no longer occur. You can even arrive at the conclusion that the risk management approach is not appropriate.

Controlling risks is the continuous process of monitoring risks, risk responses, and risk management processes. This control may include the following activities:

- Reassessing risks to determine if their probabilities and impacts have changed
- Determining if there are new risks
- Monitoring if risk triggers occur
- Activating risk response plans
- Evaluating if the risk responses were activated as planned and if they were effective
- Changing the adopted response strategies
- Preparing a workaround when an accepted risk occurs
- Analyzing risk trends in a qualitative or quantitative perspective
- Assessing whether the schedule and cost reserves are sufficient
- Preparing change requests that arise from the adopted contingency plans or workarounds
- Closing risks that may no longer occur
- Auditing existing risk management policies and procedures
- Updating the organization historical information with the acquired risk management knowledge

The project should monitor residual risks, risks on the watch list, triggers, and implemented responses.

The output of controlling risk may be updates to the risk register, organizational process assets, and project documents. Controlling risks can also lead to a new change request.

Techniques used to control risks include:

- Risk reassessment
- Reserve analysis
- Risk audits
- Variance and trend analysis
- Technical performance measurements
- Meetings

The first three techniques will be described next.

Risk Reassessment

Risk reassessment is a periodical reevaluation of the risk rating and status, verifying if there is a change in the risk probability and impact and if the adopted responses and triggers are adequate. Risk reassessment can also include identifying, analyzing, and responding to new risks, which often arise during the project. When the risk does occur, risk reassessment can document its actual impact and likelihood in order to improve future risk management decisions. Finally, risk reassessment can also **close risks** that may no longer occur.

> Significant variances to the baselines should originate a project risk reassessment.

Reserve Analysis

Throughout the project, the project manager should monitor if the available reserve suits the existing risk. As the project moves forward, and more and better information becomes available, the reserve may be consumed, reduced, or changed through the change control mechanism. For example, if you use only 10 percent of the reserve and most of the accepted risks can no longer occur, you have an indication that the reserve was overestimated.

Risk Audits

How can you know if the project managed risks effectively? A **risk audit** assesses if the risk management procedures were adopted and are appropriate and if the risk responses were effective. Risk audits are usually conducted by an external entity to ensure a more independent analysis. However, audits may also be performed by the project management team. In any case, the team and other stakeholders should be involved in the audit. Risk audits generate knowledge that can be used in the future. The organizational process assets should be updated with the acquired audits results.

Workaround

A workaround is an unplanned response for an accepted risk or to a risk that was not previously identified by the team. For example, as a result of a flood in the team's working space, the project has rented an alternative office. A workaround can also be applicable when the risk impact was actually more severe than anticipated and the adopted contingency plan was not enough to deal with the risk.

> When the risk does occur, it becomes a problem. When there is no planned response, the first priority should be to solve the problem through a workaround.

Once the problem is fixed, the team should analyze the risk and document it in the risk register so that it can improve how the risk will be managed in the future. Additionally it might have to change the project management plan to reflect the actions that were adopted to fix the problem.

Assumptions Log

Because assumptions represent uncertainty, they should be documented. The **assumptions log** is used to record and track assumptions throughout the project. This record may be part of the scope statement or an independent document.

Change Requests

While controlling the risk, a change request might be needed to implement a contingency plan or a workaround. For example, when an air traffic controllers strike was declared, the project established as a workaround that equipment would be purchased from a local vendor. As a result, a change request was issued to change the requirements documentation.

Risk Register Updates

As discussed previously, the risk register is used throughout risk identification, qualitative analysis, quantitative analysis, response planning, and control. However, the information updated in each process is different.

Risk Register Updates

Process	Updated Information
Identify risks	Risks identified, specifying their cause, event, impact, and category Potential responses
Perform qualitative risk analysis	Risk probability and impact Risks requiring urgent response Data quality Risks requiring further analysis Prioritized list of risks Watch list of low-priority risks List of critical risks (top ten risk list) Overall project risk
Perform quantitative risk analysis	Quantitative assessment of risk probability and impact Prioritized list of quantified risks Probabilistic project analysis Quantify the project reserve
Plan risk responses	Risk responses Risk owners Triggers that warn risk is imminent Triggers that activate contingency plans Residual risks Secondary risks Contingency plans and fallback plans

Risk Register Updates (*continued*)

Process	Updated Information
Control risks	New risks
	Risk reassessment
	Close risks
	Risk responses outcome
	Updates to adopted risk responses
	Workarounds
	Identify trends

MEMORIZATION EXERCISE

This exercise was designed to facilitate the memorization of the main concepts on this chapter. Assign the following definitions to a risk management concept.

1. A hierarchically organized representation of project risks arranged by risk categories

   _____

2. An uncertain event that can have a favorable or unfavorable impact on project objectives

   _____

3. Assesses if the risk management procedures were adopted and are appropriate and if the risk responses were effective

   _____

4. Completely remove the opportunity uncertainty

   _____

5. Conditional risk response, only activated if a risk trigger is hit

   _____

6. Defines how much risk the organization is willing to accept

   _____

7. Document that includes all relevant information about the risk, including event, cause, impact, probability, impact, responses, and status

   _____

8. Enables risk quantification through a combination of probability and impact

   _____

9. Graphical representation of a decision process, highlighting the factors that may influence a decision

   _____

10. Graphical treelike representation of alternative decisions with uncertain results

_____

11. Level of uncertainty that the organization is willing to accept

_____

12. Limit beyond which stakeholders are not willing to accept the risk exposure and additional risk responses are required

_____

13. Periodical reevaluation of the risk rating and status

_____

14. Positive or negative risk inherent to the organization's operations and environment

_____

15. Provision of time or costs held by management to compensate for unknown-unknowns

_____

16. Provision of time or costs held by the project manager to deal with identified risks

_____

17. Quantitative analysis technique that determines which risks have the most potential impact on project objectives

_____

18. Response planned as an alternative, or plan B, in case the main responses are ineffective

_____

19. Risk response strategy used both for threats and opportunities, which does not change the project management

_____

20. Risks that remain after risk response planning

_____

21. Risks that were created by adopted risk responses

_____

22. Risks that were not or could not be identified on the project

_____

23. Satisfaction decreases with an increase of risk exposure

_____

24. Subsidiary plan that determines how to identify, analyze, respond to, and control project risks

_____

25. Symptoms or warning signs that the risk is about to occur

_____

26. Threat response strategy that changes the project management plan to completely avoid the risk

_____

27. Threat response strategy that reduces the risk probability and impact

_____

28. Threat response strategy that transfers the ownership and impact of the risk to another entity

_____

29. Unplanned response for an accepted risk or to a risk that was not previously identified by the team

_____

30. Used on the qualitative analysis to score and rank the different project risks

_____

Process Exercises

The following exercises were designed so you could learn how to recognize the processes and understand their logical sequence. Risk management processes are listed next, including their unique number in the *PMBOK Guide*:

- 11.1 Plan risk management
- 11.2 Identify risks
- 11.3 Perform qualitative risk analysis
- 11.4 Perform quantitative risk analysis
- 11.5 Plan risk responses
- 11.6 Control risks

PROCESS EXERCISE 1

Assign the following definitions to a risk management concept.

1. Activate the risk response plans.

_____

2. Define risk management resources and responsibilities.

_____

3. Describe the attitude toward risk adopted by stakeholders.

_____

4. Develop risk responses.

_____

5. Establish the triggers that warn that the risks are imminent.

_____

6. Estimate the probability of individual risks in percentage.

_____

7. Evaluate the quality of the data available on each risk.

_____

8. Identify critical risks.

_____

9. Identify potential responses.

_____

10. Identify residual risks that remain after response planning.

_____

11. Identify risk events.

_____

12. Identify risks that require a short-term response.

_____

13. Identify secondary risks that resulted from the planned responses.

_____

14. Identify the categories used to classify risks and prepare the risk breakdown structure.

_____

15. Identify the schedule and cost contingency reserves.

_____

16. Make informed projects decisions under uncertainty.

_____

17. Numerically assess the impact of the individual risks on the project objectives.

_____

18. Perform a risk audit.

_____

19. Prepare a risk watch list.

20. Prepare a workaround when an accepted risk occurs.

21. Prepare fallback plans to implement if the main responses are not effective.

22. Qualitatively assess the probability and impact of the identified risks.

23. Rank risks according to risk factors.

24. Review the risk ranking once priority risks have been quantitatively analyzed.

25. Select risks for further analysis and response.

26. Specify the contingency plans and the triggers that activate those plans.

27. Transfer risks to external entities and define the contract terms that best respond to project risks.

28. Update the assumptions log and technical documentation according to the adopted risk responses.

29. Update the project management plan to transpose the adopted risk responses to the schedule, budget, and subsidiary plans.

30. Use probabilistic models to calculate the schedule or budget in order to provide an acceptable level of confidence.

31. Use probabilistic models to determine the likelihood of meeting specific duration or budget.

32. Use the probability and impact matrix to assign a score to each risk.

   _____

33. Verify if responses were activated as planned and if they were effective.

   _____

PROCESS EXERCISE 2

> **Assign processes to the following inputs.**

1. Work performance data _____
2. Procurement documents _____
3. Scope baseline _____
4. Stakeholders' register _____
5. Risk register _____

CHAPTER 11 EXAM

> The following questions were designed to test your knowledge on this chapter's topic. Read each question carefully, and choose the option that most accurately answers the question. Once you have completed the exam, compare your answers with the solution and read through the justification provided. Note the topics where you have the most difficulty, and make sure you dedicate enough study time to them.

1. Serious errors were found in the product during a test cycle in a software development project. Management is worried because the project CPI is 0.8 and the SPI is 0.75. Additionally, the project is struggling with a lack of resources. Which of the following is the MOST likely cause?
   A. Poor scope definition
   B. Inadequate quality management planning
   C. Lack of a staffing management plan
   D. Unidentified risks

2. The project manager has just determined communication requirements. What should be done NEXT?
   A. Risk identification
   B. Risk management plan
   C. WBS
   D. Stakeholders' register

3. Which of the following is LEAST relevant when comparing two risks?
   A. Owner
   B. Quality of the available data
   C. Impact
   D. Trend

4. The project manager wants to organize project risks by category to facilitate their management. What tool should be used?
   A. Decision tree
   B. Probability impact matrix
   C. Risk breakdown structure
   D. Risk tree

5. All of the following are part of risk identification EXCEPT:
   A. Identifying risk causes
   B. Identifying the critical risks
   C. Analyzing assumptions
   D. Identifying the risks potential responses

6. The risk register is part of which processes?
   A. Identify risks
   B. Plan risk responses
   C. Control risks
   D. All of the above

7. After preparing the risk management plan, the project manager identified the project risks and documented them in the risk register. What has the project manager done wrong?
   A. Risks should be identified by the team.
   B. The risk management plan can only be defined once the risks have been identified.
   C. Risks should be identified with stakeholders.
   D. Risks should be documented in the risk management plan.

8. Which of the following is NOT an output of a qualitative risk assessment?
   A. Risk scores
   B. Risk thresholds
   C. Selection of risks for further analysis and response
   D. Selection of risks requiring an urgent response

9. In which of the following contexts can the Delphi technique be particularly useful to identify project risks?
   A. There is no experience in the subject.
   B. The team is collocated in a common physical space.
   C. The team is spread across multiple countries.
   D. Risks are organized into categories.

10. You have identified risks, assessed them using a probability impact matrix, and ranked them according to their priority. What should you do NEXT?
    A. Plan risk responses.
    B. Approve the project management plan.
    C. Prepare the top ten list.
    D. Identify secondary risks.

11. The team is determining an overall project risk score. In which process is the team involved?
    A. Plan risk management
    B. Identify risks
    C. Perform qualitative risk assessment
    D. Control risks

12. How should you manage risks included in the watch list?
    A. Inform management.
    B. Perform a quantitative risk analysis.
    C. Document them for future monitoring.
    D. Mitigate them.

13. Quantitative risk analysis is MOSTLY concerned with:
    A. Performing a feasibility analysis
    B. Deepening the understanding of project risk
    C. Determining the budget required for risk management activities
    D. Using a decision tree analysis

14. What is the risk expected value if the project quantitative risk analysis identified two risks with the following probabilities and impacts?

    - Risk A with a 10 percent probability of a 5,000 increase in materials costs
    - Risk B with a 10 percent probability of a decrease of 2,000 in travel expenses

    A. 700
    B. 7,000
    C. 300
    D. 500

15. What tool would you use to assess the probabilities and impacts of available alternatives?
    A. Expected monetary value
    B. Monte Carlo
    C. Sensitivity analysis
    D. Decision tree analysis

16. A restaurant estimated that it needed 10 to 40 minutes to fulfill customer orders. What is the standard deviation of the estimate?
    A. 5 minutes
    B. 30 minutes
    C. 10 minutes
    D. Not enough information

17. The Monte Carlo technique analyzes the schedule risk based on:
    A. Work breakdown structure (WBS)
    B. Contingency reserve
    C. PERT estimates
    D. Gantt chart

18. The plan risk responses process includes:
    A. Developing contingency plans and identifying the responses' triggers
    B. Preparing a risk breakdown structure
    C. Determining risk causes
    D. Prioritizing risks

19. What is the output of risk response planning?
    A. Project schedule updates
    B. WBS updates
    C. Establishing contract terms and conditions
    D. All of the above

20. To address solution complexity in a major international engineering program, a large project has been broken down into several midsize projects. What type of risk response strategy has been used?
    A. Contingency plan
    B. Mitigate
    C. Decomposition
    D. Workaround

21. Fearing airline strikes, your company has decided to cancel all onsite meetings scheduled for the month of April. Web meetings have been scheduled instead. What type of risk response strategy has been used?
    A. Accept
    B. Mitigate
    C. Transfer
    D. Avoid

22. In a two-year project, the project manager has intentionally delayed a solution design activity. The project manager and the team are expecting that in the next few months, a new and more effective technology might be available on the market. This is an example of:
    A. Enhance risk
    B. Contingency plan
    C. Mitigate risk
    D. Exploit risk

23. A secondary risk is defined as:
    A. A risk that results from a risk response
    B. A risk that remains after risk response planning
    C. A risk that was accepted during risk response planning
    D. A risk identified during risk monitoring

24. Accepting a risk is a reasonable response strategy when:
    A. There is not enough information to accurately analyze the risk
    B. The risk has never occurred before in the organization
    C. There are no workarounds available
    D. It is not possible to transfer, mitigate, or avoid the risk

25. Which of the following statements regarding unknown-unknowns is correct?
    A. There should be project funds to respond to unknown-unknowns.
    B. Unknown-unknowns are documented in the risk register.
    C. The contingency reserve should account for unknown-unknowns.
    D. The project manager should identify and manage all project risks.

26. The project manager has identified, analyzed, and prioritized risks, as well as completed the risk response plan. What should be done NEXT?
    A. Estimate the risks' impact on project objectives.
    B. Determine workarounds.
    C. Prepare a risk management plan.
    D. Analyze risk trend.

27. Which of the following options is NOT part of the plan risk responses process?
    A. Contingency plans
    B. Triggers
    C. Residual risks
    D. Workarounds

28. The purpose of controlling risks is to:
    A. Prepare workarounds when accepted risks occur
    B. Identify new project risks
    C. Analyze risks trend
    D. All of the above

29. Which of the following options is a poor risk management practice?
    A. A new risk was identified during a risk monitoring meeting.
    B. The team reassessed the likelihood of a previously identified risk.
    C. The team will plan responses to all project risks to avoid future risk monitoring.
    D. Some risk responses did not impact the project management plan.

30. Which of the following statements regarding risk reassessment is NOT true?
    A. It is part of the control risks process.
    B. It assesses how well risk management processes were implemented in the project.
    C. It should be performed regularly.
    D. It may result in risk register updates.

31. A risk with a significant impact occurred. The risk was not previously identified, so there is no risk response available. What should the project manager do FIRST?
    A. Reevaluate the risk probability and impact.
    B. Accept the risk.
    C. Implement a contingency plan.
    D. Establish a workaround.

32. All of the following processes are applied to every project, EXCEPT:
    A. Plan risk management
    B. Identify risks
    C. Perform quantitative risk analysis
    D. Control risks

ANSWERS

Review Exercise 1

1. Identify the events that may impact the project.
2. Anticipate problems.
3. Reduce the exposure to project threats.
4. Explore project opportunities.
5. Reduce costs and chaos.
6. Define more feasible objectives and understand the likelihood of meeting specific objectives.
7. Adapt the methodology, or even the project manager, to the project risk.
8. Monitor the project risk trend.
9. Make "go-no-go" decisions.
10. Involve and commit stakeholders to risk responses.

11. Establish expectations.
12. Prioritize projects according to risk.
13. Obtain management support.

Review Exercise 2

1. Unidentified risks occur.
2. Risks do not have a planned response.
3. Responses were not implemented or were poorly implemented.
4. Responsibilities for implementing the responses were not defined.
5. Stakeholders have little engagement or commitment.
6. Risks occur without warning.
7. Risks are not prioritized.
8. There is not enough budget for managing risks.
9. There is a lack of risk monitoring throughout the project.
10. Risk impact and probability were poorly assessed.

Review Exercise 3

Scope

1. The team may not have identified all the work required to complete the approved scope.
2. There may not be a technical solution to the agreed-upon requirement.
3. Decisions of a project area may compromise a solution adopted on another area.

Time

1. The suppliers may be delayed in delivering materials.
2. There can be delays in other projects that the project is dependent on.
3. There may be delays in project decisions.

Resources

1. Resources may not be allocated to the project on time.
2. Resources may not have the availability or productivity required.
3. There may be cuts in financing.

Review Exercise 4

1. The event that may or may not happen
2. The risk probability and impact
3. The moment on the project life cycle when the risk can occur
4. The frequency that the risk occurs
5. The risk trend throughout time
6. The information available about the risk
7. The organization risk tolerance
8. The urgency of the risk response

Review Exercise 5

1. Risk A is the priority because it has a higher costs expected value (50% × 6,000 = 3,000) than risk B (20% × 4,000 = 800).
2. Risk B is the priority because it has a higher schedule expected value (20% × 20 = 4) than risk A (50% × 6 = 3).

Review Exercise 6

The "without the company" option has an expected cost of 5,240 that resulted from adding 1,560 and 3,680.

Speed	Probability	Additional Cost	Cost	Total Cost	Expected Value (Probability × Total Cost)
Fast	0.6		2,600	2,600	1,560
Slow	0.4		9,200	9,200	3,680

The "with the company" option has an expected cost of 5,150 that resulted from adding 4,500 and 650. Therefore, the cost of the "with the company" option is lower.

Speed	Probability	Additional Cost	Cost	Total Cost	Expected Value (Probability × Total Cost)
Fast	0.9	5,000	0	5,000	4,500
Slow	0.1	5,000	1,500	6,500	650

Review Exercise 7

1. Avoid
2. Exploit
3. Enhance
4. Share
5. Accept
6. Avoid
7. Mitigate

Review Exercise 8

1. What is the risk severity or expected monetary value?
2. What are the costs of the risk response?
3. What is the consensus around the response?
4. Who is accountable for the risk response?
5. What information do we have about the response effectiveness?

Memorization Exercise

1. Risk breakdown structure (RBS)
2. Risk
3. Risk audits

4. Exploit risk
5. Contingency plan
6. Risk tolerance
7. Risk register
8. Expected monetary value (EMV)
9. Influence diagram
10. Decision tree
11. Risk appetite
12. Risk threshold
13. Risk reassessment
14. Business risk
15. Management reserve
16. Contingency reserve
17. Sensitivity analysis
18. Fallback plan
19. Accept risk
20. Residual risk
21. Secondary risk
22. Unknown-unknown
23. Risk averse
24. Risk management plan
25. Triggers, symptoms, or risk warning signs
26. Avoid risk
27. Mitigate risk
28. Transfer risk
29. Workaround
30. Probability and impact matrix

Process Exercise 1

1. 11.6
2. 11.1
3. 11.1
4. 11.5
5. 11.5
6. 11.4
7. 11.3
8. 11.3
9. 11.2
10. 11.5
11. 11.2
12. 11.3
13. 11.5
14. 11.1
15. 11.5
16. 11.4
17. 11.4
18. 11.6
19. 11.3

20. 11.6
21. 11.5
22. 11.3
23. 11.3
24. 11.4
25. 11.3
26. 11.5
27. 11.5
28. 11.5
29. 11.5
30. 11.4
31. 11.4
32. 11.3
33. 11.6

Process Exercise 2

1. 11.6
2. 11.2
3. 11.2, 11.3
4. 11.1, 11.2
5. 11.3, 11.4, 11.5, 11.6

Chapter 11 Exam

1. **D** The project is facing problems across the time, costs, quality, and human resource management areas. Only poor risk management would explain why the project is facing generalized performance problems. All other options are not enough to explain the project situation.
2. **A** If the project manager is planning communications management, the risk management plan (answer B), the WBS (answer C), and the stakeholders' register (answer D) should be defined already. Risk identification is the only feasible option.
3. **A** The risk owner is accountable for monitoring the risk and implementing the risk responses. All other options are factors that might be used to analyze and compare different risks.
4. **C** A risk breakdown structure is a hierarchical representation of project risks grouped into categories. Decision trees (answer A) and probability impact matrix (answer B) would not organize risks by category. Risk tree (answer D) is not a project management technique.
5. **B** Identifying critical risks is part of a qualitative risk analysis. All other options are part of the identify risks process.
6. **D** The risk register is used in all alternative options.
7. **C** Risks should not be identified exclusively by the project manager. The customer, the team, and other stakeholders should also be involved. Answer A will always be less complete than answer C. Answer B is not correct because the risk management plan is defined before risk identification. Answer D is not correct because risks are not documented in the risk management plan.
8. **B** Risk thresholds are determined by the plan risk management process. All other options are an output of the perform qualitative risk assessment process.

9. **C** The Delphi technique would allow a facilitator to collect the risks identified by experts from various countries. Risks would be collected, summarized, and sent back to the experts. The process would be repeated until a reasonable consensus was achieved.

10. **C** The project manager is performing a qualitative risk analysis. Preparing the top ten list is the only option that is still part of this process.

11. **C** Determining the overall project risk score is part of the perform risk qualitative risk analysis.

12. **C** Low severity risks are monitored in the watch list. These risks should not be forgotten because there is still some possibility of occurring. There is no need to inform management (answer A). Low severity risks do not usually require a quantitative analysis (answer B). Risks in the watch list are typically accepted (answer D).

13. **B** Quantitative risk analysis deepens the understanding of project risk by numerically assessing individual risks as well as overall project risk. A feasibility analysis is not a project management process (answer A). The risk management budget is determined in risk management planning (answer C). The decision tree is a quantitative risk analysis technique. It is not the purpose of quantitative analysis (answer D).

14. **C** The first risk has an expected monetary value (EMV) of $10\% \times 5,000 = 500$. The second risk has an EMV of $10\% \times (-2,000) = -200$. The overall EMV should be the sum of the individual EMVs.

15. **D** A decision tree is a graphical treelike representation of alternative decisions with uncertain results. The other answers are not used to represent uncertain alternatives.

16. **A** Using the PERT technique, the standard deviation is calculated by (pessimistic − optimistic) / 6. If the optimistic estimate is 10 minutes and the pessimistic estimate is 40 minutes, the standard deviation will be 5 minutes.

17. **C** Monte Carlo is based on PERT estimates. The remaining options are not used by the Monte Carlo analysis.

18. **A** Developing contingency plans and identifying the responses' triggers are part of the plan risk responses process. Preparing a risk breakdown structure (answer B) is part of the plan risk management process. Determining risk causes (answer C) is part of the identify risks process. Prioritizing risks (answer D) is part of the perform qualitative risk analysis process.

19. **D** All options available are part of the plan risk responses process. Updates to the schedule (answer A) and WBS (answer B) are frequently a result of a risk response. The contract terms and conditions (answer C) are responses to previously identified risks that were incorporated in the contract.

20. **B** Mitigation is taking actions to reduce the risk probability and impact. The program minimized the risk of solution complexity by breaking down the project into smaller projects.

21. **D** The risk was avoided because the Web meetings cannot be impacted by a potential airline strike.

22. **A** Enhance risk is adopting a decision that increases the likelihood or the impact of a project opportunity.

23. **A** Secondary risks are risks that result from the planned risk responses.

24. **D** If it's not possible to transfer, mitigate, or avoid the risk, risk acceptance is the only available option.

25. **A** Management reserve is used to manage unknown-unknowns and is part of the project budget. The remaining statements are not correct.

26. **D** Estimate the risk's impact on project objectives (answer A) and prepare a risk management plan (answer C) should already have been completed. Determining workarounds (answer B) will only be needed when a risk occurs that does not have a

planned risk response. Analyzing risk trend, as part of the continuous risk monitoring effort, is the best available option.

27. **D** A workaround is defined in the control risks process. All other options are part of the plan risk responses process.

28. **D** All options available are part of the control risks process.

29. **C** Planning risk responses would not remove all project risks. The residual risks would still have to be monitored throughout the project.

30. **B** Risk reassessment is a periodical reevaluation of the risk rating and status, verifying if there is a change in the risk probability and impact, and if the adopted responses and triggers are adequate. This reassessment is part of the control risks process (answer A), should be performed regularly (answer C), and may lead to risk register updates (answer D). Assessing how well risk management processes were implemented is performed through a risk audit, not by a risk reassessment.

31. **D** When the risk occurs and there is no planned response, the first priority should not be to reevaluate the risk (answer A). The priority cannot be to implement a contingency plan (answer C) because the risk has not been identified yet. Accepting the risk (answer B) is not an option because the risk has already occurred. The project manager's main priority should be to solve the problem through a workaround.

32. **C** The project risk may not justify a quantitative risk analysis, which typically requires a lot of time and effort. All other options should be applied to every project.

12 Procurement Management

Procurement management includes all the processes required to acquire products and services from external sources, and administer the contracts or agreements associated with those acquisitions. The procurement management area also covers contract management from the supplier's side.

> When answering procurement management questions in the exam, unless otherwise specified, assume you are on the buyer side.

Procurement

Are you familiar with procurement management activities? Many project managers do not have hands-on experience in this project management knowledge area. Some examples of procurement management activities are:

- Defining procurement management activities
- Preparing a request for proposal
- Reviewing a proposal sent by the supplier
- Negotiating the contract terms and conditions
- Meeting with the supplier to clarify a claim
- Assessing the supplier's performance
- Providing a formal written note accepting that the contract has been completed
- Identifying the procurement process successes and failures

Procurement management activities are not performed similarly in all organizations. Some organizations **centralize procurement** activities within the procurement business function, benefiting from better negotiating skills, higher professional specialization regarding procurement management, career plans, standards, and templates. Other organizations choose to **decentralize procurement**, transferring a large part of these activities to the project. Decentralized procurement processes benefit from faster access to whoever is performing procurement management activities and better ability to adapt procurement decisions to the project's interests.

Unlike other knowledge areas, the project manager is not accountable for procurement management activities. A procurement manager is often accountable for managing acquisitions and its legal implications. The project manager's role is to participate and support, providing all the required information and establishing a bridge between the procurement department and the project.

REVIEW EXERCISE 1

What is the project manager's role in procurement management?

1. _____

2. _____

3. _____

4. _____

5. _____

6. _____

7. _____

8. _____

9. _____

10. _____

Contract

A contract is a mutual agreement in which parties voluntarily accept being legally bound. In a project context, the contract establishes that the supplier (also known as the seller) and buyer (also known as the customer) agree that the supplier should provide a specific product in exchange for payment.

> You can apply procurement management processes to manage the life cycle of one or more contracts.

For a contract to be legal, some conditions must be guaranteed:

- **Offer and acceptance** One entity makes an offer that is accepted by another.
- **Consideration** The supplier delivers something of value in exchange for compensation.
- **Legal capacity** Both parties have the ability to establish such legal agreement.
- **Legal purpose** The contracted product or service is conformant with the law.
- **Intention** Both parties wish that the agreement is enforced by a court.

Project contracts belong to one of the following generic categories, or to some sort of combination of them: fixed-price contracts, cost-reimbursable contract, and time and material contracts.

Fixed-Price Contract

The **fixed-price contract (FP)** is a generic contract category that fixes a payment amount for a specific product or service. Hence, the supplier is holding most of the cost variance risk. This category may include different types of contracts:

- **Firm fixed price (FFP)** Most popular type of fixed-price contract where the price is defined from the start and may not be changed without a formal contract change. Any cost increase caused by performance problems is covered by the supplier.
- **Fixed price incentive fee (FPIF)** Defines a fixed price plus an incentive mechanism. Incentives are adjusted to mutually agreed-upon performance objectives, such as duration, costs, or quality targets. These incentive mechanisms enable some price variation within limits.
- **Fixed price with economic price adjustment (FPEPA)** Type of fixed-price contract, usually used in multiyear procurements, where the price is defined but may be adjusted yearly according to economic changes, such as inflation or oil prices.

> The firm fixed-price contract is the most widely used contract.

Fixed-Price Contract

Advantages to the buyer	No need to control the supplier's actual costs
	Has a lower cost risk than other contract types
	Easier financial planning because the final price is known
	May include incentives
Disadvantages to the buyer	Requires a significant effort to define scope before the contract is signed
	Typically leads to a higher price because price must cover the cost risk
	Not a flexible contract
	Without a clear scope definition, there is a risk that potential change requests will increase the buyer's costs
Application	Clear understating about what is required
	Not enough resources to control the supplier's actual costs

Cost-Reimbursable Contract

The cost-reimbursable contract is a generic contract category where the supplier is reimbursed for allowable actual costs plus a profit fee. Although most cost variance risk belongs to the buyer, it's possible to establish incentive mechanisms that limit the buyer's risk exposure.

This generic category may include different contract types:

- **Cost plus fixed fee (CPFF)**   All allowable costs are reimbursed, plus a fixed fee. This fee is not changed unless there is a contract change.
- **Cost plus incentive fee (CPIF)**   All allowable costs are reimbursed, plus a fixed fee, plus an incentive fee linked to performance objectives. Any difference between the agreed-upon target price and the actual cost will be shared between the supplier and the buyer according to an established sharing ratio.
- **Cost plus award fee (CPAF)**   All allowable costs are reimbursed, plus a fixed fee, plus an award fee based on performance. This award fee will depend on previously established subjective criteria. For example, the buyer may agree in the contract that if he is satisfied with the project, he can be used as a reference for future commercial campaigns organized by the supplier.

Cost-Reimbursable Contract

Advantages to the buyer	Can start quickly because there is no need to define a very precise scope
	Might be less expensive than fixed-price contracts because the price does not incorporate the cost risk
	May include incentives
	Is a flexible contract
Disadvantages to the buyer	Requires a significant administration effort because the buyer has to make sure that the supplier is using only the resources absolutely needed and is invoicing only the resources used
	Higher cost risk than other alternatives
	More difficult financial planning because costs are not known upfront
Application	Scope not defined precisely

Time and Material Contract (T&M)

The time and material contract is a generic contract category that establishes a price for all resources used for the project on a per-day or per-item basis, without establishing the quantity that will be used for each resource. To limit the buyer's risk, this type of contract may have a specified ceiling and is typically used on low-value contracts.

Time and Material Contract

Advantages to the buyer	Work may start immediately because there is no need to understand the scope upfront
	Contract may have established a limit for time and costs
Disadvantages to the buyer	Supplier's profit will increase with a cost overrun
	Contract will not bind the supplier to project success
	The buyer must manage the supplier's resources
Application	There is an urgency
	The item procured is needed for a short period of time
	The buyer wants to maintain absolute control over the work
	The procured item has low monetary value
	The buyer needs to procure resources instead of scope

REVIEW EXERCISE 2

> **Assign each situation to a specific contract.**

1. Price = Actual costs + 20 _____

2. Price = 800 _____

3. Price = Actual costs + 20 + 50% of the variance toward the target cost of 100

_____

4. Price = Actual costs + 20 + additional 20 if the product is delivered without errors

_____

5. Price = 200 + additional 2 for each week before the target date _____

6. Price = Days of a programmer × 500, with a ceiling of 20 days _____

Purchase Order

A purchase order is a simple form of fixed-price contract where one party unilaterally issues a purchase request specifying product quantities and agreed-upon prices. The contract is established when the supplier formally accepts the purchase order or delivers what was requested.

Contract Incentives

The contract incentives are contract mechanisms used to synchronize the buyer's and supplier's objectives. Several instruments may be used to establish incentives:

- **Ceiling price**   Maximum price that can be paid by the buyer under the contract
- **Target cost**   Cost used as a reference to establish contract incentives. Cost variances in relation to this target will be shared between the buyer and the supplier.
- **Sharing ratio**   Describes how variances between the actual cost and the target cost will be shared between the buyer and the supplier. For example, a sharing ratio of 80%/20%, means that 80 percent of the savings (or additional costs) belong to the buyer and 20 percent belong to the seller.
- **Fixed fee or target fee**   Profit obtained by the supplier if there is no incentive compensation
- **Incentive fee**   Positive or negative compensation for variances between the actual cost and the target price
- **Price**   Total value paid by the buyer

$$\text{Price} = \text{actual cost} + \text{fixed fee} + \text{incentive fee}$$

- **Target price**   Total value paid by the buyer under the contract if the actual costs are exactly the same as the target cost

$$\text{Target price} = \text{actual cost} + \text{fixed fee}$$

- **Point of total assumption (PTA)**   Above this value, the supplier supports all costs. In other words, above the PTA additional costs are shared with a 0 to 100 percent ratio and the contract is similar to a firm fixed price. The PTA is associated with FPIF contracts.

$$\text{PTA} = \left[\frac{(\text{ceiling price} - \text{target price})}{\text{sharing ratio}} \right] + \text{target cost}$$

Example of Cost Plus Incentive Fee Contract (CPIF)

A CPIF contract was negotiated with the following target cost, fixed fee, and sharing ratio:

Target cost: 200
Fixed fee: 20
Sharing ratio: $\frac{60\%}{40\%}$ (60% to buyer and 40% to supplier)

If the contract actual cost is 180, the final price will be determined by:

Actual cost: 180
Incentive fee $= (200 - 180) \times 0.4 = 8$
Total fee $=$ fixed fee $+$ incentive fee $= 20 + 8 = 28$
Final price $=$ actual cost $+$ total fee $= 180 + 28 = 208$

Terms and Conditions

Some of the contract terms and conditions are used recurrently on similar projects (standard terms), and others are established specifically for each project (special terms).

A contract typically includes terms such as statement of work, price, roles and responsibilities, limitation of liability, penalties, incentives, contract change procedures, contract termination procedures, and claim administration procedures.

> The terms and conditions are planned responses to the procurement risks. Common responses to most procurement initiatives are reflected in the standard terms and conditions. Specific responses to one procurement initiative are reflected in the special terms and conditions.

The following table displays the procurement management processes with their respective process group:

Procurement Management Processes

Process	Process Group
Plan procurement management	Planning
Conduct procurements	Executing
Control procurements	Monitoring and controlling
Close procurements	Closing

Plan Procurement Management

Plan procurement management covers many activities. The first step is deciding if the requirements may be developed internally or if they should be acquired externally. This decision is usually known as "make or buy." Then you need to select the most adequate procedures to manage procurement and document them within a procurement management plan. Plan procurement management also prepares a procurement statement of work that later will be used by potential suppliers to determine if they have the ability to provide such elements. Finally, procurement documents that describe the buyer's needs to potential suppliers need to be provided.

Make or Buy Decision

The make or buy decision determines if the requirements will be delivered internally or will be acquired externally. All the remaining procurement management activities will only be applicable if the organization decides to procure the requirements externally. Complete the following exercise to identify reasons that can lead to "make" or "buy."

REVIEW EXERCISE 3

What are the motives that may justify making instead of buying?

1. _____

2. _____

3. _____

4. _____

REVIEW EXERCISE 4

What are the motives that may justify buying instead of making?

1. _____

2. _____

3. _____

4. _____

Procurement Management Plan

The **procurement management plan** is a subsidiary plan that establishes the rules used to manage procurement including:

- How to procure
- Selection process
- Prequalified sellers
- Contract types used
- Activities performed by the project team and activities performed by the procurement department
- Metrics used to assess the suppliers' performance
- Criteria used to select suppliers' proposals
- Criteria used to exclude suppliers

Procurement Statement of Work (SOW)

A **procurement statement of work (SOW)** is a narrative description of products or services to be acquired from an external supplier under contract. A clear SOW will enable potential suppliers to decide if they are able to deliver the items required. A SOW also establishes the performance requirements needed to administer the contract.

Depending on factors such as uncertainty and the nature of the product, a SOW may specify:

- Product specification
- Solution required to develop the product
- Delivery schedule
- Adopted standards
- Acceptance criteria

Procurement Documents

The **procurement documents** describe the buyer's needs to potential suppliers. These documents may include:

- SOW
- Type of contract that should be adopted
- Terms and conditions
- Suppliers' selection criteria
- Criteria used to exclude suppliers
- Procedures used to develop proposals

The main procurement documents are:

- **Request for proposal (RFP)**   Used to acquire elements that are not very standardized. In an RFP, the buyer specifies the product requirements and lets the supplier determine the solution and the price. The supplier responds with a **proposal** that specifies a price and a solution. For example, you can request a proposal to develop a payroll application solution.
- **Invitation for bid (IFB)**   Used to acquire products or services when the buyer can specify in detail the work that will be performed. In an IFB, the buyer specifies the product and the solution. The supplier responds with a bid that specifies the price. For example, you can issue an invitation for a bid for procuring steel for a construction project.
- **Request for quotation (RFQ)**   Used to acquire standardized elements that do not typically involve a solution and have low value. In an RFQ, the buyer specifies the product. The supplier responds with a quotation that specifies the price. For example, you can request a quotation for hotel accommodation.
- **Request for information (RFI)**   The buyer requests information about one product.

Conduct Procurements

There is a path to follow from the moment when you specify what you wish to acquire in the procurement documents, until the moment the contract is negotiated. Suppliers must be informed and their questions should be answered. Proposals must be evaluated and contracts negotiated.

The **conduct procurements** process is the procurement execution process that includes the activities required to translate procurement needs into contracts with suppliers. To move from procurement documents to a negotiated contract, the conduct procurements process may:

- Advertise the procurement process to attract potential suppliers
- Search the Internet for potential suppliers
- Hold meetings to clarify any questions that the suppliers may have
- Generate independent estimates that may be used as references while assessing proposals
- Create a short list of suppliers that will be subject to a more detailed analysis
- Receive proposals, bids, or quotations
- Review proposals
- Apply the weighting system according to the source selection criteria to select a single supplier or rank suppliers for a future negotiation process
- Apply a screening system to a procurement process to remove suppliers that do not meet the source selection criteria
- Participate in negotiations with suppliers about the contract terms and conditions, helping to clarify requirements and project risks
- Negotiate a contract with a supplier without consulting other suppliers
- Issue a letter of intent
- Award a contract

Bidder Conferences or Pre-Bid Conference

Preparing a SOW and procurement documents might not be enough to clearly communicate the procurement requirements to potential suppliers. The buyer can organize **bidder conferences** to guide the potential bidders through the procurement documents and clarify any questions. Bidder conferences can also be used to detect any inconsistency in the procurement documents.

> When meeting with potential suppliers, the buyer should make sure that all suppliers have the same information. This minimizes the risk that the best supplier was not chosen because it did not have access to adequate information. Responses provided individually to suppliers should be documented and shared with the rest of the bidders.

Prequalified Sellers

Prequalified sellers are suppliers that were selected by the buyer to move on to the next phase of the procurement process. For example, the buyer may choose to contact only suppliers that have references in the project's application area.

Proposal Evaluation Techniques

Proposals may be selected according to one set of **source selection criteria** that were previously defined in the procurement management plan. Each criterion may be scored according to its weight, or importance, for the organization. This **weighting system** enables the organization to select a single supplier or rank suppliers for a future negotiation process. Using source selection criteria, the project can have a logical and justifiable selection of suppliers and avoid conflicts and team disorientation.

Source Criteria	Weight	Score Supplier XYZ	Weighted Score Supplier XYZ
References provided	2	4	8
Financial status	3	4	12
Technical capability	4	5	20
Project management	4	4	16
Price	4	4	16
Final score			72

A **screening system** is another proposal evaluation technique that eliminates from the selection process those suppliers that do not meet the source selection criteria. For example, the screening system may exclude suppliers that do not have a minimum level of experience in the proposed area. The screening system is usually used in combination with other source selection criteria.

The team may compare the supplier's estimate to an **independent estimate**, developed internally or externally by an independent entity. Significant variances between the two estimates may indicate that the supplier's response is not adequate or that the procurement SOW was not well defined.

Procurement Negotiations

During procurement negotiations, proposals or bids are revised through bargaining in order to define contract elements such as price, incentives, penalties, procedures, and the limitations of liability. (See Figure 12.1.)

> A negotiation should concentrate on dealing with the previously identified risks.

> The main objective of this negotiating is to establish one fair and mutually favorable contract that fosters a future sustainable relationship.

Noncompetitive Procurement

Not all procurement processes operate in a competitive environment. Examples of procurement processes without competition include:

- **Sole-source procurement** The buyer chose to acquire one product that is provided by only a single supplier. The main risks of conducting a sole-source procurement concern the supplier's economic feasibility and market conditions.
- **Single-source procurement** The buyer chose to acquire a preferred supplier without consulting other alternatives. The risk of single-source procurement is assuming that a previous positive experience implies good performance in the future.
- **Joint venture** There is a previously established agreement to assign the work to a specific supplier.

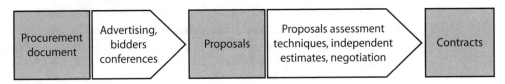

Figure 12.1 Contract cycle

Letter of Intent

A letter of intent enables the buyer to declare an intention to buy before an actual contract acceptance is completed. This commitment enables the supplier to work before the contract is accepted. However, a letter of intent does not usually legally obligate the parties to perform the contract.

Control Procurements

The **control procurements** process is the procurement monitoring and controlling process. It includes all the activities required to ensure that both supplier and buyer meet the contract requirements and that any contract changes are duly managed. From the buyer's perspective, this process includes the following activities:

- Monitoring suppliers' performance
- Inspecting and auditing suppliers' work and taking corrective actions when needed
- Having regular status meetings with the suppliers
- Authorizing the start of the work
- Reviewing invoices
- Managing contract changes
- Administering claims or disputes
- Notifying suppliers in writing whenever they underperform
- Managing contract breaches
- Waiving a contract right
- Enforcing a warranty or a performance bond
- Managing force majeure events
- Authorizing payments according to the contract performance
- Providing all the information required by the procurement department
- Updating the contract record management system with the procurement administration information

Procurement Performance Review

A procurement performance review is a formal assessment of the supplier's capacity to perform the project according to the contract conditions. Besides providing evidence of the supplier's performance, it can also identify areas of improvement and nonconformity. A procurement performance review can be used as an input when preparing a prequalified sellers list for future projects.

Contract Change Control System

Any changes to the contract must naturally be managed. Rules, forms, responsibilities, and levels of authority should be documented in the contract change control system. For example, the contract change control system can have a change control board to review changes above a specific amount.

Claims Administration or Dispute

A **claim** is a request for compensation according to the contract terms and conditions. Administering claims is the activity of reviewing and reaching agreements on pending claims through the use of a contract change control system.

> All decisions prior to the contract, written or not, that were not included or specified by the contract, do not legally bind the parties.

Contract Breach or Default

A contract breach or default occurs when one contract requirement is not met. A **contract material breach** may release the innocent organization from its contractual obligations. Usually this type of breach leads to financial compensations. A contract breach may generate **punitive damages**, or contractual fines used to compensate for contract breach losses.

> When there is a breach, the other party should issue a letter formalizing it. Additionally, the buyer should work collaboratively with the supplier so that the breach can be corrected.

Waiver

A waiver is a buyer's voluntary surrender of a contract privilege. A waiver is usually issued when the contract privilege does not compensate for the required effort to achieve it. The waiver prevents a contract breach but does not necessarily avoid financial compensations.

Warranty

Sometimes, contracting parties need an assurance from the other party that the contract conditions will occur. A warranty is a contractual guarantee provided during a period of time, ensuring that the products and services will be delivered according to contract requirements. The warranty may later be used to enforce a legal compensation if the contract requirements are not met.

Performance Bond

A buyer may suffer significant losses if the vendor does not complete the project or fails to meet some contract requirements. A performance bond is a contract tool that guarantees satisfactory compensation if the vendor fails to deliver the contracted value. If the contract requirements are not met, a performance bond issued by a bank or other financial institution guarantees a payment up to the performance bond value.

Force Majeure

Some risks lay beyond the control of the contracting parties. Force majeure is a contract clause that releases parties from contract obligations when a predefined uncontrollable event occurs. Examples of force majeure motives are wars, crime, earthquake, flooding, and hurricanes. Often, the contract release will only be applicable while the force majeure conditions prevail.

Payment Authorizations

Invoices sent from the supplier for payment, according to the products and services delivered, go through an accounts payable system. In many organizations, this system is centralized within a financial or accounts payable department. Other organizations decentralize this function in projects. On such cases, before authorizing the payment, the project management team may have to confirm that the performance has met contracted specifications.

REVIEW EXERCISE 5

> **What are the differences between conduct procurements and control procurements?**

1. The conduct procurements process performs all the activities required to ensure that

   _____

2. The control procurements process performs all the activities required to ensure that

   _____

Close Procurements

Close procurements is the procurement management closing process. This process closes the project acquisitions in a controlled manner, ensuring that the work was performed according to requirements and following all the adopted contract closing procedures.

Procurement closing activities may include:

- Provide a formal written notice accepting that the contract is closed
- Manage the contract early termination
- Negotiate remaining claims or disputes through mediation or arbitration
- Conduct an audit on the procurement process
- Perform lessons learned
- Update final records
- Archive records

The contract should specify the criteria used for formal acceptance.

Contract Early Termination

Early termination is a contract interruption before it has been fulfilled. Contract early termination may be:

- **Termination for convenience**   When one of the parties unilaterally terminates the contract. In such cases, the other party usually can claim financial compensations.
- **Termination for cause or default**   When the contract is terminated because one party did not fulfill its contract obligations
- **For mutual understanding**   When both parties agree to terminate the contract

Contract early terminations are managed by the close procurements process.

Procurement Audits

A procurement audit is a review of the procurement processes to verify if they are being performed as planned and if they meet the need for which they were implemented. The final purpose of a procurement audit is to identify lessons learned and improve future procurement initiatives. A procurement audit should cover all the procurement management activities, including planning, conducting, and controlling.

MEMORIZATION EXERCISE

> The following exercise was designed to facilitate the memorization of the main concepts on this chapter. Assign the following definitions to a procurement management concept.

1. A contract requirement was not met.

   _____

2. A type of proposal evaluation technique that assigns a specific weight to each procurement criterion, enabling the organization to select a single supplier or rank suppliers for a future negotiation process

   _____

3. A type of proposal evaluation technique that eliminates from the selection process those suppliers that do not meet the source selection criteria

   _____

4. Above this value, the supplier supports all costs

   _____

5. Contract mechanisms used to synchronize the buyer's and supplier's objectives

   _____

6. Cost-reimbursable type of contract that reimburses all allowable costs, plus a fixed fee, plus an incentive fee linked to performance objectives

   _____

7. Describes how variances between the actual cost and the target cost will be shared between the buyer and the supplier

   _____

8. Documents that describe the buyer's needs to potential suppliers

   _____

9. Estimate developed internally or externally by an independent entity that can be compared to the suppliers' estimates

   _____

10. Formal assessment of the supplier's capacity to perform the project according to the contract conditions

    _____ Performance Review _____

11. Generic contract category that establishes a price for all resources used for the project on a per-day or per-item basis, without establishing the quantity that will be used for each resource

    _____ T & M _____

12. Generic contract category that fixes a payment amount for a specific product or service

    _____ Fixed Price _____

13. Meeting organized by the buyer to help potential suppliers understand the procurement documents

    _____

14. Narrative description of products or services to be acquired from an external supplier under contract

    _____ SOW _____

15. Procurement department that performs most of the procurement management activities

    _____ ~~SOW~~ Centralized _____

16. Procurement document used to acquire elements that are not very standardized. The buyer specifies the product requirements and lets the supplier determine the solution and the price.

    _____ RFP _____

17. Procurement document used to acquire products or services when the buyer can specify in detail the work that will be performed. The buyer only requests a price from the supplier.

    _____ ~~RFQ~~ IFB _____

18. Procurement document used to acquire standardized elements that do not typically involve a solution and have low value

    _____ RFQ _____

19. Request for compensation according to the contract terms and conditions

    _____

20. Review of the procurement processes to verify if they are being performed as planned and if they meet the need for which they were implemented

    _____

21. Seller's formal response to the buyer's need, specifying a price for performing the work described in the procurement document

BID

22. Seller's formal response to the procurement document, including a solution and a price

Proposal

23. Simple form of fixed-price contract where one party unilaterally issues a purchase request

24. Subsidiary plan that establishes the rules used to manage procurement

PMP

25. The buyer chose to acquire one product that is provided only by a single supplier.

Sole Source

Process Exercises

The following exercises were designed so you could learn how to recognize the processes and understand their logical sequence. Procurement management processes are listed next, including their unique number in the *PMBOK Guide*:

- 12.1 Plan procurement management
- 12.2 Conduct procurements
- 12.3 Control procurements
- 12.4 Close procurements

PROCESS EXERCISE 1

Assign processes to the following activities.

1. Administer claims or disputes.

3

2. Advertise the procurement process to attract potential suppliers.

2

3. Apply a screening system to a procurement process to remove suppliers that do not meet the source selection criteria.

2

4. Apply the weighting system according to the source selection criteria.

2

5. Archive records.

_____4_____

6. Authorize payments.

_____3_____

7. Authorize the start of the supplier's work.

_____3_____

8. Conduct an audit on the procurement process.

_____4_____

9. Create a short list of suppliers that will be subject to a more detailed analysis.

_____2_____

10. Decide whether to make or buy.

_____1_____2_____

11. Define potential suppliers.

_____1_____2_____

12. Define the source selection process.

_____1_____

13. Describe what, when, and how to procure.

_____1_____

14. Establish the source selection criteria.

_____1_____2_____

15. Generate independent estimates that may be used as references while assessing proposals.

_____2_____

16. Hold meetings to clarify any questions that the suppliers may have.

_____2_____

17. Inspect and audit the supplier's work, and take corrective actions when needed.

_____3_____

18. Manage contract changes.

_____3_____

19. Manage the contract early termination.

_____4_____

20. Monitor the suppliers' performance.
_____3_____

21. Negotiate a contract with a supplier without consulting other suppliers.
_____2_____

22. Negotiate remaining claims or disputes through mediation or arbitration.
_____4_____

23. Participate in negotiations with suppliers about the contract terms and conditions, helping clarify requirements and project risks.
_____2_____

24. Prepare request for proposals, request for quotations, and invitation for bids.
_____1 2_____

25. Provide a formal written notice accepting that the contract is closed.
_____4_____

26. Provide all the information required by the procurement department.
_____2 all_____

27. Receive proposals, bids, or quotations.
_____2_____

28. Review invoices.
_____3_____

29. Review proposals.
_____2_____

30. Search the Internet for potential suppliers.
_____2_____

31. Select which contracts to adopt.
_____1_____

32. Update final records.
_____4_____

33. Update the contract record management system with the procurement administration information.
_____3_____

PROCESS EXERCISE 2

> **Assign processes to the following inputs.**

1. Contracts _____
2. Source selection criteria _____
3. Procurement statement of work _____
4. Procurement documents _____
5. Requirements documentation _____
6. Suppliers' proposals _____
7. Activity resource requirements _____

CHAPTER 12 EXAM

> The following questions were designed to test your knowledge on this chapter's topic. Read each question carefully, and choose the option that most accurately answers the question. Once you have completed the exam, compare your answers with the solution and read through the justification provided. Note the topics where you have the most difficulty, and make sure you dedicate enough study time to them.

1. What is the project manager's MAIN responsibility in procurement management?
   A. Establishing a bridge between the project and the procurement department
   B. Preparing request for proposals
   C. Helping potential suppliers understand the procurement documents
   D. Approving changes

2. Which of the following is one advantage of decentralizing procurement management processes?
   A. The professionals performing procurement activities have a high professional expertise.
   B. The professionals performing procurement activities have well-defined careers.
   C. The contract is more easily adapted to project needs.
   D. There are standards and templates available for the procurement activities.

3. All of the following are defined in the plan procurement management process EXCEPT:
   A. Contract negotiation
   B. Make or buy decision
   C. Statement of work (SOW)
   D. Procurement management plan

4. How would you define a procurement management plan?
   A. Describes how contracts should be managed within the organization
   B. Is developed by the procurement department for all procured items
   C. Is a subsidiary of the project management plan
   D. Is an output of the conduct procurements process

5. A team member does not know what the supplier should deliver under a contract. Which document should you direct the team member to?
   A. Proposal
   B. Contract special terms
   C. Procurement SOW
   D. The project WBS

6. You are about to develop the procurement documentation and send it to potential suppliers. You wish to receive a response with an approach and a price. Which of the following should you prepare?
   A. Request for proposal
   B. Invitation for bid
   C. SOW
   D. Proposal

7. You need to procure a standard material, equally available from a number of suppliers. Which procurement document should be prepared?
   A. RFQ
   B. IFB
   C. RFP
   D. RFI

8. Which of the following is the buyer's MAIN concern in a fixed-price (FP) contract?
   A. Preventing the seller from reducing scope
   B. Auditing all costs invoiced
   C. Defining a clear SOW
   D. Administering the contract closely to prevent a cost overrun

9. You are trying to decide which contract to use in a procurement process. Which of the following is NOT a good reason to choose a cost-reimbursable over a fixed-price contract?
   A. It requires less time to prepare.
   B. The price is usually cheaper.
   C. It requires less effort to audit the supplier's invoices.
   D. It is more flexible.

10. Which contract type transfers most of the risk to the buyer?
    A. Cost-reimbursable
    B. Fixed price
    C. Fixed price plus incentive fee
    D. Purchase order

11. The project manager and the procurement department are trying to decide which contract type to adopt. The project manager is arguing the contract should include an incentive system. What is the MAIN advantage of contract incentives?
    A. Providing a reference for assessing the vendor's performance at the end of the project
    B. Aligning the objectives of the seller with the objectives of the buyer
    C. Reducing the required contingency reserve
    D. Reducing the final price

12. On a cost plus incentive fee contract, the target cost is 100,000, the target fee is 10,000, the sharing ratio is 60/40, the ceiling price is 120,000, and the final actual cost was 120,000. What is the final price paid by the buyer?
    A. 110,000
    B. 120,000
    C. 122,000
    D. 128,000

13. After collecting the sellers' proposals, the project team is struggling to select the supplier. Which of the following options would be of MOST help?
    A. Source selection criteria
    B. Screening system
    C. Prequalified sellers
    D. Bidder conference

14. What should be the buyer's MAIN concern during contract negotiation?
    A. Establishing fair and sustainable terms and conditions
    B. Reducing the price to pay
    C. Managing claims
    D. Defining a clear scope of work

15. What is the buyer's MAIN concern on a bidder conference?
    A. Verifying that the deliverables were completed according to the contract
    B. Negotiating conditions that are acceptable to both parties
    C. Formalizing the decisions made
    D. Making sure that all parties have access to the same information

16. After issuing and advertising an RFP for a major procurement, the team is facing too many sellers' responses and is struggling to select the supplier. Which of the following options would be of LEAST help?
    A. Contract SOW
    B. Screening system
    C. Contract negotiation
    D. Bidder conference

17. Which of the following is the buyer's MAIN concern if choosing to single-source the procurement process?
    A. Dependency on the supplier
    B. Quality
    C. Vendor not being qualified for this project
    D. Vendor's financial status

18. Which of the following activities is NOT part of the control procurements process?
    A. Claims administration
    B. Review of proposals
    C. Authorization of the start of the supplier work
    D. Review of contract changes

19. The MAIN purpose of the control procurements process is:
    A. Receiving proposals and negotiating contracts
    B. Making sure that the other contracting party is meeting contract requirements
    C. Establishing a contract change control system
    D. Formally accepting the contract

20. The seller provided a component that did not meet the contract requirements. After further analysis you discovered that the contract requirements are incoherent. You also noticed that the component delivered actually fits your business need. What is the BEST thing to do?
    A. Complete a detailed requirement analysis, update the requirements documentation, and then accept the deliverable.
    B. Reject the deliverable.
    C. Request a change to the contract.
    D. Accept the deliverable as is.

21. The seller has just informed the buyer that an important contract milestone date will not be met. How should the buyer proceed?
    A. Move to the close procurements process.
    B. Change the procurement management plan.
    C. Issue payments as established within the contract.
    D. Issue payments but deduct the impact of the schedule delay from the payment amount.

22. A _____ is a formal request, issued by the seller, for loss compensation under a contract.
    A. Letter of intent
    B. Bond
    C. Letter of default
    D. Claim

23. A procurement audit is part of:
    A. Plan procurement management
    B. Conduct procurements
    C. Control procurements
    D. Close procurements

24. Your company has decided that a large ongoing product development project is no longer feasible and the contract with the supplier will be terminated. Which processes can help you manage the situation?
    A. Close project and phase and contract closure
    B. Closing and close procurements
    C. Close project or phase, and close procurement
    D. Perform integrated change control and close project and phase

25. Which process generates a formal written notice that the contract has been completed?
    A. Close project or phase
    B. Contract verification
    C. Close procurements
    D. Control procurements

ANSWERS

Review Exercise 1

1. Assess proposals.
2. Manage the relationship with suppliers.
3. Help select suppliers.
4. Help prepare procurement documents.
5. Approve payments.
6. Review contract change orders.
7. Incorporate procurement activities in the schedule.
8. Integrate the supplier in the team.
9. Control the supplier's deliverables.
10. Provide support to the contract closing activities.

Review Exercise 2

1. CPFF
2. FFP
3. CPIF
4. CPAF
5. FPIF
6. T&M

Review Exercise 3

1. There is capacity available.
2. It is strategic (proprietary information, retain knowledge, etc.).
3. There is an obligation (legislation, agreements, etc.).
4. The cost may be shared with other projects.

Review Exercise 4

1. There is a patent.
2. Internal resources are scarce.
3. There is an urgency to complete the product.
4. There is an opportunity to acquire knowledge.

Review Exercise 5

1. The conduct procurements process performs all the activities required to ensure that procurement documents lead to negotiated contracts.
2. The control procurements process performs all the activities required to ensure that the supplier and the buyer perform according to the contract.

Memorization Exercise

1. Contract breach or default
2. Source selection criteria
3. Screening system
4. Point of total assumption (PTA)
5. Contract incentives
6. Cost plus incentive fee (CPIF) contract
7. Sharing ratio
8. Procurement documents
9. Independent estimate
10. Procurement performance review
11. Time and material (T&M) contract
12. Fixed-price (FP) contract
13. Bidder conferences
14. Procurement statement of work (SOW)
15. Centralized procurement
16. Request for proposal (RFP)
17. Invitation for bid (IFB)
18. Request for quotation (RFQ)
19. Claim
20. Procurement audit
21. Bid
22. Proposal
23. Purchase order
24. Procurement management plan
25. Sole-source procurement

Process Exercise 1

1. 12.3
2. 12.2
3. 12.2
4. 12.2
5. 12.4
6. 12.3
7. 12.3
8. 12.4
9. 12.2
10. 12.1
11. 12.1
12. 12.1
13. 12.1
14. 12.1
15. 12.2
16. 12.2
17. 12.3
18. 12.3
19. 12.4
20. 12.3

21. 12.2
22. 12.4
23. 12.2
24. 12.1
25. 12.4
26. All processes
27. 12.2
28. 12.3
29. 12.2
30. 12.2
31. 12.1
32. 12.4
33. 12.3

Process Exercise 2

1. 12.3
2. 12.2
3. 12.2
4. 12.2, 12.3, 12.4
5. 12.1
6. 12.2
7. 12.1

Chapter 12 Exam

1. **A** The project manager is not accountable for procurement management work. The project manager should provide all the required information and establish a bridge between the procurement department and the project. The project manager may be involved in preparing requests for proposals, explaining procurement documents to potential suppliers, and approving changes. However, a procurement manager is typically accountable for these activities.

2. **C** If the procurement activities are performed by team members, the adopted decisions and contract can more easily respond to project needs. The remaining options are not advantages of decentralizing the procurement management activities.

3. **A** The contract is negotiated in the conduct procurements process. All other options are performed in the plan procurement management process.

4. **C** The procurement management plan is part of the project management plan. Answer A is not correct because it is referring to an organizational contract management policy. Answer B is not correct because the procurement management plan is not typically developed by the procurement department and may be specific to each procured item. Answer D is not correct because the procurement management plan is an output of the plan procurement management process.

5. **C** The procurement SOW is a narrative description of the products and services that will be acquired under a contract.

6. **A** A request for proposal is used when the buyer wishes to receive a solution and a price for a specific need.

7. **A** The request for quotation (RFQ) is the document used to request a price for a standardized item.

8. **C** Without a clear scope definition, potential change requests within a fixed-price contract might increase the buyer's costs. A is not the best answer because the scope is defined within the contract. B is not a correct answer because auditing all costs invoices is a typical concern within a cost-reimbursable contract. Answer D is not correct because the buyer is relatively protected from a cost overrun when working with a fixed-price contract.

9. **C** The cost-reimbursable contract requires a considerable administration effort from the buyer because the buyer has to make sure that the supplier is using only the resources absolutely needed and is invoicing only the resources used. All other options are advantages of a cost-reimbursable contract.

10. **A** With a cost-reimbursable contract the supplier is reimbursed for allowable actual costs plus a profit fee. Thus most of the cost risk belongs to the buyer. In all other options, the buyer is not holding most of the risk.

11. **B** Contract incentives are a contractual mechanism used to synchronize the buyer and supplier objectives.

12. **B** The first step is calculating the incentive fee:

    Fee = target fee + (target cost − actual cost) × sharing ratio

    $$= 10,000 + (100,000 - 120,000) \times 0.4$$

    $$= 2,000$$

    Once we know the fee, we can calculate the final price:

    Final price = actual cost + fee

    $$= 120,000 + 2,000$$

    $$= 122,000$$

    Because 122,000 is higher than the ceiling price, the final price is 120,000.

13. **A** Source selection criteria assign specific "weights" to each procurement criteria in order to evaluate suppliers and prepare a logical and justifiable selection. The screening system (answer B) and the prequalified sellers (answer C) could be useful, but they are not the main source selection techniques. Bidder conferences (answer D) are used to help potential suppliers understanding the procurement documents.

14. **A** The main objective of contract negotiation is to establish a fair contract, which protects a future sustainable relationship.

15. **D** In a bidder conference, the buyer should make sure that all suppliers have the same information. The goal is to minimize the risk that the best supplier is not chosen because it did not have access to adequate information.

16. **D** A bidder conference could lead to better proposals but would not have an impact on the number of proposals received. All the remaining options could be useful.

17. **C** The buyer chose to acquire from a preferred supplier without consulting other alternatives. The main risk of single-source procurement is assuming that a previous positive experience implies good performance in the future.

18. **B** Reviewing proposals is part of the conduct procurements process. All other options are part of the control procurements process.

19. **B** The control procurements process includes all the activities required to ensure that both supplier and buyer meet the contract requirements. Receiving proposals and negotiating contracts (answer A) are part of the conduct procurements process. Establishing a contract change control system (answer C) is part of the plan procurement management process. Formally accepting the contract (answer D) is part of the close procurements process.

20. **C** Accepting the deliverable (answer D) and performing a detailed requirements analysis (answer A) would not be possible without changing the contract. Rejecting the deliverable (answer B) would be a worse option than requesting a formal contract change.

21. **C** There is no information to support an assumption that the contract is breached (answer A), that compensation is due (answer D), or that the procurement management plan should be changed (answer B). Payments should be made according to the contract terms.

22. **D** A claim is a request for compensation according to the contract terms and conditions.

23. **D** A procurement audit is part of the close procurements process.

24. **C** The close project or phase process manages terminated projects. The close procurements process manages terminated contracts.

25. **C** A formal written notice that the contract has been completed is generated during the close procurements process.

13 Stakeholder Management

As discussed earlier, stakeholders are individuals or groups that may influence or be influenced by the project. Stakeholder management includes the processes required for meeting stakeholders' expectations. Some examples of stakeholder management activities are:

- Identifying stakeholders
- Analyzing their needs, wishes, concerns, and authority
- Determining the most adequate strategy to manage each stakeholder or group of stakeholders
- Managing identified problems jointly with stakeholders
- Promoting the engagement of stakeholders with the project
- Communicating proactively with stakeholders to monitor their needs and expectations
- Influencing expectations

The following table displays the stakeholder management processes with their respective process group:

Stakeholder Management Processes

Process	Process Group
Identify stakeholders	Initiating
Plan stakeholder management	Planning
Manage stakeholder engagement	Executing
Control stakeholder engagement	Monitoring and controlling

Identify Stakeholders

To manage the project, the project manager should be able to understand and influence the project environment, creating positive relationships with stakeholders and managing their expectations. Identifying stakeholders enables the project management team to concentrate on what is critical for project success. The **identify stakeholders** process may include:

- Identifying project stakeholders
- Collecting additional stakeholder information in a stakeholder register
- Analyzing their needs, wishes, concerns, roles, and level of knowledge about the project
- Mapping project stakeholders according to their power, influence, and project support

Stakeholder Register

The stakeholder register can hold relevant information about the individuals and groups that influence or are influenced by the project. This information may include contacts, requirements, expectations, power, interests, and attitude toward the project. (See Figure 13.1.)

Mapping Stakeholder Influence

Stakeholder analysis can be performed around multiple criteria:

- **Authority versus interest**   Relating the stakeholders' capacity to influence project decisions with the impact that these decisions have on their interests
- **Authority versus attitude**   Relating the level of stakeholders' authority with the type of attitude they have toward the project

Authority

Attitude	High	Medium	Low
Favorable			
Neutral			
Unfavorable			

Name	Role	Contact	Requirements	Power	Interest	Attitude	Knowledge

Figure 13.1 Example of a stakeholder register

Influence Curve

The **influence curve** illustrates that the ability to influence a change is relatively high at the project's beginning and low at its end. Simultaneously, the cost of a potential change is relatively low at the project's beginning and high at its end.

> Engaging stakeholders from the beginning of the project, particularly those that have more power and influence, is the best way to minimize the risk of negative or constant changes.

Plan Stakeholder Management

Stakeholders' attitudes, engagement, commitment, and availability to accept project objectives are not independent of the attitudes of project managers. Nor are they independent of the adopted communication approach and the project manager's availability to adapt the project to stakeholders' needs.

Planning stakeholder management or preparing a **stakeholder management plan** is an opportunity to think in advance about the strategies that best promote engagement and commitment to the project. The **plan stakeholder management** process may include:

- Analyzing how stakeholders will be impacted by the project
- Classifying the level of stakeholders' support
- Determining the strategies that will generate a positive engagement from stakeholders

A **stakeholder engagement assessment matrix** can be used to map specific stakeholders to levels of engagement, such as unaware, resistant, neutral, supportive, and leading. By adding information about the current and the desired levels of stakeholder engagement, this matrix can be used to identify engagement gaps and guide the plan stakeholder management process.

REVIEW EXERCISE 1

How can you distinguish a stakeholder register, a stakeholder management plan, and a communications management plan?

Stakeholder register _____

_____

_____

_____

Stakeholder management plan _____

_____

_____

_____

Communications management plan _____

_____

_____

_____

Manage Stakeholder Engagement

Lack of engagement and expectations management is one of the main causes of project failures. The main purpose of the manage stakeholder engagement process is to prevent the project from going off track due to unmanaged expectations and problems. The stakeholder management process may include:

- Establishing and influencing expectations
- Communicating proactively with stakeholders
- Managing expectations
- Influencing changes
- Promoting the stakeholders' engagement in the project
- Solving problems
- Generating corrective actions
- Creating lessons learned
- Maintaining a project issue log, documenting and tracing problems, obstacles, and expectations, from identification to resolution

> The engagement and expectations should be managed throughout the entire project, even when the project is nearly finished. If there is a conflict of interests between different project stakeholders, the project manager is most accountable to the customer.

REVIEW EXERCISE 2

> **What are the potential consequences of lack of stakeholder management?**

1. _____

2. _____

3. _____

4. _____

5. _____

6. _____

7. _____

Control Stakeholder Engagement

It is important to monitor the relationship with the stakeholders to verify if the adopted management strategies require improvement. The **control stakeholder engagement** process keeps the adopted strategies aligned with project needs throughout the project. Controlling stakeholder engagement also includes updating the stakeholder register when new stakeholders are identified or when there are updates required to the registered stakeholders.

As with other stakeholder management processes, control stakeholder engagement is accomplished through constant communication.

MEMORIZATION EXERCISE

> **The following exercise was designed to facilitate the memorization of the main concepts in this chapter. Assign the following definitions to a stakeholder management concept:**

1. Determines the strategies that best promote engagement and commitment to the project

   _____

2. Illustrates how the ability to influence a change is relatively high at the project's beginning and low at its end. Simultaneously, it highlights how the cost of a potential change is relatively low at the project's beginning and high at its end.

   _____

3. Project document that holds relevant information about stakeholders, including contacts, requirements, expectations, power, interests, and attitude toward the project

   _____

Process Exercises

The following exercises were designed so you could learn how to recognize the processes and understand their logical sequence. Stakeholder management processes are listed next, including their unique number in the *PMBOK Guide*:

- 13.1 Identify stakeholders
- 13.2 Plan stakeholder management
- 13.3 Manage stakeholder engagement
- 13.4 Control stakeholder engagement

PROCESS EXERCISE 1

> **Assign processes to the following activities.**

1. Analyze the stakeholders' needs, wishes, concerns, and authorities. _____
2. Change the adopted stakeholder management strategies. _____
3. Communicate proactively with stakeholders. _____
4. Determine the most suitable strategy to manage each group of stakeholders. _____
5. Identify stakeholders. _____
6. Manage expectations. _____

7. Position project stakeholders according to their power, influence, and project support.

_____

8. Promote the stakeholders' engagement in the project. _____

9. Solve problems. _____

PROCESS EXERCISE 2

Assign processes to the following inputs:

1. Communications management plan _____

2. Change log _____

3. Stakeholder register _____

4. Project charter _____

CHAPTER 13 EXAM

The following questions were designed to test your knowledge on this chapter's topic. Read each question carefully, and choose the option that most accurately answers the question. Once you have completed the exam, compare your answers with the solution and read through the justification provided. Note the topics where you have the most difficulty, and make sure that you dedicate enough study time to them.

1. Project stakeholders are identified during which process group?
   A. Executing
   B. Initiating
   C. Planning
   D. Stakeholders management

2. A project has been dealing with significant scope changes. Which of the following is the LEAST likely cause?
   A. Some deliverables only recently decomposed into work packages
   B. Lack of a change control system
   C. Poor stakeholders' identification
   D. Lack of management support

3. While preparing a stakeholder register, you are focused on analyzing stakeholders' influence. Which of the following statements regarding stakeholders' influence is correct?
   A. Stakeholders should be able to influence project decisions throughout the project.
   B. Stakeholders' influence remains steady throughout the project.
   C. Stakeholders' influence is usually lower in the beginning of the project.
   D. Stakeholders' influence should decrease throughout the project, along with the impact of potential changes.

4. All of the following options are included in a stakeholder register EXCEPT:
   A. Stakeholders' requirements and interests
   B. Stakeholders' power and influence over the project
   C. Stakeholders' identification
   D. Stakeholder management strategy

5. At the early stages of the project, you noticed a high level of resistance from a number of stakeholders. How should you approach the situation?
   A. Establish a responsibility assignment matrix defining the stakeholders' roles.
   B. Review the project charter according to stakeholders' expectations.
   C. Meet with stakeholders to understand their issues and expectations and remove any existing obstacles.
   D. Meet with the sponsor to prevent these stakeholders from negatively influencing the project.

6. The project manager has just been informed that one stakeholder is unhappy about a specific deliverable. The project manager believes that the stakeholder's concern should not be an issue because the deliverable will fully address the need. What should the project manager do?
   A. Inform management.
   B. Send the requirements documentation to the stakeholder to prove that the adopted scope meets the need.
   C. Set up a meeting with the stakeholder to discuss his concerns.
   D. Ask the stakeholder to clearly document his requirement and issue a change request.

7. Which of the following is NOT part of stakeholder management?
   A. Exceeding expectations
   B. Influencing expectations
   C. Determining stakeholders' roles and knowledge about the project
   D. Managing issues proactively

8. During scope verification you notice that a critical deliverable does not meet its requirements. The customer did not notice it and is about to validate the deliverable. You are worried because the correction can compromise the project schedule. What should you do NEXT?
   A. Complete scope verification without correcting the defect. Correct the defect later at a more appropriate time.
   B. Correct the deliverable and review the project schedule.
   C. Inform the customer.
   D. Issue a change request.

9. Whenever there is a conflict of interests between different project stakeholders, the project manager should be more accountable to:
   A. Sponsor
   B. Steering
   C. Customer
   D. PMI

10. Which of the following should NOT be part of stakeholder management?
    A. Completing work outside the project's scope
    B. Using an issue log
    C. Issuing change requests
    D. Influencing stakeholders

11. Which of the following is LEAST related to stakeholder management?
    A. Issue log
    B. Assumptions log
    C. Changes log
    D. Influence curve

12. A critical resource was removed from the project a few weeks before the project due date. Which of the following is the LEAST likely reason?
    A. Lack of a staffing management plan
    B. The functional manager not being included in the communications management plan
    C. Lack of a work authorization system
    D. Lack of management support

13. A project is facing major changes during project execution. Which of the following would have been the BEST option to avoid this situation?
    A. Involve all available stakeholders in the project charter development.
    B. Review the WBS carefully with the team.
    C. Formally approve a requirements register.
    D. Spend more time managing stakeholders.

14. The project has a history of changes to the approved scope statement. Which of the following would have been LEAST helpful in preventing this situation?
    A. Configuration management system
    B. Stakeholder management plan
    C. Issue log
    D. Project charter

15. While managing an IT integration project, the team informed the project manager that the technical architecture, previously approved by the customer, can be significantly improved. Such change would meet the customer's initial expectations but could compromise the adopted schedule. How should the project manager proceed?
    A. Discuss the issue with the customer.
    B. Inform the customer and review the project WBS.
    C. Review the project scope to reflect the improvement in the technical architecture.
    D. Do not inform the customer and capture lessons learned.

16. One month before the project's scheduled completion, the customer requested an additional critical requirement. What should the project manager do NEXT?
    A. Request management support.
    B. Inform the customer that the requirement will be delivered by a future project.
    C. Approve a change request before working on the new requirement.
    D. Initiate integrated change control.

17. The project is nearly finished, and the team is completing the last technical deliverable. One week before the due date, the team informed the project manager that it will not be possible to complete the project within the schedule. What is the BEST option?
    A. Inform the customer that the project will be late.
    B. Inform management.
    C. Review the communications management plan.
    D. Analyze available alternatives.

18. Manage stakeholder engagement belongs to the _____ process group.
    A. Planning
    B. Executing
    C. Monitoring and controlling
    D. Closing

19. Which of the following processes does NOT use an audit?
    A. Perform quality assurance
    B. Control risks
    C. Control stakeholder engagement
    D. Control procurements

ANSWERS

Review Exercise 1

Concept	Description
Stakeholder register	Documents relevant information about stakeholders, including contacts, requirements, expectations, power, interests, and attitude toward the project
Stakeholder management plan	Defines the strategies that best promote engagement and commitment to the project
Communications management plan	Identifies communication requirements and determines how communications will be managed throughout the project

Review Exercise 2

1. Constant project changes
2. Low project support
3. Delays on project decisions
4. Less time dedicated to the project by stakeholders
5. Conflict
6. Low morale
7. Unrealistic demands

Memorization Exercise

1. Stakeholder management plan
2. Influence curve
3. Stakeholder register

Process Exercise 1

1. 13.1
2. 13.4
3. 13.3
4. 13.2
5. 13.1
6. 13.3
7. 13.1
8. 13.3
9. 13.3

Process Exercise 2

1. 13.3
2. 13.3
3. 13.2
4. 13.1

Chapter 13 Exam

1. **B** Project stakeholders are identified during the initiating process group.
2. **A** A progressive elaboration of project deliverables is a normal scope planning approach. Without a change control system (answer B) and management support (answer D), the project would have a difficult time enforcing change control. Poor stakeholders' identification (answer C) can lead to changes, because stakeholders may not feel committed to the adopted scope.
3. **A** Stakeholders should be able to influence project decisions during the whole project. Their ability to influence change is usually higher at the project beginning and progressively decreases throughout the project (answers B and C). The impact of potential changes usually increases throughout the project (answer D).
4. **D** The stakeholder management strategy is part of the stakeholder management plan. All other options may be included in the stakeholder register.
5. **C** To manage a project, you need to understand the stakeholders' issues and expectations and remove any existing obstacles.
6. **C** A meeting can clarify if the deliverable meets the stakeholder's need as well as show concern with his interests. Answers A and B do not clarify if the deliverable meets the need. Answer D does not show the stakeholder the same concern with his interests as answer C.
7. **A** Exceeding expectations is often the outcome of either offering extra work or failing to translate expectations into requirements. In either case, exceeding expectations is not a good project management practice. All the other options are part of stakeholder management.
8. **C** The deliverable should be corrected because it does not meet its specification. However, correcting the deliverable would lead to a schedule delay. Therefore, there is a conflict between schedule and scope. The project manager should inform the customer so that the best decision can be made. Answer A is not an ethical option. Answer B would lead to a schedule delay. Answer D would not be the first step.
9. **C** If there is a conflict of interests between different project stakeholders, the project manager is most accountable to the customer.

10. **A** The team cannot complete work outside the project's scope. All the other options are part of stakeholder management.

11. **B** The assumptions log documents the project assumptions to ensure traceability. Updates to the issue log (answer A) and the changes log (answer C) are often the result of stakeholder management. The influence curve describes how the stakeholders' ability to influence decreases throughout the project (answer D).

12. **C** The fact that a critical resource was removed from the project suggests a problem with human resource management planning. Maybe the project does not have a staffing management plan (answer A) or the plan is not being implemented by lack of management support (answer D). Maybe the resource allocation problems are caused by inadequate communication with the functional manager (answer B). The lack of a work authorization system should not lead to the resource allocation problems.

13. **D** Lack of stakeholder management is one of the main causes of constant project changes.

14. **A** A configuration management system can help to keep track of changes, but cannot avoid them. All the other options can help prevent constant and significant changes.

15. **A** The project manager should disclose that there is a potential change that can significantly improve the project value.

16. **D** Changes should be managed, however inappropriate and harmful. If a potential change is unfavorable, the negative impacts should be reflected on the change request impact analysis.

17. **D** Before informing management or informing the customer, the project manager should analyze alternative solutions to meet the due date.

18. **B** Manage stakeholder engagement is part of the executing process group.

19. **C** The control stakeholder engagement process does not use audits as a tool. All the other options use audits.

14 Full-Length Practice Exam

The following exam simulates the complete range and duration of the PMP exam. Give yourself four hours to answer the following 200 exam questions.

Read each question carefully and choose the option that most accurately answers the question. Once you have completed the exam, compare your answers with the solutions and read through the provided justifications.

Note the topics where you have the most difficulty to make sure you will dedicate enough study time to them.

1. The seller has failed to provide the buyer a contracted deliverable. How should the buyer proceed?
   A. Send a letter formalizing the default and meet with the supplier to identify a corrective action.
   B. Terminate the contract.
   C. Inform the supplier that such conduct is unacceptable.
   D. Request a contract change to remove the deliverable from the contract.

2. Your team has collected requirements from stakeholders and is about to prepare requirements documentation. Which of the following should NOT be part of the requirements documentation?
   A. Functional requirements
   B. Requirements management approach
   C. Quality requirements
   D. Business need

3. The estimate costs process is defined as:
   A. Adding up cost estimates to create a cumulative time-phase budget
   B. Estimating all costs according to the resources required to perform the project activities
   C. Comparing actual cost performance to the plan and managing changes to the cost baseline
   D. A project management technique for measuring project performance, combining and integrating scope, schedule, and cost assessment

4. Lessons learned are part of which process group?
   A. Planning
   B. Executing
   C. Closing
   D. All of the above

5. The customer has requested a scope change that can be implemented with no impact on the project schedule. You are also aware that implementing such change could greatly improve your relationship with the customer. What should be done NEXT?
   A. Implement the change and update the project management plan.
   B. Analyze the impact of the change.
   C. Request an approval for the change.
   D. Implement the change and issue a change request to ensure traceability.

6. All of the following are part of the control costs process EXCEPT:
   A. Identify changes to the cost baseline.
   B. Monitor cost risks.
   C. Determine actual costs.
   D. Forecast future costs.

7. Calculating late start and late finish dates by working backward through the network diagram is known as:
   A. Schedule compression
   B. Backward pass
   C. Reverse scheduling
   D. Reverse leveling

8. Earned value (EV) minus planned value (PV) equals _____.
   A. Schedule variance (SV)
   B. Cost variance (CV)
   C. Estimate to complete (ETC)
   D. Schedule performance index (SPI)

9. Standard compensation, additional to direct wages, formally given to all employees is also known as _____.
   A. Rewarding authority
   B. Fringe benefits
   C. Perquisites
   D. Recognition and rewards systems

10. Which of the following is TRUE regarding a control account?
    A. It's a WBS numbering system.
    B. It's used to manage cost at specific levels of the WBS.
    C. It's used to prevent the project from going through the next phase without formal approval.
    D. It's part of the company chart of accounts.

11. Activity A has a duration of 8 and can start anytime. Activity B has a duration of 10 and can start after activity A. Activity C has a duration of 4 and can start after activity A. Activity D has a duration of 8 and can start after activity C. Activity E has a duration of 6 and can start after activity C. Activity F has a duration of 4 and can start after activities B, D, and E. If the project deadline were 24, what would be the float of activity E?
    A. 0
    B. 4
    C. 2
    D. 6

12. Which of the following is an example of a cost management assumption?
    A. Technology will be available to support an advanced requirement.
    B. Hardware will be delivered in late August.
    C. There are enough funds to complete the project.
    D. Resources will be trained before starting the project.

13. Which of the following would NOT help develop a project team?
    A. Hold a kickoff meeting.
    B. Organize a milestone party.
    C. Develop a project logo.
    D. Use virtual teams.

14. Which of the following is NOT an input to the identify risks process?
    A. Expert judgment
    B. Scope baseline
    C. Organizational process assets
    D. Risk management plan

15. While painting your house, you know the paint takes four hours to dry. Once the paint is dry, you will hang the pictures on the wall. To correctly sequence the work, you need to do which of the following?
    A. Add a lag time of four hours to the painting activity.
    B. Add a lead time of four hours to the painting activity.
    C. Remove the dependency between the two activities, and manually supervise them.
    D. Build a slack of four hours to the painting activity.

16. Which of the following is NOT an output of the define activities process?
    A. Milestone list
    B. Activity attributes
    C. Work packages
    D. Activity list

17. An organization that has typical characteristics of a matrix organization and yet is partially projectized is known as a _____.
    A. Performing organization
    B. Project management office (PMO)
    C. Composite organization
    D. Strong matrix

18. A project deliverable is often developed by multiple organizational units. Which WBS element can be used to assign work responsibilities to organizational units?
    A. Control accounts
    B. Organizational breakdown structure (OBS)
    C. Responsibility assignment matrix (RAM)
    D. Work packages

19. During scope definition meetings, your team is facing conflict among key stakeholders. Your key concern is to find a long-term resolution for the scope definition conflicts. Which of the following is your BEST option?
    A. Compromise
    B. Consensus
    C. Collaborate
    D. Withdraw

20. A project with a baseline cost of 100,000 and a total funding of 115,000 has a _____ of 15,000.
    A. Management reserve
    B. Negative cost variance
    C. Profit
    D. Positive cost variance

21. How does a risk reassessment differ from a risk audit?
    A. A risk audit is conducted only at the end of the project.
    B. A risk reassessment is focused on the overall project risk, while a risk audit is focused on the individual risk.
    C. A risk reassessment is focused on individual risks, while the risk audit is focused on the risk management process.
    D. A risk reassessment is normally conducted by an external team, while a risk audit is conducted by team members.

22. Requiring a certified PMP to award a contract is an example of:
    A. Weighting system
    B. Screening system
    C. Performance requirement
    D. Constraint

23. Which of the following is NOT part of the executing process group?
    A. Completing work packages
    B. Distributing information about the project
    C. Holding a project kickoff meeting
    D. Using an issue log to manage project issues

24. Which of the following BEST describes successful quality management?
    A. A happy customer
    B. Meeting requirements
    C. High conformance costs
    D. Low nonconformance costs

25. The contracting officer wants to exempt the company from fulfilling their obligations should certain uncontrollable events occur. The contract should:
    A. Specify unknown unknowns
    B. Include a force majeure clause
    C. Include a termination for convenience cause
    D. Include an incentives system

26. An activity has an optimistic duration of 10 days, a most likely duration of 13 days, and a pessimistic duration of 22 days. What is the PERT standard deviation of the activity?
    A. 2
    B. 4
    C. 12
    D. 14

27. Which of the following is LEAST relevant for reviewing a procurement claim?
    A. Negotiation meeting minutes
    B. Approved contract changes
    C. Contract
    D. Procurement management plan

28. You need to quickly provide a preliminary cost estimate of a construction project. How should you proceed?
    A. Provide an analogous estimate.
    B. Estimate the work packages' costs and aggregate them into an overall estimate.
    C. Wait until there is enough information for an accurate and detailed estimate.
    D. Collect historical data and work with the PMO to develop a parametric model.

29. Variance analysis is a tool and technique for:
    A. Collecting requirements
    B. Defining scope
    C. Validating scope
    D. Controlling scope

30. In which circumstances would you use a nominal group technique (NGT)?
    A. When you need to present a model to key stakeholders and obtain feedback
    B. When you need to gather information from large populations
    C. When you need to reach a consensus through an anonymous process
    D. When you need to make a decision quickly by vote, but want everyone's opinions taken into account

31. A project is running out of funds. Who has the responsibility to manage the situation?
    A. Project manager
    B. Senior management
    C. Functional manager
    D. Sponsor

32. The product scope:
    A. Is progressively elaborated throughout the project
    B. Defines the complete scope of work
    C. Is defined in the project work breakdown structure (WBS)
    D. Defines the project business need

33. How does data quality impact risk management?
    A. It impacts the overall project risk ranking.
    B. It provides information on the risk impact on quality objectives.
    C. It provides information on the likelihood of meeting project objectives.
    D. It provides information on how much you know about the risk.

34. Which of the following communication types is MORE suited to deal with conflict between two team members?
    A. Formal written
    B. Formal oral
    C. Informal written
    D. Informal oral

35. Which of the following options is NOT an input of the collect requirements process?
    A. Scope management plan
    B. Scope statement
    C. Requirements management plan
    D. Stakeholders' register

36. The control scope process can include all of the following activities EXCEPT:
    A. Validating deliverables
    B. Identifying scope changes
    C. Preventing the team from completing work that is not included in the project scope
    D. Comparing actual scope performance with the baseline

37. You have already completed activity sequencing, what should you do NEXT?
    A. Estimate activity durations.
    B. Estimate activity resources.
    C. Develop the project schedule.
    D. Compress the project schedule.

38. After completing the WBS, the activity list, and the network diagram, the project manager estimated activity durations. What has he done wrong?
    A. Forgot to level the resources
    B. Did not optimize the project schedule
    C. Did not involve the project team
    D. Forgot to analyze the overall schedule risk

39. A fixed price incentive fee contract has been established with the following parameters:

    • Target cost: 2,000,000   Target fee: 100,000
    • Sharing ratio: 60%/40%   Price ceiling: 2,200,000

    What is the point of total assumption?

    A. 2,166,667
    B. 2,200,000
    C. 2,225,000
    D. 2,500,000

40. To provide good customer service in a restaurant, a table should be thoroughly prepared before a new customer is seated. This is an example of:
    A. A mandatory dependency
    B. A discretionary dependency
    C. Lag
    D. Start-to-start dependency

41. Which statement best describes the role of assumptions in the project management effort?
    A. Assumptions are documented in the scope statement or in an independent log, and are used for risk identification and risk monitoring purposes.
    B. Assumptions are documented in the project charter and are used for risk monitoring purposes.
    C. Documenting assumptions removes the project uncertainty.
    D. Assumptions represent restrictions imposed by stakeholders or by the project environment.

42. What is the MAIN benefit of colocating project team members within a matrix organization environment?
    A. Reduces communications costs and improves team building
    B. Improves resource allocation
    C. Improves change control
    D. Reduces conflict

43. Team members are starting to feel uneasy. They have all been hired on a contract basis, and the project is approaching its completion date. The project is running in _____.
    A. A projectized organization
    B. A functional organization
    C. A matrix organization
    D. A program context

44. Earned value (EV) is also known as:
    A. Budgeted cost of work scheduled
    B. Actual cost of the work completed
    C. Budgeted cost of work completed
    D. Net present value of the project cash flows

45. You have just been nominated to manage your first project. To manage it more effectively, you should rely on organizational process assets. Which of the following options is NOT an organizational process asset?
    A. Corporate knowledge base
    B. Project management procedures and templates
    C. Lessons learned
    D. Organizational infrastructure

46. You are about to move on to determining the budget estimate. Which of the following do you NOT need as an input?
    A. WBS
    B. Cost baseline
    C. Basis of estimate
    D. Project schedule

47. What is the role of focus groups in the collect requirements process?
    A. Stakeholders discuss ideas to generate a solution with the help of a moderator.
    B. Requirements are organized into groups for easier management.
    C. Requirements are collected based on an unrestrained exchange of ideas.
    D. Requirements are generated by presenting a model to key stakeholders and obtaining feedback.

48. How can the management reserve be used in risk management?
    A. Manage unknown-unknowns.
    B. Manage risks identified by management.
    C. Manage known-unknowns.
    D. Account for profit.

49. Activity A has a duration of 8 and can start anytime. Activity B has a duration of 10 and can start after activity A. Activity C has a duration of 4 and can start after activity A. Activity D has a duration of 8 and can start after activity C. Activity E has a duration of 6 and can start after activity C. Activity F has a duration of 4 and can start after activities B, D, and E. What is the project critical path?
    A. A-B-F
    B. A-C-D-F
    C. A-C-E-F
    D. A-B-F and A-C-E-F

50. _____ can help define what is accepted and what is not accepted as team behavior, reducing conflict and improving productivity.
    A. Staffing management plan
    B. Recognition and rewards system
    C. Ground rules
    D. Roles and responsibilities

51. What does a negative float mean?
    A. A schedule delay is affecting another project on the same program.
    B. The project has high risk.
    C. The project started before the planned date.
    D. The scheduled completion date is after an imposed deadline.

52. Risks that remain after risk response planning are:
    A. Force majeure risks
    B. Residual risks
    C. Pure risks
    D. Secondary risks

53. Which of the following is NOT TRUE regarding reserve analysis?
    A. The project manager should prevent changes to the established reserve.
    B. It is part of the control risk process.
    C. It can be applied to both time and cost.
    D. It compares the amount of contingency reserves available to the amount of risk.

54. A team member determines that a new approach is needed to complete a work package. Who has the responsibility to manage the situation?
    A. Project manager
    B. Management
    C. Functional manager
    D. Team member accountable for the work package

55. All of the following are correct for a process under control EXCEPT:
    A. Measurements are within control limits.
    B. It does not require further inspection.
    C. It can be improved.
    D. It has variation caused by common causes.

56. All of the following are benefits of using risk categories in risk management EXCEPT:
    A. Defining an approach for managing risks
    B. Easier reporting
    C. Easier access to risk historical information
    D. Displaying risks in a risk breakdown structure

57. The profit in a CPIF contract is:
    A. Known from the start of the contract
    B. Determined by fixed fee plus incentive fee
    C. The target fee
    D. Determined by the difference between the actual cost and target cost

58. Which of the following is LEAST related to schedule risk?
    A. A complex and risky activity is on the critical path
    B. Multiple critical paths
    C. Multiple paths converging into a single activity
    D. An activity with a free float of zero

59. Which of the following is NOT a control quality tool or technique?
    A. Run chart
    B. Sampling
    C. Inspection
    D. Benchmarking

60. A product development project requires the help of a senior marketing expert to design the communication campaign. How should the project manager proceed if the only available expert can be assigned to the project only in a specific time frame?
    A. Use the critical chain method.
    B. Use the Monte Carlo analysis.
    C. Perform a resource leveling according to the expert's availability.
    D. Perform a resource smoothing.

61. In which of the following options is your contract complete?
    A. All deliverables have been completed as contracted, but the customer is not happy.
    B. All deliverables have been completed as contracted, but there are still open claims.
    C. Some contracted project management deliverables have not been completed.
    D. There was a breach in the contract.

62. Before starting the development phase of an IT project, you are working to ensure that the design phase was completed according to the project management plan. You are involved in:
    A. Initiating
    B. Executing
    C. Monitoring and controlling
    D. Closing

63. The project with an initial budget of 50,000 has an estimate at completion of 60,000. If a new change request is authorized with a budget of 5,000, what is the revised budget for the project?
    A. 50,000
    B. 55,000
    C. 60,000
    D. 65,000

64. Which of the following tools is NOT used to define responsibilities?
    A. Responsibility assignment matrix
    B. Organizational breakdown structure
    C. Staffing management plan
    D. Resource breakdown structure

65. In a project running in a matrix organization, who is accountable for the overall procurement process?
    A. The project team member performing the procurement activities
    B. The project manager
    C. Management
    D. The procurement manager

66. The customer is extremely pleased with the quality of the project that went well beyond what was planned. How would you describe the project's performance?
    A. There is not enough information.
    B. It was a success because the customer is happy.
    C. It was unsuccessful.
    D. It was a success because the quality exceeded what was planned.

67. When should you use a weighting system instead of a screening system?
    A. When you need faster results
    B. When you want to exclude suppliers that do not meet a specific requirement
    C. When you need to prioritize suppliers according to criteria
    D. When you want to contact a short list of suppliers

68. Which of the following sets of processes is part of the planning process group?
    A. Develop project management plan and identify stakeholders
    B. Estimate costs and perform quantitative risk analysis
    C. Plan procurement and perform quality assurance
    D. Plan communications management and acquire project team

69. Activity A has a duration of 8 and can start anytime. Activity B has a duration of 10 and can start after activity A. Activity C has a duration of 4 and can start after activity A. Activity D has a duration of 8 and can start after activity C. Activity E has a duration of 6 and can start after activity C. Activity F has a duration of 4 and can start after activities B, D, and E. What is the float of activity E?
    A. 0
    B. 2
    C. −2
    D. 12

70. A formal document that describes the products and services that should be provided by the project is known as:
    A. Business case
    B. WBS
    C. SOW
    D. Scope statement

71. Which of the following options regarding a rough order of magnitude (ROM) estimate is NOT TRUE?
    A. It usually ranges from −50 percent to +50 percent from the most likely estimate.
    B. It establishes expectations.
    C. Its precision level may be defined in the cost management plan.
    D. It's prepared during the planning process group.

72. Which of the following statements regarding analogous estimating is FALSE?
    A. It is not a type of expert judgment.
    B. It can be applied to both project and activity levels.
    C. It establishes management expectations.
    D. It uses information regarding similar projects.

73. How does quality management classify quality costs?
    A. Plan quality, quality assurance, and quality control costs
    B. Conformance and nonconformance costs
    C. Fixed and variable costs
    D. Direct and indirect costs

74. All of the following are true about quality management EXCEPT:
    A. The team focus should be on designing quality into the project instead of inspecting.
    B. The quality assurance team is the ultimate responsible for project quality.
    C. Quality may refer to project, process, or product.
    D. The project team should pursue a continuous process improvement.

75. The project schedule should be distributed:
    A. To the customer and the team
    B. To the customer and the sponsor
    C. To all stakeholders
    D. According to the communications management plan

76. Which of the following aims to eliminate causes of quality defects?
    A. Plan quality management
    B. Perform quality assurance
    C. Control quality
    D. Process analysis

77. You have prepared a WBS and a project schedule. What should you do NEXT?
    A. Send the schedule for approval.
    B. Determine the budget.
    C. Estimate costs.
    D. Reconcile funding limits.

78. Which of the following statements regarding scope management is correct?
    A. Scope changes should be avoided.
    B. Workshops enable a swift collection of requirements.
    C. The WBS is a list of activities.
    D. The sponsor should approve all scope changes.

79. In order to collect project requirements, the project manager has sent questionnaires to a number of stakeholders. Once the ideas have been collected and processed, they will be sent back to stakeholders for a new feedback iteration. The process will be repeated until a meaningful consensus is obtained. The technique used by the project manager is known as:
    A. Focus group
    B. Nominal group technique
    C. Delphi technique
    D. Iteration technique

80. All of the following are part of configuration management EXCEPT:
    A. Identify and document specific product elements
    B. Audit specific product elements to verify their conformance to requirements
    C. Identify risks regarding the development of product elements
    D. Control the development of specific product elements

81. Which of the following is NOT included in the change management plan?
    A. Which project documents are subject to formal change control
    B. Role of the change control board
    C. A list of approved change requests
    D. Procedure that enables an automatic approval of changes in case of emergency

82. You want to use a steady amount of resources each month, but you do not want to change the project completion date. What technique should you use?
    A. Crashing resources
    B. Resource smoothing
    C. Resource leveling
    D. Histogram

83. You have just completed the project schedule. Before submitting it for approval, you should prepare:
    A. Contingency reserve
    B. WBS
    C. Schedule data
    D. All of the above

84. Which of the following options is NOT a possible result of a contract breach?
    A. Letter of default
    B. Punitive damages
    C. Terminated contract
    D. Letter of intent

85. All of the following can approve the project charter EXCEPT:
    A. Senior management
    B. Program manager
    C. Portfolio manager
    D. Project manager

86. Which of the following is a disadvantage of a matrix organization?
    A. Team members possibly losing their jobs at the end of the project
    B. Lack of a clear career path
    C. Specialized resources duplicated by project
    D. Difficulty in allocating resources

87. You have just obtained the final sign-off on your 12-month project, after completing all the work required by the customer. You are now updating the organization historical information knowledge base. Which of the following statements is correct?
    A. The project is closed because formal acceptance has been obtained.
    B. You are performing a planning activity because the information knowledge base should have been updated in the beginning of the project.
    C. The project is closed because updating the organization knowledge base is not project work.
    D. You are performing a closing activity.

88. Which of the following contracts would minimize the buyer's cost risk if the project scope is well known?
    A. Cost plus incentive fee (CPIF)
    B. Cost plus award fee (CPAF)
    C. Firm fixed price (FFP)
    D. Cost plus percentage of cost

89. If the CPI is 0.8, SPI is 1.1, and BAC is 10,000, what is the project EAC?
    A. 8,000
    B. 20,000
    C. 12,500
    D. There is not enough information.

90. Helping the team build consensus through discussion and the use of multiple perspectives from the different team members is an example of what type of conflict resolution technique?
    A. Consensus management
    B. Compromise
    C. Problem solve
    D. Smooth

91. The stimulus for initiating a project can be all of the following EXCEPT:
    A. Project charter
    B. Customer request
    C. Process improvement opportunities
    D. Political decision

92. Which of the following is NOT a legal requirement to consider a contract valid?
    A. Legal purpose
    B. Offer and acceptance
    C. Consideration
    D. Negotiation

93. You have just collected the following project performance information:

    - PV = 1,500,000
    - EV = 1,100,000
    - AC = 1,000,000

    If the project BAC = 2,000,000, what is the project ETC?

    A. 818,182
    B. 828,182
    C. 1,818,182
    D. 1,828,182

94. A numbering system used to provide a unique identification number to each element of the WBS is a:
    A. Chart of accounts
    B. Control account plan
    C. Code of accounts
    D. WBS dictionary

95. The main concern of the collect requirements process is:
    A. Identifying stakeholders and managing their engagement
    B. Understanding and prioritizing stakeholders' needs
    C. Establishing an agreement on project scope with relevant stakeholders
    D. Defining resource requirements

96. All of the following can be used to calculate EAC, EXCEPT:
    A. BAC / CPI
    B. ETC + AC
    C. AC + (BAC − EV) / CPI
    D. ETC + (BAC − EV)

97. Which of the following statements regarding the project scope statement is correct?
    A. It is developed by the customer and used as an input during scope definition.
    B. It describes the buyers' needs to potential suppliers.
    C. It is prepared by the project management team with the input of relevant stakeholders and is used as an input during the development of the WBS.
    D. It establishes the contract scope.

98. The WBS can help:
    A. Manage scope
    B. Communicate with project stakeholders
    C. Develop project team
    D. All of the above

99. The project is behind schedule. Who has the responsibility of managing the situation?
    A. Project manager
    B. Senior management
    C. Project management team
    D. Team

100. A buyer wants to send a formal invitation to potential vendors. The buyer wishes to receive offers similar in scope and make a selection based on price. Which of the following should he prepare?
    A. Request for proposal
    B. Invitation for bid
    C. Statement of work
    D. Request for quotation

101. How can a workaround help the risk management process?
    A. It's an unplanned response to a specific risk.
    B. It's a contingency reserve.
    C. It's a contingency plan for low severity risks.
    D. It's an alternative response in case the adopted planned responses fail to work.

102. You have been asked to manage the implementation of improvements to an existing billing system. To help you analyze the process, which of the following tools would you use?
    A. Cause-and-effect diagrams
    B. Value analysis
    C. Flowcharts
    D. Benchmarking

103. Which of the following statements regarding procurement control is NOT true?
    A. The control procurements process is performed by the buyer and supplier.
    B. The buyer may inspect and audit the supplier's work.
    C. The supplier may issue claims.
    D. The project manager is the main person responsible for contract change management.

104. Which of the following is the best approach for planning change management?
    A. There is no point in planning change because changes are not predictable.
    B. A specific change management approach has to be determined for each change because the environment is dynamic.
    C. Better planning avoids the need for changes.
    D. The change management plan establishes a common approach to manage change.

105. Where can team members obtain information about activity descriptions, dependencies, resource requirements, imposed dates, estimates, and activity constraints and assumptions?
    A. Schedule
    B. Activity attributes
    C. WBS
    D. Activity list

106. The team is ready to start estimating the project costs. Which of the following is LEAST reliable?
    A. Lessons learned from past projects
    B. External databases on resource productivity
    C. Team knowledge
    D. Cost records of previous projects

107. Which of the following is NOT a collect requirements tool or technique?
    A. Prototypes
    B. Interviews
    C. Workshops
    D. Product breakdown

108. In a _____ contract, the seller agrees to deliver a product at an established contract price plus a predefined fee for exceeding selected project objectives.
    A. FPIF
    B. FFP
    C. CPIF
    D. FPAF

109. _____ can be documented in the project scope statement.
    A. Project cost-benefit analysis
    B. Work packages
    C. Scope management approach
    D. Product acceptance criteria

110. Assumption analysis is mainly used to:
    A. Plan risk management
    B. Plan risk responses
    C. Identify risks
    D. Perform qualitative risk analysis

111. Using legitimate power to deal with conflict is an example of which conflict resolution technique?
    A. Autocratic
    B. Force
    C. Mandating
    D. Confronting

112. All of the following are part of the communication model EXCEPT:
    A. Sender and receiver
    B. Message and mean
    C. Noise
    D. Idea

113. All of the following can be inputs to initiating a project EXCEPT:
    A. The project charter
    B. Enterprise environmental factors
    C. Statement of work
    D. Organizational process assets

114. You want to determine the combination of resources that minimizes project costs. What technique should you use?
    A. Design of experiments
    B. Staffing management plan
    C. Resource breakdown structure
    D. Cost breakdown structure

115. Which of the following tools analyzes the relationship between two variables?
    A. Pareto diagram
    B. Cause-and-effect diagrams
    C. Scatter diagram
    D. Control chart

116. In which team development stage is the team more efficient?
    A. Forming
    B. Norming
    C. Performing
    D. Planning

117. A location used as project command center to improve project communication is known as:
    A. Colocation
    B. War room
    C. PMO
    D. Project management information system

118. Which of the following is a closing activity?
    A. Authorize the start of the next project phase.
    B. Accept a deliverable.
    C. Verify a deliverable.
    D. Manage the project termination before completion.

119. The scope baseline in an output of:
    A. Collect requirements
    B. Define scope
    C. Create WBS
    D. Control scope

120. A large process reengineering project is halfway done and is showing a CPI of 1.3 and a SPI of 0.75. How should the project manager proceed to realign the project with its baselines?
    A. Use the management reserve.
    B. Crash the schedule.
    C. Reduce the product scope.
    D. Issue a change request to extend the project schedule.

121. A contingency reserve is _____.
    A. An active risk acceptance response
    B. Determined by a risk audit
    C. A passive risk acceptance response
    D. Not a risk response strategy

122. Which of the following statements regarding change management is NOT true?
    A. The change request status should be updated in the change log.
    B. Changes should be communicated to project stakeholders.
    C. The project manager does not have the authority to approve project changes.
    D. The change management system is part of the configuration management system.

123. _____ is a particularly helpful technique for acquiring project team members.
    A. Ground rules
    B. Resource negotiation
    C. Networking
    D. Expert judgment

124. Which of the following communication methods is MORE suited to distribute information to a large numbers of recipients?
    A. Interactive
    B. Push
    C. Formal
    D. Passive

125. While reviewing the cost estimates sent by team members, you noticed that one estimate was higher than what you expected. How should you proceed?
    A. Correct the estimate using the PERT method.
    B. Request the basis of the estimate.
    C. Accept the estimate because it was developed by the team.
    D. Ask the team member to use an analogous estimate for the duration of the activity.

126. Inspections are used in all of the following processes EXCEPT:
    A. Control scope
    B. Control quality
    C. Manage project team
    D. Validate scope

127. The project manager is responsible for all the following EXCEPT:
    A. Providing project job descriptions
    B. Developing organizational project management processes
    C. Establishing the project recognition and rewards system
    D. Negotiating resources with the functional manager

128. All of the following are tools and techniques used to close a procurements process EXCEPT:
    A. Updating final records
    B. Negotiating open claims
    C. Performing a procurement performance review
    D. Performing a procurement audit

129. Risk thresholds can help:
    A. Measure the effectiveness of the risk response plan execution
    B. Identify who is the owner of the risk responses
    C. Determine how risk management will be performed
    D. Warn that the risks are about to occur

130. The outputs of risk response planning include:
    A. Risk triggers and project management plan updates
    B. Fallback plans, project document updates, and contingency reserves
    C. Residual risks, secondary risks, and risk response owners
    D. All of the above

131. Which of the following statements regarding the project life cycle is TRUE?
    A. A project phase includes multiple life cycles.
    B. The project life cycle includes the phases of initiating, planning, executing, monitoring and controlling, and closing.
    C. The project life cycle extends from product conception until the product phaseout.
    D. The complete set of phases of a project is known as a project life cycle.

132. Which of the following is LEAST useful in developing a project team?
    A. Involving the team in planning
    B. Organizing milestone parties
    C. Establishing rules of acceptable and unacceptable behavior
    D. Using issue logs

133. Although the seller delivered with a defective performance, the buyer knowingly accepted that performance. The contract is considered to be:
    A. Breached
    B. Terminated by default
    C. Valid with rights waived
    D. Valid with a claim

134. Management is asking for a 5 percent cut on project estimates. What should the project manager do?
    A. Change the estimates but explain why you disagree and document the risks involved.
    B. Change the estimates but ask management to keep the estimates confidential.
    C. Refuse to change the estimates.
    D. Change the estimates.

135. Which of the following is an advantage of a functional organization?
    A. Loyalty to the project
    B. Project manager with little formal authority
    C. Team members organized and grouped by functions
    D. Better support from multiple functional areas

136. Key resources left the project without the project manager's knowledge. Which of the following is the LEAST likely reason?
    A. Lack of a staffing management plan
    B. Lack of a communications management plan
    C. Lack of a recognition and rewards systems
    D. Changes on resource allocation have not been validated by the functional manager

137. All of the following can be used to perform a root cause analysis EXCEPT:
    A. Flowcharts
    B. Run charts
    C. Cause-and-effect diagrams
    D. Ishikawa diagram

138. What does a TCPI represent?
    A. Expected total cost at project completion
    B. Ratio between earned value and actual cost
    C. Estimate of cost to complete the project
    D. The performance required in the future to achieve a previously defined objective

139. _____ is an example of a Herzberg hygiene factor.
    A. Work environment
    B. Self-fulfillment
    C. Performance recognition
    D. Perquisite

140. Which of the following is NOT part of the control risks process?
    A. Monitoring unknown-unknowns
    B. Performing a risk audit
    C. Closing risks
    D. Assessing if the responses were implemented as planned and if they were effective

141. Which of the following should NOT be used to measure accomplished work?
    A. Milestones with weighted values
    B. Actual cost
    C. Percent complete
    D. 50-50 rule

142. You are trying to make sure that potential suppliers have a clear and common understanding of the procurement need. Which of the following is your BEST option?
    A. Statement of work
    B. Procurement management plan
    C. Bidder conference
    D. Request for proposal

143. In a back-office system implementation project, the team is unable to plan in detail the development phase until all the design work is complete. Which project management approach would BEST address the situation?
    A. Rolling wave
    B. Contingency reserve
    C. Critical chain
    D. Float

144. The system that includes the tools required to collect, register, process, and disseminate information among project stakeholders is known as the:
    A. Work authorization system
    B. Information distribution system
    C. Change control system
    D. Project management information system (PMIS)

145. How can a recognition and rewards system support project management?
    A. Assesses project performance
    B. Selects the best resources for the project
    C. Establishes a clear link between project performance and reward
    D. Assesses team performance

146. A project has the following performance data:

    - $AC = 2,000,000$
    - $CV = -250,000$
    - $SPI = 1.12$
    - $BAC = 10,000,000$

    What is the project earned value?
    A. 1,750,000
    B. 1,562,500
    C. 2,250,000
    D. There is not enough information.

147. Which of the following is NOT part of the quantitative risk analysis process?
    A. Calculating the expected monetary value of project decisions
    B. Assessing the impact of risks on project objectives
    C. Performing a quantitative assessment of the risk response
    D. Statistically analyzing the schedule and budget risk

148. A matrix organization can be classified as weak, balanced, or strong depending on:
    A. The customer's level of involvement in the project
    B. The size of its projects
    C. The project manager's level of project authority
    D. The sponsor's level of project authority

149. Which of the following is part of the perform qualitative risk analysis process?
    A. Reserve analysis
    B. Risk urgency assessment
    C. Risk reassessment
    D. Assumptions analysis

150. Which of the following is NOT part of the close procurements process?
    A. Indexing all contract documents
    B. Closing open claims
    C. Preparing a final report documenting what was contractually agreed and what was delivered
    D. Conducting a procurement inspection

151. Which risks should be analyzed by the perform quantitative risk analysis process?
    A. Only the risks in the watch list
    B. Only risks ranked as a priority by the qualitative risk analysis
    C. Only risks that could not be managed by the plan risk responses process
    D. All project risks

152. Which of the following is NOT part of the conduct procurements process?
    A. Applying screening criteria
    B. Negotiating with suppliers
    C. Comparing the supplier's estimate to an independent estimate
    D. Authorizing the start of the supplier's work

153. One project activity must start with a one-week delay from the start of another. What method should be used to represent that dependency in a network diagram?
    A. Critical path method
    B. Activity on arrow
    C. Activity on line
    D. Activity on node

154. To estimate the duration of a construction design activity, you have used the duration of a relatively similar activity on a previous project and increased it by 10 percent. What estimate activity duration technique are you using?
    A. Analogous
    B. Heuristic
    C. Three-point estimating
    D. Parametric

155. You are using a flowchart to understand and estimate the cost of quality in a process. Before moving on to the next process, you should:
    A. Complete a process improvement plan
    B. Complete a quality audit
    C. Complete the project budget
    D. Complete a quality inspection

156. Bidder conferences should be performed during:
    A. Plan procurement management process
    B. Planning
    C. Control procurements process
    D. Conduct procurements process

157. When can project lessons learned be collected?
    A. At project closure
    B. Throughout the project, at project closure, and sometime after the project has closed
    C. At the end of each meeting
    D. At project closure and sometime after the project has closed

158. Your company needs to urgently contract the service of an interior design company to design and furnish the new office building. With no time to complete a detail scope analysis, the company should rely on:
    A. A fixed-price contract
    B. A time and material contract
    C. Contract incentives
    D. The supplier's experience

159. The project management team is about to start developing responses to identified risks. After reading the risk management plan, one team member is worried because she does not understand the concept of a fallback plan. You should explain to the team member that a fallback plan is:
    A. A provision of time or costs for unforeseeable events
    B. An alternative risk response, or plan B, activated if the main risk response is ineffective
    C. A planned course of action implemented if the specified risk events occur
    D. An action to reduce the probability or impact of the risk by revising the project management plan

160. A large industrial project adopted control events at the end of a phase, when the sponsor and steering committee have the opportunity to review the project performance and major deliverables, as well as terminate the project if needed. These control events are known as:
    A. Change control board meetings
    B. Steering meetings
    C. Stage gates
    D. Sign-off meetings

161. Which of the following options is NOT part of a business case?
    A. Business need
    B. Framing the project in the organization strategy
    C. Product scope description
    D. Cost-benefit analysis

162. In which of the following options is historical information typically used as an input?
    A. Monitoring performance
    B. Creating lessons learned
    C. Creating the WBS
    D. Producing project deliverables

163. The EV = 600, PV = 500, AC = 550, and BAC = 1,000. After analyzing the project cost variance, the project manager determined that past performance had been influenced by specific factors that should not resurface in the future. What is the project EAC?
    A. 400
    B. 917
    C. 950
    D. 1,050

164. _____ uses arrows to represent dependencies.
    A. Activity-on-arrow (AOA)
    B. Precedence diagramming method (PDM)
    C. PERT
    D. Organizational breakdown structure (OBS)

165. All of the following are tools and techniques of the estimate costs process EXCEPT:
    A. Expert judgment
    B. Cost of quality
    C. Three-point estimate
    D. Earned value management (EVM)

166. The customer is complaining that a critical deliverable was not included in the approved scope statement. How should the project manager proceed?
    A. Include the deliverable in the scope statement and WBS, and use the project contingency reserve to accommodate the additional work.
    B. Analyze the impact of the change.
    C. Tell the customer that the deliverable is out of scope and cannot be completed.
    D. The scope statement does not require an update because the project objectives have not changed.

167. Which of the following statements regarding a change control board is NOT correct?
    A. Some project changes should not be reviewed by the change control board.
    B. The change control board should approve major deliverables.
    C. The change control board role and responsibility are defined in the change management plan.
    D. The change control board should approve or reject change requests when required.

168. Which of the following is part of a staffing management plan?
    A. Description of roles and responsibilities
    B. Project hierarchies
    C. How staff will be acquired to the project
    D. Team performance assessment

169. Your company has decided to procure a service through a fixed-price contract to manage cost risk. What was the adopted risk response strategy?
    A. Transfer
    B. Explore
    C. Workaround
    D. Avoid

170. Which of the following is NOT an output of the estimate costs process?
    A. Basis of estimate documentation
    B. Cost of the quality conformance and nonconformance work
    C. Cost reserves
    D. The procedure that determines how to report cost performance

171. A document that tracks requirements along the project life cycle is known as:
    A. Requirements documentation
    B. Requirements traceability matrix
    C. Requirements management plan
    D. Requirements log

172. The team is analyzing proposals and applying weighting criteria. Which process are they performing?
    A. Plan procurement management
    B. Conduct procurements
    C. Control procurements
    D. None. Evaluating proposals and applying weighting criteria are part of the procurement department function.

173. Management is worried that the project will not be delivered according to planned quality. The project manager should:
    A. Review the quality management plan
    B. Meet with management and provide information regarding the adopted quality management approach
    C. Prepare a quality inspection
    D. Prepare a quality audit

174. What is the name of an organization that defines project management methodologies and templates, as well as provides project management guidance?
    A. Steering committee
    B. Projectized organization
    C. Tight matrix
    D. PMO

175. Minimizing the importance of what is under conflict is an example of which technique?
    A. Compromise
    B. Smooth
    C. Good leadership skills
    D. Collaborate

176. Which of the following statements regarding the use of sampling in quality management is TRUE?
    A. Sampling is used during plan quality management to assess if all elements are in conformance to requirements.
    B. Variable sampling shows the degree of conformance to requirements.
    C. Sampling is used during a quality audit to assess if a process is under control.
    D. Attribute sampling shows the degree of conformance to requirements.

177. Which of the following options is NOT part of the control schedule process?
    A. Fast tracking the remaining work to correct a schedule delay
    B. Analyzing schedule variances
    C. Analyzing schedule reserves
    D. Forecasting schedule performance

178. A risk response strategy that completely removes the opportunity uncertainty is known as:
    A. Avoid
    B. Accept
    C. Exploit
    D. Enhance

179. Value analysis is performed during:
    A. Project charter development
    B. Integrated change management
    C. Scope definition
    D. Closure

180. As a result of quality control, the need for a defect repair was identified. To repair such defect you should:
    A. Follow the configuration management plan
    B. Follow the change management plan
    C. Follow the organization quality police
    D. Follow the quality management plan

181. What is estimate at completion (EAC)?
    A. It is a forecast of cost to complete the project.
    B. It is a forecast of cost variance at the end of the project.
    C. It is a forecast of total cost at the end of the project based on project performance.
    D. It is a forecast of total cost at the end of the project based on historical data.

182. You have just finished identifying stakeholders and mapping them according to their power, interest, and support. You are worried about a specific powerful stakeholder that can strongly impact the project performance. What is the BEST course of action?
    A. Ask the stakeholder to approve the project charter.
    B. Avoid involving the stakeholder in key project meetings.
    C. Ask the sponsor to deal directly with the stakeholder.
    D. Involve the stakeholder as soon as possible.

183. The sponsor has asked for a four weeks' reduction on the project schedule. All of the following can be used to reduce project duration EXCEPT:
    A. Reduce quality
    B. Fast track the project
    C. Use more resources
    D. Revise the project baseline

184. One team member informed the project manager that key users from the system development project are unhappy. Key users are arguing that some key system functionalities should be included in the product scope. The project manager remembers that the customer decided not to include these functionalities in the product scope. What should the project manager do FIRST?
    A. Ask the stakeholders for a document describing the functionalities.
    B. Discuss the issue in the next status meeting with the customer.
    C. Remind the customer that the product scope does not include the functionalities.
    D. Discuss the issue with the stakeholders.

185. Which of the following is NOT a valid reason to use risk management?
    A. Project threats can be minimized.
    B. There is always risk aversion.
    C. Feasible objectives should be defined.
    D. Contingency plans can be planned ahead to avoid chaos.

186. Which technique are team members using when they increase the activities' duration estimates to account for problems?
    A. Float
    B. Risk mitigation
    C. Padding
    D. Reserve analysis

187. Reporting project performance is part of which project management process?
    A. Control communications
    B. Direct and manage project work
    C. Manage communications
    D. Plan communications management

188. A project stakeholder consistently makes decisions to avoid decisions with high-risk exposure. The stakeholder is known as:
    A. Risk seeking
    B. Risk avoiding
    C. Risk averse
    D. Risk managing

189. The project charter of a new engineering project has just been approved. The project manager should start working on the:
    A. Risk register
    B. Project management plan
    C. Requirements documentation
    D. Performance report

190. Which of the following is NOT a good reason to gather project lessons learned?
    A. To identify team members accountable for product defects
    B. To develop the project team
    C. To improve and share company knowledge
    D. To improve future project performance

191. Which of the following is NOT an example of an enterprise environmental factor?
    A. Organizational structure
    B. Industry standards
    C. Market conditions
    D. Historical information

192. What is the most demanding level of quality an organization can try to achieve?
    A. 1 Sigma
    B. 2 Sigma
    C. 3 Sigma
    D. 6 Sigma

193. Which of the following statements regarding cost aggregation is correct?
    A. The budget is determined aggregating costs according with the scope statement.
    B. The budget is determined aggregating costs according with the resource breakdown structure.
    C. The budget is determined aggregating costs according with the work breakdown structure.
    D. Cost aggregation is used in the estimate costs process.

194. What is the impact of using a lead within a network diagram?
    A. Establishes a float between activities
    B. Sets a waiting time between activities
    C. Reduces the duration of an activity
    D. Accelerates the schedule

195. The concept of _____ describes three concurrent project objectives that must be simultaneously accomplished, namely scope, time, and cost.
    A. Three-point estimate
    B. Baselines
    C. EVM
    D. Triple constraint

196. Schedule compression should be focused on:
    A. Minimizing risk
    B. Critical activities
    C. Minimizing costs
    D. Noncritical tasks

197. You are preparing your weekly status meeting to report the project performance to management. How should you model communication?
    A. Vertical
    B. Formal
    C. Interactive
    D. All of the above

198. Which of the following is NOT defined in a WBS dictionary?
    A. Detailed information regarding work packages
    B. Acceptance criteria
    C. Critical path
    D. Code of accounts

199. You have decided to use the PERT approach to estimate activity durations. Which of the following estimates has the highest standard deviation?
    A. Activity A with an estimate ranging from 4 to 9 days
    B. Activity B with an estimate of optimistic = 3, most likely = 6, pessimistic = 9
    C. Activity C with a most likely estimate of 6 and a standard deviation of 1.5
    D. Activity D with an estimate of optimistic = 4, most likely = 6, pessimistic = 11

200. Which of the following is used as an input to the estimate activity durations process?
    A. Contingency reserves
    B. Expert judgment
    C. Parametric estimates
    D. Resource calendars

ANSWERS

1. **A** When there is a breach, the other party should issue a letter formalizing it. Additionally, the buyer should work collaboratively with the supplier so that a corrective action can be identified.

2. **B** The requirements management approach is defined in the requirements management plan. All other options can be part of the requirements documentation.

3. **B** The estimate costs process involves estimating all costs according with the resources required. Answer A is referring to the determine budget process. Answer C is referring to the control costs process. Answer D is referring to earned value management.

4. **D** Lessons learned are transferred to organizational process assets in the closing process group. As part of the organizational process assets, they are inputs to multiple project management processes, influencing decisions during initiating, planning, executing, monitoring and controlling, and closing process groups.

5. **B** Once a change is identified, it should first be analyzed before it can be approved (answer C) or implemented (answers A and D).

6. **B** Monitor cost risks is part of the control risks process. All other options are part of the control costs process.

7. **B** The backward pass calculates the late start and late finish dates of project activities by moving backward throughout the network diagram.

8. **A** The schedule variance is the difference between the earned value and the planned value.

9. **B** Fringe benefits are standard compensation, additional to direct wages, formally given to all employees.

10. **B** The control account establishes the level of WBS detail where the project performance will be assessed. All other statements are not correct.

11. **C** The alternative paths are:

    A-B-F with 22 days
    A-C-D-F with 24 days
    A-C-E-F with 22 days

    Activity E is in the path A-C-E-F. Therefore it has a float of 2 days (24 − 22). If there is a deadline of 24 days, the float of activity E does not change.

12. **C** The project is assuming that there will be enough funds to complete the project, although there is some uncertainty involved.

13. **D** Virtual teams can reduce communication costs and allow geographically scattered team members to be involved in project decisions. Nevertheless, virtual teams do not contribute to team development. All other options have a direct impact on team development.

14. **A** Expert judgment is a tool used by the identify risks process. It is not an input. All the other answers can be used as inputs to the identify risks process.

15. **A** A lag is a waiting time between two sequential activities.

16. **C** Work packages are determined in the create WBS process. All the other answers are an output of the define activities process.

17. **C** A composite organization adopts characteristics of different organization types.

18. **D** Work packages can be used to assign work responsibilities to individuals or organizational units.

19. **C** Collaboration is usually considered to be the best conflict resolution technique, promoting long-lasting resolutions in which all stakeholders win.

20. **A** The budget is the sum of the baseline cost plus the management reserve. Therefore: management reserve = budget − baseline cost = 115,000 − 100,000 = 15,000.

21. **C** Risk reassessment is a periodical reevaluation of identified risks and their responses. It is therefore not focused on overall project risk (answer B). A risk audit assesses if the risk management procedures were adopted and are appropriate and if the risk responses were effective. It is therefore focused on the risk management process. A risk audit can be conducted throughout the project (answer A). A risk reassessment is usually conducted inside the team, and a risk audit is usually performed by an external entity (answer D).

22. **B** A screening system eliminates from the selection process those suppliers that do not meet the source selection criteria.

23. **C** A kickoff meeting is part of planning. All the other options are part of the executing process group.

24. **B** Quality management includes the activities required to ensure that the project, product, and adopted processes meet requirements.

25. **B** Force majeure is a contract clause that releases parties from contract obligations when a predefined uncontrollable event occurs.

26. **A** The PERT standard deviation is calculated based on the optimistic (O) and pessimistic (P) estimates. The PERT standard deviation is calculates as $(P - O) / 6$. Therefore, the standard deviation is 2.

27. **A** All decisions prior to the contract, which were not included in the contract, do not legally bind the parties.

28. **A** The project manager needs to prepare a quick and preliminary estimate. Therefore, an analogous estimate is the best choice available. A bottom-up estimate (answer B) and developing a parametric model (answer D) would be very time consuming. Waiting for an accurate and detailed estimate (answer C) is not a reasonable choice when a preliminary estimate is requested.

29. **D** Variance analysis is used as a scope control technique.

30. **D** NGT quickly reaches a decision through vote. Each member ranks each opinion, and the highest ranked opinion is selected.

31. **D** The sponsor is the manager who provides the financial resources.

32. **A** The product scope can be progressively elaborated as more and better information becomes available. The project scope (not the product scope) is defined in the WBS. Therefore, answers B and C are incorrect. The project business need is established during initiation before planning the product scope. Therefore, answer D is not correct.

33. **D** Data quality assesses how much is known about the risk.

34. **D** Oral and informal communication supports the interactivity needed to reach a conflict resolution.

35. **B** The scope statement will be defined only in the define scope process. Therefore, it cannot be an input of the collect requirements process. All the other options can be used as inputs when collecting requirements.

36. **A** Validating deliverables is part of the validate scope process. All the other options are part of the control scope process.

37. **B** The estimate activity resources process is performed immediately after the sequence activities process.

38. **C** Involving team members in activity estimating would have increased the team members' engagement.

39. **A**

PTA = ((ceiling price – target price) / sharing ration)) + target cost

Target price = target cost + target fee
    = 2,000,000 + 100,000
    = 2,100,000

PTA = ((2,200,000 – 2,100,000) / 0.6)) + 2,000,000
    = 2,166,667

40. **B** That a table should be thoroughly prepared represents a good practice. It is not physically mandatory. Therefore, it is a discretionary dependency.

41. **A** Assumptions should be recorded within a project assumptions log for improved traceability. This log may be part of the scope statement or an independent assumptions log. Assumptions hold a certain degree of uncertainty. They should, therefore, be used for risk management purposes. Answer B is not an incorrect statement. It is, however, a worse choice than answer A because assumptions are not primarily recorded in the project

charter and are often used to identify risks. Answer C is not correct, because documenting assumptions facilitates risk management, but does not eliminate risk. Answer D is not correct, because imposed restrictions are known as constraints.

42. **A** The colocation technique concentrates team members in a single physical space, facilitating communication and developing a sense of teamwork.

43. **A** At the end of each project, the projectized organization's resources are mobilized for another project, allocated to a resource pool, or released from the organization.

44. **C** Earned value assesses the progress performed up to a specific date. This value is calculated by analyzing the budget cost of the work completed by that date.

45. **D** Organizational infrastructure is an enterprise environmental factor. All the other options are organizational process assets.

46. **B** The cost baseline is an output of the determine budget process. All the other options can be inputs to the determine budget process.

47. **A** In a focus group, stakeholders discuss ideas and generate a solution with the help of a moderator.

48. **A** A management reserve is a provision of time or costs, held by management, to compensate for unforeseen events. Management reserve is created to manage unknown-unknowns.

49. **B** The alternative paths are:

    A-B-F with 22 days
    A-C-D-F with 24 days
    A-C-E-F with 22 days

    Therefore, the path A-C-D-F is critical.

50. **C** Ground rules are unwritten rules that define what behaviors are accepted and what behaviors are not accepted during the project.

51. **D** A negative float shows how many days have to be recovered to meet a deadline or baseline.

52. **B** Residual risks are risks that remain after response planning.

53. **A** As the project moves forward, and more and better information becomes available, the reserve may be changed through the change control mechanism. Therefore, answer A is not correct. All the other statements are correct.

54. **D** A different approach is needed to complete a work package. However, we have no information regarding a change to the scope baseline. The project manager is not necessarily responsible for reviewing and validating modifications to work packages that do not imply a scope baseline change. Often, the team has enough authority to decide on such modifications. If a team member is accountable for the deliverable, he or she should have the responsibility to manage the situation.

55. **B** Quality control is a continuous process. Therefore, a process under control does not mean there will be no future inspections. All the other statements are correct.

56. **A** The risk management approach is not defined by risk categories. The risk management approach is established in the risk management plan.

57. **B** In the cost plus incentive fee contract (CPIF), the profit is determined by the fixed fee plus an incentive fee.

58. **D** The free float is the time frame during which an activity can be delayed without delaying the early start of a successor activity. A free float of zero does not necessarily represent significant risk. The activity might not be critical or might have a low level of uncertainty. All other options are strongly related to schedule risk.

59. **D** Benchmarking is a quality management planning technique.

60. **C** Resource leveling can be used to adapt utilization to temporary resource constraints (e.g., a resource that is available only in a specific time frame).

61. **A** If all deliverables have been completed as contracted, the contract is complete.

62. **D** You are working to obtain the formal acceptance to close the phase. You are, therefore, involved in the closing process group.

63. **B** The budget can be changed only with an approved change request. If 5,000 were added to the initial budget of 50,000, the revised budget is 55,000.

64. **C** A staffing management plan determines how the resource requirements, identified while planning the time management knowledge area, will be acquired by the project. A responsibility assignment matrix (answer A), an organizational breakdown structure (answer B), and a resource breakdown structure (answer D) can document responsibilities.

65. **D** The procurement manager is accountable for procurement management activities.

66. **C** The project experienced score creep because it went beyond requirements. Therefore, the project was unsuccessful.

67. **C** The weighting system enables the organization to rank suppliers according to previously defined source selection criteria. A screening system eliminates from the selection process those suppliers that do not meet the source selection criteria.

68. **B** Estimating costs and performing quantitative risk analysis are part of planning. Identifying stakeholders (answer A) is part of the initiating process group. Performing quality assurance (answer C) and acquiring project team (answer D) are part of the executing process group.

69. **B** The alternative paths are:

    A-B-F with 22 days
    A-C-D-F with 24 days
    A-C-E-F with 22 days

    Activity E is in the path A-C-E-F. Therefore, it has a float of 2 days (24 − 22).

70. **C** A project SOW is a formal document that describes the products and services that should be provided by the project.

71. **D** A ROM estimate is prepared during initiation. All the other statements are correct.

72. **A** Selecting which historical information to use and adapting it to the project context depend on the estimator's expert judgment. Therefore, analogous estimating is a type of expert judgment. All the other statements are correct.

73. **B** Quality costs can be classified as conformance or nonconformance costs.

74. **B** The project manager is accountable for the overall project quality. All the other statements are correct.

75. **D** The communications management plan identifies and documents communication requirements. These communication requirements can include who receives the project schedule.

76. **C** Defect repair, including eliminating the defect cause, is part of the control quality process.

77. **C** The project management team should first estimate costs before determining the budget (answer B), reconciling funding limits (answer D), and approving the project management plan (answer A).

78. **B** Stakeholders meet in workshops to discuss ideas and generate consensus, allowing for a swift collection of information. All the other statements are not true.

79. **C** The Delphi technique reaches consensus by repeatedly consulting experts, usually through an anonymous process.

80. **C** Product development risks are not identified in the configuration management system. They are identified, along with all other risks, during the identify risks process. All the other options are part of configuration management.

81. **C** The change management plan includes the rules used to manage changes. Those rules can include procedures (answer D) and responsibilities (answer B), and identify which project documents are subject to formal change control (answer A). Answer C is not correct, because change requests should not be recorded in the change management plan. They can be recorded in the change log.

82. **B** The resource smoothing's priority is promoting constant resource utilization, using the flexibility provided by the activities' float. Resource smoothing outcome cannot change the project duration or change the project critical path.

83. **C** Supporting data used while developing the schedule should be documented for future reference. The contingency reserve (answer A) and WBS (answer B) should already exist before submitting the schedule for approval.

84. **D** A letter of intent enables the buyer to declare an intention to buy before an actual contract acceptance is completed. All other options can be the result of a contract breach.

85. **D** The project charter cannot be authorized by the project manager.

86. **D** In a matrix organization there are frequent authority and priority conflicts over resources, which can lead to staffing issues. All the other options are disadvantages of a projectized organization.

87. **D** The project is not closed until all project work has been completed. Therefore, answers A and C are not correct. Updating the organization's historical information knowledge base is a typical closing activity. Therefore, answer B is not correct.

88. **C** A firm fixed price contract minimizes the buyer's risk if the project scope is well known.

89. **C** The estimate at completion (EAC) can be calculated as BAC / CPI. Therefore, EAC = 10,000/0.8 = 12,500.

90. **C** In the problem solve technique, also known as collaborate, the conflict situation is managed as a problem. Throughout the process, team members should maintain an open atmosphere where different opinions can be discussed and combined.

91. **A** The project charter is the document used to formally initiate the project. It is not a stimulus or reason to launch a project. All other options can be a stimulus for initiating a project.

92. **D** Contract negotiation is a technique used in the conduct procurements process.

93. **A** Because there is no information regarding the cause of prior performance, assume a typical estimate when calculating the project estimate to complete (ETC):

$$EAC \text{ (typical)} = BAC / CPI$$
$$= (2,000,000 / (1,100,000 / 1,000,000))$$
$$= 1,818,182$$

$$ETC = EAC - AC$$
$$= 1,818,182 - 1,000,000$$
$$= 818,182$$

94. **C** The code of accounts is a numerical system used to assign a unique number to each WBS element.

95. **B** During the collect requirements process, the team should analyze and prioritize requirements. Identifying stakeholders and managing their engagement (answer A) is part of the stakeholder management processes. Establishing an agreement on project scope (answer C) is part of the define scope process. Defining resource requirements (answer D) is part of the estimate resource requirements process.

96. **D** ETC + (BAC − EV) does not represent EAC. There are several methods to calculate the EAC, including a new estimate (answer B) or a typical estimate (answers A and C).

97. **C** The scope statement is prepared by the project management team during scope definition and is used as an input during WBS development. A scope statement is not a statement of work (answer A), a procurement document (answer B), or a contract statement of work (answer D).

98. **D** There are many advantages of using a WBS, including managing the scope (answer A), facilitating communication (answer B), and helping develop a project team (answer C).

99. **A** The project manager is accountable for managing the project and meeting project objectives.

100. **B** In an invitation for bid, the buyer specifies the product and the solution and requests a price from the potential supplier.

101. **A** A workaround is an unplanned response for an accepted risk or to a risk that was not previously identified by the team.

102. **C** A flowchart is a graphical representation of process steps that can be used to identify process improvements.

103. **D** Unlike other knowledge areas, the project manager is not accountable for procurement management activities.

104. **D** The rules used to manage changes are defined in the change management plan. Even though changes are unpredictable, the rules used to manage changes can be defined in advance in a change management plan. Therefore, answers A and B are not correct. Answer C is not correct because changes cannot be fully avoided.

105. **B** Defining activities also includes documenting relevant information that may be used by the team while completing the work. This additional information is known as activity attributes.

106. **C** Team knowledge is subject to personal subjective elements, such as attitude, interests, memory, and agenda. Therefore, it is a less reliable source of information.

107. **D** Product breakdown decomposes the product into deliverables to facilitate an agreement among project stakeholders. It is used as a scope definition technique. All other options can be used as tools or techniques of the collect requirements process.

108. **A** A FPIF contract defines a fixed-price plus an incentive mechanism. Incentives are adjusted to mutually agreed-upon performance objectives.

109. **D** Product acceptance criteria can be part of a scope statement. None of the other options are part of a scope statement.

110. **C** Assumptions have, by definition, some level of uncertainty. The project team can identify risks by reviewing the consistency and information quality of the documented assumptions.

111. **B** In the force conflict resolution technique, someone's perspective is imposed on others.

112. **D** The idea is not part of the communication model. The model includes sender, encoding, message, medium, receiver, decoding, feedback, and noise.

113. **A** The project charter is the document used to formally initiate the project. It is therefore an output of the initiating process group. All other options can be inputs to initiating a project.

114. **A** The design of experiments is a quality planning tool that statistically analyzes the influence of different variables on a specific overall result. In this example, the analyzed variables are resources and the overall result is the project cost.

115. **C** A scatter diagram is a graphical representation of the measurements of two variables along two axes, to verify if they are statistically correlated.

116. **C** Tuckman's team development theories states that teams reach their performance peak in the performing phase.

117. **B** A war room is a location used as the project command center.

118. **D** Managing the project termination before completion is a closing activity. Authorizing the start of the next project phase is an initiation activity (answer A). Accepting and verifying a deliverable is a monitoring and controlling activity (answers B and C).

119. **C** The scope baseline is an output of the create WBS process.

120. **B** The project has a favorable cost performance and an unfavorable schedule performance. The project manager can reduce the schedule duration through an increase in project resources. The project manager does not have the authority to use the management reserve (answer A), reduce scope (answer C), or extend the schedule (answer D).

121. **A** A contingency reserve is an active risk acceptance response.

122. **C** Depending on the rules established in the change management plan, the project manager might have the authority to approve some types of change requests. All the other statements are true.

123. **B** Resource negotiation is the only available acquire project team technique.

124. **D** In passive communication, information is placed in a repository that can be accessed by receivers.

125. **B** Your first step should be to understand the information provided by the team members. The basis of estimates can provide additional details that support and justify the estimates.

126. **C** The manage project team process is not performed through inspections. All other available processes use inspections.

127. **B** Organizational project management processes would not be defined within the project. They are typically developed by the project management office. The project manager can be responsible for all other options.

128. **C** A procurement performance review is a formal assessment of the supplier's capacity to perform the project according to the contract conditions. A procurement performance review is a control procurements technique. All the other options are tools and techniques used to close a procurements process.

129. **A** A risk threshold is the limit beyond which stakeholders are not willing to accept the risk and additional risk responses are required. Risk thresholds can be used to assess the effectiveness of risk responses.

130. **D** All available options are outputs of the plan risk responses process.

131. **D** The project life cycle is the collection of phases that the project must go through from its beginning to its closing. A phase does not include a life cycle (answer A). It is actually the other way around. Process groups are not phases (answer B). A project life cycle is not the same as a product life cycle (answer C).

132. **D** There are many ways to develop a project team, including involving team members in planning decisions (answer A), organizing milestone parties (answer B), and setting ground rules (answer C). Using an issue log is particularly relevant when you need to remove obstacles that may impact team performance. Managing team performance is part of the manage project team process.

133. **C** A waiver is a buyer's voluntary surrender of a contract privilege. The buyer knowingly accepted that performance. Therefore the contract is not breached (answer A) and is not terminated (answer B). There is no information regarding claims (answer D).

134. **C** Reviewing the estimates, without changing other project management constraints (answers A, B, and D), would not be an ethical alternative.

135. **C** A functional organization is organized around resources' functional expertise, which makes it easier to develop and share knowledge. In a functional organization there is no significant loyalty to the project (answer A). The fact that the project manager has little formal authority is not an advantage (answer B). Better support from multiple functional areas is an advantage of a matrix organization (answer D).

136. **C** The recognition and rewards systems may influence the team members' motivation. Nevertheless, team members left the project without the project manager's knowledge. Therefore, it is more likely that the problem's root cause is inadequate staffing management planning or poor communication with the functional manager.

137. **B** A run chart displays time-phased data in order to detect a trend and forecast future performance. It cannot be used to perform a root cause analysis.

138. **D** TCPI is the performance required in the future to achieve a previously defined objective (the budget or a revised objective).

139. **A** Hygiene factors may destroy motivation if they are not met, but they cannot increase motivation. Poor work environment can be an example of a hygiene factor.

140. **A** Unknown-unknowns were not identified as risks. Therefore, they cannot be monitored.

141. **B** Actual cost should not be used to assess the performance of accomplished work. All the other options are commonly used to assess performance.

142. **C** Bidder conferences are meetings organized by the buyer to help potential suppliers understand the procurement documents.

143. **A** The team is facing a problem of lack of detailed information regarding a future project phase. Rolling wave planning is a progressive elaboration planning technique that plans for the short term in detail and prepares a high-level plan for the long run. The plan is detailed as more and better information becomes available.

144. **D** The PMIS includes the tools required to collect, record, process, and disseminate information across project stakeholders.

145. **C** The purpose of a recognition and rewards system is to establish a clear relationship between individual performance and reward and thereby increase motivation and performance.

146. **A** If:

CV = EV − AC = −250,000 and AC = 2,000,000
Therefore:

EV = CV + AC = 1,750,000

147. **C** The perform quantitative risk analysis process analyzes risks, not responses.

148. **C** Depending whether the authority is more concentrated on the functional manager or on the project manager, the matrix organization may be classified as weak, balanced, or strong.

149. **B** The importance of a risk may depend on the time available to develop and implement a risk response. The perform qualitative risk analysis process assesses the risk urgency.

150. **D** Conducting a procurement inspection is part of the control procurements process.

151. **B** The perform quantitative risk analysis consumes time and resources. The qualitative risks analysis should identify the risks that require quantitative analysis.

152. **D** Authorizing the start of the supplier's work is part of the control procurements process. All the other options are performed during the conduct procurements process.

153. **D** The described situation requires a start-to-start dependency. The activity on arrow method (answer B), also known as activity on line (answer C), does not support start-to-start dependencies. The critical path method (answer A) is not used to represent dependencies in a network diagram.

154. **A** An analogous estimate estimates the duration or costs using historical information accumulated in the organization. An analogy estimate can be adjusted considering the project complexity.

155. **A** You are estimating the cost of quality in a process. Therefore, you are planning quality management. The only available option that is still part of planning quality management is completing a process improvement plan.

156. **D** A bidder conference is part of the conduct procurements process. Conduct procurements is an execution process. Therefore, answer B is not correct.

157. **B** Lessons learned should be generated throughout the project and at project closure. There may also be postmortem lessons learned, issued after the project is finished. Therefore, answer B is the best choice.

158. **C** The new contract will include scope (design and furnish). Therefore, a time and material contract should not be used (answer B). The scope of that contract will not be well defined. Therefore, a fixed price contract should not be used (answer A). Supplier's experience would not be enough to establish a sustainable contract. Your company should use a cost-reimbursable contract with contract incentives to synchronize objectives with the supplier.

159. **B** A fallback plan is an alternative risk response, or plan B, activated if the main risk response is ineffective.

160. **C** A stage gate is a predefined event in the project, typically at the end of a phase, where the sponsor and steering committee have the opportunity to review the project performance and major deliverables, as well as decide whether to proceed to the next phase.

161. **C** A product scope description can be a part of a project statement of work, but typically would not be part of a business case. All the other options can be part of a business case.

162. **C** Lessons learned are typically used as an input during planning as part of organizational process assets. Creating the WBS is the only planning activity available.

163. **C** Because prior performance has been influenced by specific factors that should not resurface in the future, the project manager should use an atypical estimate at completion.

$$EAC\ (atypical) = AC + (BAC - EV) = 550 + (1,000 - 600) = 950$$

164. **B** The PDM represents activities by nodes and dependencies by arrows.

165. **D** EVM is a control costs technique. All other options are tools and techniques of the estimate costs process.

166. **B** There is a potential scope change that should be managed through the change control process. Therefore answers A and D are not correct. The change should not be ignored. Therefore, answer C is not correct.

167. **B** The change control board does not approve deliverables. All other statements are correct.

168. **C** The staffing management plan establishes how staff will be acquired to the project. Roles and responsibilities (answer A) and project hierarchies (answer B) are part of the human resource management plan but are not included in a staffing management plan. A team performance assessment (answer D) is an output of the develop project team process.

169. **A** The company transferred the cost risk to the supplier.

170. **D** The procedure that determines how to report cost performance is part of the cost management plan.

171. **B** A requirements traceability matrix traces requirements implementation throughout the project life cycle.

172. **B** Analyzing proposals and applying weighting criteria is part of the conduct procurements process.

173. **D** A quality audit is an independent evaluation of project compliance led by internal or external auditors. It can effectively raise stakeholders' confidence regarding the project's quality. Before completing a quality audit, there is no information to sustain that the quality management plan needs to be reviewed (answer A). Meeting with management and providing information regarding the adopted quality management (answer B) could not offer the same independence and structure as a quality audit. A quality inspection (answer D) would help determine if specific deliverables meet requirements but is not enough to provide confidence regarding the project quality management.

174. **D** A PMO is the organizational unit responsible for project management throughout the organization.

175. **B** The smooth technique is concerned with maintaining a comfortable environment instead of seeking a more sustainable conflict resolution.

176. **B** In variable sampling, a measurement is classified on a continuous numerical scale that rates the degree of conformance or nonconformance. Sampling is not used in plan quality management (answer A). Sampling is not used in quality audits (answer C). Attribute sampling classifies each measurement as either conforming or nonconforming to requirements (answer D).

177. **C** Analyzing schedule reserves is not part of the control schedule process.

178. **C** The exploit risk response strategy changes the project management plan to completely remove the opportunity uncertainty.

179. **C** Value analysis is a product analysis technique used during scope definition.

180. **D** The quality management plan should establish the procedures used in quality control.

181. **C** The EAC is the expected total cost of an activity or project when the work is completed.

182. **D** Involving stakeholders from the project start, particularly those that have a higher influence, is the best option to minimize the risk of unfavorable changes.

183. **D** Reducing the schedule duration without redefining other project constraints is not an acceptable project management alternative.

184. **D** Stakeholders should be managed. There is a potential scope change that must be identified and analyzed.

185. **B** There will not always be risk aversion from project stakeholders.

186. **C** Padding is an estimating technique that attempts to manage risk by inflating the estimate.

187. **C** Reporting project performance is part of the manage communications process.

188. **C** The stakeholder demonstrated evidences of being risk averse; that is, his level of satisfaction decreases with an increase of risk exposure.

189. **B** The project management plan is the first document to work on during planning.

190. **A** The main purpose of lessons learned is to improve future performance (answer D). Lessons should be shared within the organization (answer C), so that everyone understands the root causes of prior successes and failures. Indirectly, generating lessons learned can also foster a project team's development (answer B).

191. **D** Historical information is part of the organizational process assets. All other options are enterprise environmental factors.

192. **D** The sigma level defines the probability of delivering a product without defects. 1 Sigma = 68.26%, 2 Sigma = 95.46%, 3 Sigma = 99.73%, 6 Sigma = 99.99%. Therefore, 6 Sigma is the most demanding level of quality.

193. **C** The budget is determined aggregating costs according to the work breakdown structure. All the other options are not correct.

194. **D** A lead is used when you need to accelerate the schedule by overlapping activities.

195. **D** *Triple constraint* is a term used to describe three concurrent project constraints that must be simultaneously accomplished.

196. **B** Schedule compression should be focused on critical activities. Compressing noncritical activities (answer D) would not have an impact on the overall project duration. The schedule compression purpose is not minimizing risks (answer A) or minimizing costs (answer C).

197. **D** A reporting meeting is an example of vertical, formal, and interactive communication.

198. **C** The critical path is part of a network diagram. All the other options can be defined in a WBS dictionary.

199. **C** The PERT standard deviation, or sigma, is calculated as (pessimistic – optimistic) / 6. Therefore, the activities standard deviations (sigma) are:

Sigma A = 0.83
Sigma B = 1
Sigma C = 1.5
Sigma D = 1.16

Therefore, activity C has the highest standard deviation.

200. **D** Resource calendars are used to estimate durations according to resource availability. Contingency reserves (answer A) are an output of estimating activity durations. Expert judgment (answer B) and parametric estimates (answer C) are techniques of estimating activity durations.

AC	actual cost
ACWP	actual cost of work performed
ADM	arrow diagramming method
AOA	activity on arrow
AON	activity on node
BAC	budget at completion
BCR	benefit-cost ratio
BCWP	budgeted cost of work performed
BCWS	budgeted cost of work scheduled
CAP	control account
CBS	cost breakdown structure
CCB	change control board
CM	configuration management
CMMI	Capability Maturity Model Integration
COQ	cost of quality
CPAF	cost plus award fee
CPFF	cost plus fixed fee
CPI	cost performance index
CPIF	cost plus incentive fee
CPM	critical path method
CV	cost variance
DOE	design of experiments
EAC	estimate at completion
EMV	expected monetary value
ETC	estimate to complete
EV	earned value
EVM	earned value management
FFP	firm fixed price
FP	fixed price
FPAF	fixed price award fee
FPEPA	fixed price economic price adjustment
FPIF	fixed price incentive fee
IFB	invitation for bid
IRR	internal rate of return
JIT	just in time
LF	late finish
LS	late start
NPV	net present value
OBS	organizational breakdown structure
PBS	product breakdown structure
PDM	precedence diagramming method
PERT	Program Evaluation and Review Technique
PMIS	project management information system

PMO	project management office
PTA	point of total assumption
PV	present value or planned value
QA	quality assurance
QC	quality control
RACI	responsible, accountable, consulted, and informed
RAM	responsibility assignment matrix
RBS	resource breakdown structure or risk breakdown structure
RFI	request for information
RFP	request for proposal
RFQ	request for quotation
ROM	rough order of magnitude
SOW	statement of work
SPI	schedule performance index
SV	schedule variance
TCPI	to-complete performance index
TF	total float
TQM	total quality management
VAC	variance at completion
WBS	work breakdown structure
WP	work package

The following tables organize processes by knowledge area. The number used refers to their unique number in the *PMBOK Guide,* 5th edition.

Initiating

Process		Area
4.1	Develop project charter	Integration management
13.1	Identify stakeholders	Stakeholder management

Planning

Process		Area
4.2	Develop project management plan	Integration management
5.1	Plan scope management	Scope management
5.2	Collect requirements	Scope management
5.3	Define scope	Scope management
5.4	Create WBS	Scope management
6.1	Plan schedule management	Time management
6.2	Define activities	Time management
6.3	Sequence activities	Time management
6.4	Estimate activity resources	Time management
6.5	Estimate activity durations	Time management
6.6	Develop schedule	Time management
7.1	Plan cost management	Cost management
7.2	Estimate costs	Cost management
7.3	Determine budget	Cost management
8.1	Plan quality management	Quality management
9.1	Plan human resource management	Human resource management
10.1	Plan communications management	Communications management
11.1	Plan risk management	Risk management
11.2	Identify risks	Risk management
11.3	Perform qualitative risk analysis	Risk management
11.4	Perform quantitative risk analysis	Risk management
11.5	Plan risk responses	Risk management
12.1	Plan procurement management	Procurement management
13.2	Plan stakeholder management	Stakeholder management

Executing

Process		Area
4.3	Direct and manage project work	Integration management
8.2	Perform quality assurance	Quality management
9.2	Acquire project team	Human resource management
9.3	Develop project team	Human resource management
9.4	Manage project team	Human resource management
10.2	Manage communications	Communications management
12.2	Conduct procurements	Procurement management
13.3	Manage stakeholder engagement	Stakeholder management

Monitoring and Controlling

Process		Area
4.4	Monitor and control project work	Integration management
4.5	Perform integrated change control	Integration management
5.5	Validate scope	Scope management
5.6	Control scope	Scope management
6.7	Control schedule	Time management
7.4	Control costs	Cost management
8.3	Control quality	Quality management
10.3	Control communications	Communications management
11.6	Control risks	Risk management
12.3	Control procurements	Procurement management
13.4	Control stakeholder engagement	Stakeholder management

Closing

Process		Area
4.6	Close project or phase	Integration management
12.4	Close procurements	Procurement management

Glossary

Accept risk   Risk response strategy, used for both threats and opportunities, which does not change the project management.

Accuracy   Assesses if repeated quality control measurements show the same results.

Active communication   The sender unilaterally sends the message without requesting a response.

Activity   Actions required to produce deliverables and work packages.

Activity attributes   Additional relevant information regarding activities, such as assumptions and constraints.

Activity list   Logical organization of decomposed activities, used to improve manageability.

Activity resource requirements   Resources required to perform project activities.

Activity templates   Historical information regarding activities, can be standardized for future reuse.

Actual cost   Costs actually incurred up to a specific date.

Actual schedule   Schedule updated throughout the project with information about the actual start and finish dates of the project activities.

Affinity diagram   Diagram that organizes existing ideas into groups according to their similarities, in order to improve their manageability.

Analogous estimate   Estimate of durations or costs using historical information accumulated in the organization.

Application area   Category of projects that share specific characteristics.

Arbitration   A formalized and agreed-upon system for administering justice through a third party.

Arrow diagramming method (ADM)   A network diagram used to sequence activities, with the arrows representing activities and the nodes, or circles, representing dependencies.

Assignable cause   Variation outside a process control limit, requiring an effort to identify the causes that led to the nonconformities.

Assumptions   Factors that although uncertain are considered as givens for planning purposes.

Assumptions analysis   Technique that identifies risks by reviewing the consistency of the established assumptions, as well as the quality of the information available about these assumptions.

Assumptions log   Document used to record and track assumptions throughout the project.

Attribute sampling   Each measurement is classified as either conforming or nonconforming to requirements, according to the existence of predefined attributes.

Avoid risk   Threat response strategy that changes the project management plan to completely avoid the risk.

Backward pass   Technique that calculates the late start and late finish dates of project activities by moving backward throughout the network diagram.

Balanced matrix organization   Matrix organization where the authority is evenly shared between functional manager and project manager.

Baseline Formally approved version of project objectives used to assess performance.

Basis of estimate Additional details that support and justify the estimates.

Benchmarking Technique that analyzes other projects, internal or external to the organization, in order to establish references, generate improvement ideas, and create a basis for comparison.

Benefit-cost ratio (BCR) Ratio of the benefits of a project, relative to its costs.

Beta distribution Distribution ranging between a minimum and a maximum value, concentrating around the most likely value, that is often skewed to one of the sides of the distribution.

Bid Seller's formal response to the buyer's need, specifying a price for performing the work described in the procurement document.

Bidder conference or pre-bid conference Meeting organized by the buyer to help potential suppliers understand the procurement documents.

Bottom-up estimate Estimates the costs starting from the lowest levels of the WBS.

Brainstorming Information-gathering technique based on an unconstrained and informal exchange of ideas.

Budget at completion (BAC) Budgeted value for the project or activity total costs.

Budget estimate Estimate prepared during planning ranging from –10 percent to +25 percent from the most likely estimate.

Business case Document used to analyze the project feasibility and justify its selection.

Business risk Risk inherent to the organization's business activity where there is a possibility of loss and a possibility of gain.

Capability Maturity Model Integration Model that assesses quality processes maturity and establishes objectives and guidelines for improvement.

Cause-and-effect diagram Highlights how specific causes may lead to actual or potential problems.

Ceiling price Maximum price that can be paid by the buyer under the contract.

Centralized procurement Procurement department is performing most of the procurement management activities.

Change control board (CCB) A formal board established to review and validate change requests.

Change control meetings Meetings held to analyze change requests, review their impact, and make a decision on whether to approve or reject the change.

Change log Log used to ensure traceability over project changes.

Change management plan Plan that sets the rules on how to manage project changes.

Change management system Procedures, tools, and responsibilities implemented to manage changes to the project management plan or other documents formally controlled.

Change request Formal written request that supports the change management process.

Chart of accounts Numerical system used for accounting purposes.

Checklist List of the elements that need to be checked to ensure that the deliverables, or processes, were performed according to specifications.

Claim Request for compensation according to the contract terms and conditions.

Claims administration Reviewing and reaching agreements on pending claims, through the use of a contract change control system.

Closing   Process group that includes all the processes required to bring a formal and controlled end to the phase, project, or contract.

Code of accounts   Numerical system used to assign a unique number to each WBS element.

Coercive power   Authority based on the ability to punish.

Colocation   Concentrates team members in a single physical space to facilitate communication, focus the team on the project objectives, and develop a sense of teamwork.

Common cause   Variation inside a process control limit, which does not require an investigation effort.

Communication channels   Existing one-to-one communication relationships within the project.

Communication expeditor   Establishes and maintains formal and informal communication channels across project stakeholders.

Communication model   Two-way process of reaching mutual understanding that includes a sender, a message, a medium, a receiver, feedback, and noise.

Communication technology   Tools used to transfer information among stakeholders.

Communications management   Activities required to identify, collect, process, and distribute project information.

Communications management plan   Statement that identifies communication requirements and determines how they will be managed throughout the project.

Composite organization   Organizations that adopt characteristics of different organization types.

Compromise in conflict   Conflict resolution technique where both parties give in and reject their initial perspectives in order to reach an agreement.

Configuration management plan   Plan that sets the rules regarding how to identify, document, and change specific product components.

Configuration management system   System that provides formal and specific guidelines on how to identify, document, and change specific product components.

Conformance costs   Costs of preventing and assessing defects.

Conformance to requirements   Quality management principle that encourages providing all the specified requirements and only the specified requirements.

Consideration   The supplier delivers something of value in exchange for compensation.

Constraint   Existing limits to project management decisions.

Contingency plan   Conditional risk response, only activated if a risk trigger is hit.

Contingency reserve   Provision of time or costs held by the project manager to deal with identified risks.

Contract   Mutual agreement in which parties voluntarily accept being legally bound.

Contract breach   A contract requirement was not met.

Contract change control system   Rules, forms, responsibilities, and levels of authority implemented to manage contract changes.

Contract early termination   Contract interruption before it has been fulfilled.

Contract early termination for cause or default   The contract is terminated because one party did not fulfill its contract obligations.

Contract early termination for convenience   One of the parties unilaterally terminates the contract.

Contract early termination for mutual understanding   Both parties agree to terminate the contract.

Contract incentives   Contract mechanisms used to synchronize the buyer's and supplier's objectives.

Contract material breach   A contract breach that may release the innocent organization from its contractual obligations.

Contract record management system   Procedures, rules, systems, and standards associated with managing contract documents.

Contract special terms   Changes to the standard contract to account for specific project needs regarding scope, risk, schedule, or communications.

Contract standard terms   Predefined terms of contract used recurrently on similar projects.

Control account   Establishes the level of WBS detail where the project performance will be assessed.

Control chart   Chart that represents data over time to determine if the product, process, or project performance is under control or needs intervention.

Control limits   Limits within a control chart that define the acceptable range of process variation.

Corrective action   Action required to correct an existing variance to the project management plan.

Cost aggregation   Summing the work packages' cost estimates and risk contingency reserve along the WBS.

Cost baseline   Approved version of the authorized time-phased budget.

Cost management   Processes required for assessing the project resources in monetary values, determining the budget, and controlling the costs.

Cost management plan   Plan that specifies the procedures, tools, and techniques used for managing costs.

Cost of quality (COQ)   Technique that identifies all quality conformance and nonconformance costs.

Cost performance index (CPI)   Performance metric that represents efficiency through the ratio of earned value to actual costs.

Cost plus award fee (CPAF)   Cost-reimbursable type of contract that reimburses all allowable costs, plus a fixed fee, plus an award fee based on performance.

Cost plus fixed fee contract (CPFF)   Cost-reimbursable type of contract that reimburses all allowable costs, plus a fixed fee.

Cost plus incentive fee contract (CPIF)   Cost-reimbursable type of contract that reimburses all allowable costs, plus a fixed fee, plus an incentive fee linked to performance objectives.

Cost variance (CV)   Difference between the earned value and the actual cost.

Cost-reimbursable contract   Generic contract category where the supplier is reimbursed for allowable actual costs plus a profit fee.

Costs aggregation   Sum of the cost estimates of the WBS work packages and the risk contingency reserve along the WBS.

Crashing   Schedule compression technique that reduces the project duration through an increase in project resources.

Critical activity   Any activity on a critical path.

Critical chain method   Schedule network analysis technique that can be used as an alternative to the critical path method. This method is based on leveling resources and reducing multitasking.

Critical path   In a network diagram, the critical path is the path where all activities are critical, that is, have a zero float.

Critical path method (CPM)   Scheduling technique that plans the project duration, analyzing the longest project path, that is, the sequence of critical activities that cannot be delayed without delaying the project.

Customer   Person or group that receives the project product, using it to create value for the organization.

Dashboard   A control panel that provides an at-a-glance understanding regarding project performance.

David McClelland's theory of needs   Motivational theory that states that there are people motivated by power, people motivated by affiliation, and people motivated by results.

Decentralized procurement   The team is performing most of the procurement management activities.

Decision tree   Graphical treelike representation of alternative decisions with uncertain results.

Decomposition   The process of breaking down project deliverables into smaller, more manageable components.

Definitive estimates   Estimates prepared during project execution with a precision ranging from –10 percent to +10 percent, or even –5 percent to +5 percent.

Deliverable   Tangible and verifiable item that must be produced in order to complete the project.

Delphi technique   A consensus is reached by repeatedly consulting experts, usually through an anonymous process.

Dependency   Logical relation between activities.

Design of experiments   Quality planning tool that statistically analyzes the influence of different variables on the product, project, or process quality.

Direct costs   Costs incurred by the project in order for it to exist.

Discretionary dependency   Optional dependency, frequently recommended as part of a methodology but which may be changed at the behest of the project manager and team decisions.

Documentation reviews   Analyzing project documents and plans; the main source of risk identification.

Dummy activity   An activity of zero duration used to show a logical relationship in the arrow diagramming method that cannot be described with regular nodes.

Duration   Number of work units required to complete an activity.

Early date   Earliest date that an activity can start, or finish, because all predecessor activities have been completed.

Early finish   The earliest day that an activity can finish, completing all predecessor activities.

Early start   The earliest day that an activity can start, completing all predecessor activities.

Earned value (EV)   Budgeted cost of the work completed up to a specific date.

Earned value management (EVM)   Consistent cost control technique that analyzes project performance by combining and integrating scope, time, and costs assessment.

Earned value report   Report that integrates scope, time, and cost to assess performance.

Enhance risk   Opportunity response strategy that increases the risk probability and impact.

Enterprise environmental factors   Elements that exist around the project and may influence its performance, such as infrastructure, culture, human resource skills, and available systems.

Estimate at completion (EAC)   The expected total cost of an activity or project when the work is completed.

Estimate to complete (ETC)   Estimated cost to complete a project or activity.

Executing   Process group that includes all the processes required to execute the plan, completing project deliverables and coordinating resources.

Expectancy theory   Motivational theory that states that people are motivated if they believe that there is an expected relationship between effort, performance, and rewards.

Expected monetary value (EMV)   Enables risk quantification through a combination of probability and impact.

Expert power   Authority based on knowledge, skills, and experience.

Expert judgment   Judgment based upon expertise, typically used for planning purposes.

Exploit risk   Completely remove the opportunity uncertainty.

External dependency   Dependency from actions and decisions from external entities.

Fallback plan   Alternative risk response, or plan B, activated if the main risk response is ineffective.

Fast tracking   The schedule is reduced by overlapping activities that would normally be done sequentially.

Fee   Difference between the price and the total costs.

Feedback   Response acknowledging the reception of the message.

Finish to finish   The predecessor activity has to finish before the successor activity finishes.

Finish to start   The predecessor activity has to finish before the successor activity starts.

Firm fixed price (FFP) contract   Most popular type of fixed-price contract where the price is defined from the start and may not be changed without a formal contract change.

Fitness for use   Ability to meet the customer's need while developing a product or service.

Fixed costs   Costs that are not impacted by changes to the size of the activity or project.

Fixed-formula rule   Work performance is assessed assigning a percentage of progress when the work package starts and the rest when it finishes.

Fixed price with economic price adjustment (FPEPA)   Type of fixed-price contract, usually used in multiyear procurements, where the price is defined but may be adjusted yearly according to economic changes, such as inflation or oil prices.

Fixed price incentive fee contract (FPIF)   Type of fixed-price contract that defines a fixed price plus an incentive mechanism.

Fixed-price contract   Generic contract category that fixes a payment amount for a specific product or service.

Float   Time frame during which an activity may be delayed, from its early start, without delaying the project.

Flowchart   Graphical representation of the steps required to achieve an objective, or the steps associated with a process.

Focus groups   Stakeholders discuss ideas and generate a solution with the help of a moderator.

Force conflict   Conflict management technique where someone's perspective is imposed on others.

Force field analysis   Quality planning tool that helps highlight the favorable and unfavorable factors, or forces, that drive the quality improvement decision.

Force majeure   Contract clause that releases parties from contract obligations when a pre-defined uncontrollable motive occurs.

Forecasting   Process of making statements about events whose actual outcomes have not yet been observed.

Forecast report   Report that predicts future performance.

Formal communication   Communication that conforms to established professional rules, standards, and processes.

Forward pass   Technique that calculates the early start and early finish dates of project activities by moving forward throughout the network diagram.

Free float   Time frame during which an activity can be delayed without delaying the early start of a successor activity.

Fringe benefits   Standard compensation, additional to direct wages, formally given to all employees.

Functional manager   Manager responsible for the work of a business function, business line, or organization unit.

Functional, hierarchical, or vertical organization   Organization where the staff is grouped hierarchically by functions. The authority of the functional managers over the project is clear, with each employee having only one clear boss.

Funding limit reconciliation   Comparing the use of funds with the existing financial constraints.

Gantt chart or bar chart   Represents the activities schedule through horizontal bars, complemented with additional information such as durations and dates.

Gold plating   Offering the customer additional scope or quality.

Ground rules   Unwritten rules that define what behaviors are accepted and what behaviors are not accepted during the project.

Group creativity techniques   Methods used to facilitate creativity in a group of people, which may include brainstorming, nominal group techniques, Delphi technique, mind maps, and affinity diagrams.

Herzberg theory   Motivational theory that states that motivation may be influenced by hygiene factors and motivating agents.

Heuristic   Accepted empirical rule.

Hierarchy   Who each team member reports to during the project.

Histogram   Graphical representation of a time-phased resource allocation, usually through vertical bars.

Historical information or historical data   Knowledge accumulated by the organization that can be used as planning inputs in future projects.

Human resource management   Processes required to manage the team.

Human resource management plan   Determines how team members will be acquired and managed, establishes their roles and responsibilities, and defines the project hierarchy.

Incentive fee   Positive or negative compensation for variances between the actual cost and the target price.

Independent estimate   Estimate developed internally or externally by an independent entity that can be compared to the suppliers' estimates.

Indirect costs   Costs that are incurred for the benefit of more than one project and are therefore shared among different projects.

Individual risks   Specific project risks.

Influence curve   Illustrates how the ability to influence a change is relatively high at the project's beginning and low at its end. Simultaneously, it highlights how the cost of a potential change is relatively low at the project's beginning and high at its end.

Influence diagram   Graphical representation of a decision process, highlighting the factors that may influence a decision.

Informal communication   Communication that is not constrained to established professional rules, standards, and processes.

Information management system   Set of tools used to support project information.

Informational power   Authority based on the ability to access and use information to his or her own advantage.

Initiating   Process group that includes all the processes required to authorize the start of a project or phase, as well as establishing a common vision.

Input   Item required by the process in order to produce its output.

Inspection   Work and deliverables examination to verify if they conform to requirements.

Integration management   Includes all the processes required to ensure the coordination of the different project management knowledge areas, protecting their consistency and alignment to project constraints and stakeholders' expectations.

Integration plans   Elements of the project management plan that establish product and project change management rules.

Intention   Both parties wish that the agreement is enforced by a court.

Interactive communication   Communication method in which two or more people communicate interactively.

Internal dependency   Dependency from other activities from within the project.

Internal rate of return (IRR)   Measures the project return on a percentage basis.

Interviews   Information is collected through direct questions to project stakeholders.

Invitation for bid (IFB)   Procurement document used to acquire products or services when the buyer can specify in detail the work that will be performed. The buyer only requests a price from the supplier.

ISO 9000   Set of standards from the International Organization for Standardization (ISO) that assesses the capacity of the organization to follow its own quality procedures.

Issue log   Tool used to manage the team and other stakeholders' engagement by documenting and tracing problems, obstacles, and expectations, from identification to resolution.

Joint venture   Previously established agreement assigning the work to a specific supplier.

Just in time (JIT)   Management approach that reduces stocks to zero or nearly zero by requesting suppliers to deliver materials only when they are required.

Kaizen   Japanese continuous improvement philosophy, based on small but constant changes to obtain large results.

Kickoff meeting   Meeting where the stakeholders have an opportunity to familiarize themselves with the project baselines, management approach, and team members.

Knowledge areas   Logical organization of project management processes by topics. Knowledge areas include integration, scope, time, cost, quality, human resources, communications, risk, procurement, and stakeholders.

Known-unknowns   Risks that were identified during the project.

Lag   Waiting time between the predecessor activity and the successor.

Late date   Latest date that an activity may start, or finish, without delaying the project.

Latest finish   The latest possible date that an activity may finish without delaying the project.

Latest start   The latest possible date that an activity may start without delaying the project.

Lead   A modification of a logical relationship that accelerates the schedule by overlapping activities.

Lean manufacturing   Quality management approach focused on eliminating work that does not add value.

Learning curve   Work productivity increases as the team member becomes familiarized with the work.

Legal capacity   Both parties have the ability to establish a specific legal agreement.

Legal purpose   The contracted product or service is conformant with the law.

Legitimate power   Authority based on the hierarchical position in the organization.

Lessons learned   Assessment performed by stakeholders to capture what went well and what could have been done better in order to improve future performance.

Lessons learned report   Report that assesses what went well and what could have been improved.

Letter of intent   Enables the buyer to declare an intention to buy before an actual contract acceptance is completed.

Level of effort rule   Work performance is assessed indirectly by the performance of other work packages or proportionally to the elapsed time.

Life cycle costing   Includes within project decisions all the costs required to develop, operate, and discontinue the product.

Make or buy decision   Determines if the requirements will be delivered internally or will be acquired externally.

Management reserve   Provision of time or costs held by management to compensate for unknown-unknowns.

Mandatory dependency   Dependency that is inherent to the physical nature of the work or results from a contract or legal requirement.

Marginal analysis   Used by quality management to define the optimum level of quality costs, analyzing the savings generated by a one-unit increase in quality spending.

Maslow's hierarchy of needs   Motivational theory that states that there is a pyramid of human needs. Each individual is particularly motivated to satisfy the needs of a particular pyramid step. When those needs are met, the individual will be motivated to meet the needs of the next step.

Matrix organization   Multidimensional organization that combines the functions' vertical lines with the project's horizontal lines to better adapt to a project's challenges.

McGregor's Theory X and Theory Y   Motivational theories that state there are two types of managers. Manager X assumes that people need to be micromanaged permanently. Manager Y assumes that people should have some autonomy.

Milestone   Significant zero duration project event.

Milestone chart   High-level schedule that identifies project milestones and their specific dates.

Mind maps   Diagrams that help generate and organize ideas.

Mitigate risk   Threat response strategy that develops actions to reduce the risk probability and impact.

Monitoring and controlling   Process group that includes all the processes required to compare the actual performance against the plan, identify potential variances, issue corrective or preventive actions, and manage changes.

Monte Carlo analysis   Technique that assesses schedule risk based on the simulation of multiple project iterations.

Multicriteria decision analysis   Assessment technique based on weighting multiple criteria.

Near-critical path   Sequence of activities with a low float.

Negative float   How many days have to be recovered to meet a deadline or project baseline.

Net present value (NPV)   Present value of the future cash flows generated by the project.

Network diagram   Graphical representation of the activities, events, and dependencies.

Network diagrams templates   Historical information regarding activities, milestones, and dependencies, can be standardized for future reuse.

Network path   A series of connected activities in a network diagram.

Nominal group technique   Technique that quickly reaches a decision through vote, taking into account everyone's opinion.

Nonconformance costs   Costs of solving internal and external failures.

Nonrecurring costs   Costs that occur once throughout the project and do not tend to repeat themselves.

Nonverbal communication   Communication based on physical gestures, such as facial expressions and body language.

Observations   Requirements are collected by examining individuals within their work environment.

Offer and acceptance   One entity makes an offer that is accepted by another.

One-point estimate   The estimator generates only one value per activity.

Operation   Work with permanent characteristics, frequently repeating the same process.

OPM3   PMI's globally recognized best-practice standard for assessing the maturity of the organization's practices for managing projects, programs, and portfolios.

Opportunity cost   Cost of losing the best available alternative to the project.

Organization chart   Diagram that displays the reporting hierarchy between team members.

Organizational breakdown structure (OBS)   Hierarchical diagram that displays the relationship between the work and the organizational units.

Organizational process assets   Assets accumulated in the organization, which can be used to guide and improve the project management effort.

Ouchi's Theory Z   Motivational theory that argues that employees are motivated by a spirit of trust, commitment, and development.

Output   Item developed by a project management process.

Overall project risk   Aggregation of the project's individual risks.

Padding   Estimating technique that attempts to manage risk by inflating the estimate.

Paralingual communication   Communication based on pitch, tone, and inflections in the voice.

Parametric estimate   Estimating method that uses a statistical relationship between historical data and project variables.

Pareto diagram   In quality management, this diagram is used to graphically display the most common causes of defects, the most frequent type of defects, or the most frequent customer complaints, ordered by the number of times they occur.

Passive communication   Information is placed in a repository that can be accessed by receivers.

Payback period   Period of time required for the project to repay the original investment.

Payment systems   System used to pay suppliers' invoices.

Percentage complete rule   Work performance is assessed through a subjective assessment of the percentage of work completed.

Percentage complete with milestones gates rule   Work performance is measured through a subjective assessment of the percentage of work completion.

Performance bond   Contract tool that guarantees satisfactory completion of a project's contract.

Performance measurement baseline (PMB)   Scope, schedule, and cost baseline for the earned value management technique.

Performance reviews   Monitor the project performance regarding project objectives such as scope, schedule, or cost.

Performing organization   Organization responsible for performing the work and for managing the required resources.

Perquisites   Special compensation given to some employees for their outstanding performance.

Planned value (PV)   Budgeted cost of the work scheduled to be completed up to a specific date.

Planning   Process group that includes all the processes required to define, refine, and formalize objectives, as well as determine the necessary actions to attain them.

Planning package   Large blocks of work used to plan work in the long run, where work packages are not yet identified.

Point of total assumption (PTA)   The supplier supports all costs over this value.

Portfolio   Group of projects or programs coordinated to implement the business strategy.

Portfolio manager   Person responsible for managing the portfolio.

Practice continual improvement   Quality management principle that encourages product and process improvements through a continuous effort to introduce small enhancements.

Pre-assignment   Resources are selected for the project without any type of negotiation with the project manager.

Precedence   Logical dependency between activities or between an activity and an event.

Precedence diagramming method (PDM)   Main technique used to sequence activities, representing activities by nodes and dependencies by arrows.

Precision   Assesses if the values measured during quality control are close to the actual values.

Preliminary schedule   Schedule that is developed based on preliminary and inaccurate information.

Prequalified sellers Suppliers that were selected by the buyer to move on to the next phase of the procurement process.

Present value (PV) Expected future cash flows adjusted by a set discount rate.

Prevention is preferable to inspection Quality management principle that suggests that the cost of preventing is usually lower than the cost of correcting.

Preventive action Action required to avoid an anticipated variance to the project management plan.

Price Total value paid by the buyer.

Probabilistic distribution Graphical representation of the probability of a range of values (e.g., project costs).

Probability and impact matrix Used on the qualitative analysis to score and rank the different project risks.

Problem solve Conflict resolution technique that manages each conflict situation as a problem that requires a solution.

Process Set of related activities that generates a desired output by using specific inputs, techniques, and tools.

Process analysis Technique that executes the process improvement plan, looking for obstacles and non-value-added activities.

Process groups A logical organization of project management processes that includes initiating, planning, executing, monitoring and controlling, and closing.

Process improvement plan Planned effort to improve standard project management practices. The plan can be used as a guide to improve project management practices such as metrics, quality, issue management, change control, project tracking, and status reporting.

Process quality Efficiency and effectiveness of the adopted processes.

Procurement Acquire products and services from external sources.

Procurement audit Review of the procurement processes to verify if they are being performed as planned and if they meet the need for which they were implemented.

Procurement documents Documents that describe the buyer's needs to potential suppliers.

Procurement management All processes required to acquire products and services from external sources, and administer the contracts or agreements associated with those acquisitions.

Procurement management plan Subsidiary plan that establishes the rules used to manage procurement.

Procurement negotiation Proposals or bids are revised through bargaining in order to define contract elements.

Procurement performance review Formal assessment of the supplier's capacity to perform the project according to contract conditions.

Procurement statement of work (SOW) Narrative description of products or services to be acquired from an external supplier under contract.

Product analysis Scope definition technique that translates the product into specific deliverables.

Product breakdown Product analysis technique that decomposed the product into deliverables to facilitate an agreement among project stakeholders.

Product life cycle The complete history of a product, extending through its idea, definition, development, operation, and disposal phases.

Product quality Assesses the project's products according to its requirements.

Product scope Product functionalities or specifications established through product requirements.

Program   Set of related projects and operations that when managed in a coordinated way address a common business objective.

Program Evaluation and Review Technique (PERT)   Type of three-point estimate that uses optimistic, most likely, and pessimistic values to determine the duration or cost of an activity.

Program manager   Person responsible for managing the program.

Progress report   Report that describes what was accomplished in the reporting period.

Progressive elaboration   Providing greater levels of planning detail as the project moves toward completion and as more and better information becomes available.

Project   Temporary initiative carried out with the aim of producing a unique product.

Project charter   Formal document that authorizes the beginning of the project and provides the project manager with the authority to apply resources to project activities.

Project coordinator   Type of project manager's role in a functional, or weak, matrix organization with a low level of authority. The project coordinator has a higher level of project authority than the project expeditor, with some level of coordination authority over the team.

Project document   Documents permanently updated during planning, executing, and controlling that are not part of the project management plan.

Project expeditor   Type of project manager's role in a functional, or weak matrix, organization with a very low level of authority.

Project float   Amount of time a project can be delayed without delaying the project-imposed deadline or the project manager's baseline.

Project information   Information required to monitor and control the project and may include work performance data, work performance information, and work performance reports.

Project life cycle   Collection of phases that the project must go through from its beginning to its closing.

Project management   Professional activity that pursues project success through the structured application of initiating, planning, executing, monitoring and controlling, and closing processes.

Project management information system (PMIS)   System that includes the tools required to collect, record, process, and disseminate information across project stakeholders.

Project management office (PMO)   Organizational unit responsible for project management throughout the organization.

Project management plan   Sets the rules regarding how the project will be managed, including which processes will be used and how they will be implemented. It also includes a scope, schedule, and cost baseline.

Project management team   Members of the project team directly involved in project management work.

Project manager   With authority delegated by the sponsor, he or she is accountable for managing the project and meeting project objectives.

Project performance appraisal   Formal and informal assessment of individual team member's performance.

Project phase   A group of logically related work, for easier planning and controlling.

Project quality   Assesses if the project is meeting its schedule, costs, and scope objectives.

Project records   Organize relevant information about the project, including e-mails, meeting minutes, and contract administration documents.

Project schedule   Diagram that identifies the start and finish dates for each activity.

Project schedule network diagram   Graphical representation of activities, events, and their dependencies. It may include a time scale.

Project scope   All the work required to deliver the project's product, as well as meet other project objectives.

Project selection methods   Methods used to select and prioritize projects.

Project team   Includes everyone who is involved in executing technical and project management activities.

Projectized organization   Organization structured around and oriented toward projects. Authority over each project is exclusively assigned to a project manager.

Proposal   Seller's formal response to the procurement document. It includes a solution and a price.

Prototypes   Requirements are generated by presenting a model to stakeholders and requesting feedback.

Punitive damages   Contractual fines used to compensate for contract breaches losses.

Purchase order   Simple form of fixed-price contract where one party unilaterally issues a purchase request.

Pure risk   There is a possibility of loss, but no possibility of gain.

Quality   Assesses how well the requirements are being met.

Quality attributes   Define specific and measurable properties of the product or process, and are used to verify compliance.

Quality audit   Independent evaluation of project quality compliance, led by internal or external auditors.

Quality control measurements   Actual values obtained by the quality control inspections.

Quality grade   Used to distinguish elements with the same utility but different technical attributes.

Quality inspection   An inspection to determine if a deliverable meets specified quality criteria.

Quality management   Includes the activities required to ensure that the project, the product, and the adopted processes meet requirements.

Quality management plan   Subsidiary plan of the project management plan that describes how the organization or program quality policy will be implemented on the project.

Quality metrics   Describe the specific product or project requirements that should be achieved.

Quality policy   Set of rules and guidelines defined by the organization or by a program that should be used as a reference while preparing the project quality management plan.

Questionnaires and surveys   Requirements are generated using previously defined questions.

RACI chart   Type of responsibility assignment matrix that categorizes responsibilities as: R(esponsible), A(ccountable), C(onsulted), and I(nformed).

Rebaselining   Revising the baseline in response to project changes or to the acknowledgment that the former baseline is no longer achievable.

Recognition and reward system   Set of rules that define how team members will be recognized and compensated.

Recurring costs   Costs that occur on a repetitive basis.

Referent power   Authority based on an authority not formally assigned but that exists indirectly due to other factors such as personality.

Request for information   Procurement document used for requesting information about one product.

Request for proposal (RFP)   Procurement document used to acquire elements that are not very standardized. The buyer specifies the product requirements and lets the supplier determine the solution and the price.

Request for quotation (RFQ)   Procurement document used to acquire standardized elements that do not typically involve a solution and have low value.

Requirements documentation   Documents that describe requirements and explain how the project's business need is addressed.

Requirements management plan   Element of the project management plan that sets the rules regarding how to analyze, prioritize, document, approve, develop, verify, change, and trace requirements.

Requirements traceability matrix   Document, typically with a tabular form, that connects each requirement to one business need, a project objective, and a deliverable.

Reserve   A provision of time and costs to account for risk.

Reserve analysis   Technique used to define the contingency reserve when estimating durations and costs. This technique can also be used to compare existing reserve with remaining risk.

Residual risk   Risks that remain after risk response planning.

Resource acquisition   Resources are acquired from outside sources.

Resource breakdown structure (RBS)   Hierarchical diagram that displays the relationship between the work and the resource types.

Resource leveling   The project manager's priority is adapting resource utilization to avoid planning above capacity.

Resource negotiation   Resources are acquired for the project through a negotiation between the project manager and other entities.

Resource smoothing   Resources optimization technique that adjusts the schedule in order to promote constant resource utilization.

Responsibility   Activities required to perform the work properly.

Responsibility assignment matrix (RAM)   Assigns WBS work packages to team members to clearly define responsibilities.

Reward power   Authority based on the ability to reward.

Risk   A potential event that can have a favorable or unfavorable impact on project objectives.

Risk appetite   Level of uncertainty that the organization is willing to accept.

Risk audit   Assesses whether the risk management procedures were adopted and are appropriate and whether the risk responses were effective.

Risk averse   Satisfaction decreases with an increase of risk exposure.

Risk breakdown structure   A hierarchically organized representation of project risks arranged by risk categories.

Risk categories   Logical way to group risks, favoring and accelerating the reuse of accumulated historical information.

Risk cause   The reason that can potentially lead into the risk event.

Risk closure   The risk is closed when its occurrence can no longer happen.

Risk data quality assessment   Qualitative risk analysis technique that considers the accuracy and completeness of project data while assessing the probability and impact of project risks.

Risk event   The description of what might affect the project.

Risk factors   Elements that can influence people's perception of the risk's importance.

Risk impact   The potential consequence of the risk occurence.

Risk management   Process of identifying, analyzing, and responding to risk factors throughout the project.

Risk management plan   Subsidiary plan that determines how to identify, analyze, respond to, and control project risks.

Risk neutral   Satisfaction does not change with an increase of risk exposure.

Risk ranking or scores   Risks are ranked based on their probability and impact, as well as other risk factors.

Risk reassessment   Periodical reevaluation of the risk rating and status.

Risk register   Document that includes all relevant information about the risk, including event, cause, impact, probability, impact, responses, and status.

Risk response owner   Stakeholder in charge of the adopted risk response.

Risk score   Numerical assessment of the risk severity that can be used to prioritize risks, as well as assess if the risk responses were effective in reducing risk exposure.

Risk seeking   Satisfaction increases with an increase of risk exposure.

Risk threshold   Limit beyond which stakeholders are not willing to accept the risk exposure and additional risk responses are required.

Risk tolerance   Defines how much risk the organization is willing to accept.

Risk triggers   Symptoms or warning signs that the risk is about to occur.

Risk watch list   Noncritical risks that are marked for later review during the project.

Risks requiring further analysis   Risks that will move further on the risk management process, to quantitative analysis or response planning.

Risks requiring short-term responses   Qualitative risk analysis technique that lists the risks requiring short-term responses.

Role   Team member's function within the project.

Rolling wave planning   Progressive elaboration planning technique that plans for the short term in detail and prepares a high-level plan for the long run.

Root cause analysis   Technique that attempts to understand the underlying causes of problems or risks.

Rough order of magnitude estimate (ROM)   Estimates prepared during the initiating process group, with large upper and lower ranges of variation.

Rule of seven   Rule applied on a control chart to determine that a process is out of control. The rule is applied when there are seven measurements in a row that are on one side of the mean, even if they are within the control limits.

Run chart   Chart that displays time-phased data in order to detect a trend and forecast future performance.

S curve   Graphical representation of an authorized time-phased budget.

Sampling   Selecting part of the population in order to infer the characteristics of the entire population.

Scatter diagram   Graphical representation of the measurements of two variables along two axes, to verify if they are statistically correlated.

Schedule baseline   Approved version of the project schedule.

Schedule compression   Reduction of the overall project duration, using a combination of changes in scope, time, costs, quality, human resources, and risks.

Schedule management plan   Element of the project management plan that establishes the procedures, tools, and techniques used for managing the schedule.

Schedule network analysis   Group of schedule development techniques that includes the critical path method, the critical chain method, resource leveling, simulation, crashing, and fast tracking.

Schedule performance index (SPI)   Performance metric that represents speed through the ratio of earned value to planned value.

Schedule variance (SV)   Difference between the earned value and the planned value.

Schedule data   Data that support the project schedule.

Scope baseline   Approved version of the scope statement, WBS, and WBS dictionary.

Scope creep   Uncontrolled additions to project or product scope.

Scope management   Ensures that all the required work is performed and only the required work is performed.

Scope management plan   Plan that specifies the procedures, tools, techniques, and responsibilities required for managing scopes.

Scope statement   Document that establishes a common understanding among different stakeholders over the project and product scope.

Screening system   A type of proposal evaluation technique that eliminates from the selection process those suppliers that do not meet the source selection criteria.

Secondary risk   Risks that were created by adopted risk responses.

Sensitivity analysis   Quantitative analysis technique that determines which risks have the most potential impact on project objectives.

Share risk   Opportunity response strategy where the opportunity is shared with another entity.

Shared responsibility over quality   Quality management principle that establishes that the responsibility for quality should be shared among management, project manager, and team.

Sharing ratio   Describes how variances between the actual cost and the target cost will be shared between the buyer and the supplier.

Single-source procurement   The buyer chose to acquire a preferred supplier without consulting other alternatives.

Six Sigma   Quality management approach that aims to improve processes in order to eliminate errors.

Smooth conflict   Conflict management technique that attempts to maintain a comfortable environment instead of seeking a conflict resolution.

Sole-source procurement   The buyer chose to acquire one product that is only provided by a single supplier.

Source selection criteria   A type of proposal evaluation technique that assigns a specific weight to each procurement criterion, enabling the organization to select a single supplier or rank suppliers for a future negotiation process.

Specification limits   Limits within a control chart that define the customer specification or the contract requirements.

Sponsor   Manager who provides the financial resources and promotes the project.

Staffing management plan   Component of the human resource management plan that determines how the resource requirements will be acquired by the project and how resources will be managed.

Stage gate   Predefined event in the project, typically at the end of a phase, where the sponsor and steering committee have the opportunity to review the project performance and major deliverables, as well as decide whether to proceed to the next phase.

Stakeholder   Person or group that can be impacted positively or negatively by the project.

Stakeholder engagement assessment matrix   Matrix used to map specific stakeholders to current and desired levels of engagement.

Stakeholder management   Processes required for meeting stakeholders' expectations.

Stakeholder management plan   Determines the strategies that best promote engagement and commitment to the project.

Stakeholder register   Project document that holds relevant information about stakeholders, including contacts, requirements, expectations, power, interests, and attitude toward the project.

Standard deviation or sigma   Measures the statistical dispersion from the average.

Start to finish   The predecessor activity has to start before the successor activity finishes.

Start to start   The predecessor activity has to start before the successor activity starts.

Statement of work (SOW)   Formal document that describes the products and services that should be provided by the project.

Status report   Summarizes the project situation at a certain time.

Steering committee   Advisory group that provides project management guidance, key decision making, progress monitoring, conflict arbitration, key deliverables approval, and facilitation of resources allocation.

Strong matrix organization   Type of matrix organization where most of the authority over the project belongs to the project manager.

Subproject   Decomposition of a project into more easily manageable components.

Subsidiary plans   Elements of the project management plan used to establish management rules for a specific area.

Sunk costs   Costs that cannot be avoided even if the project was cancelled.

SWOT analysis   Information-gathering technique based on analyzing the strengths, weaknesses, opportunities, and threats associated with a specific topic.

Tailoring   Adapting the project management processes to the project needs and environment.

Target cost   Cost used as a reference to establish contract incentives.

Target fee   Profit obtained by the supplier if there is no incentive compensation.

Target price   Total value paid by the buyer under the contract if the actual costs are exactly the same as the target cost.

Target schedule   Schedule developed based on deadlines set by management or the customer.

Team-building activities   Activities developed to increase the team's overall performance.

Team performance assessment   Formal or informal evaluations of the team's performance.

Technique   Group of systematic steps required to obtain a specific outcome, using specific tools.

Three-point estimate   An estimate that uses three points to determine the duration or the cost of an activity.

Time and material contract (T&M)   Generic contract category that establishes a price for all resources used for the project on a per-day or per-item basis, without establishing the quantity that will be used for each resource.

Time management Knowledge area that includes all the processes required to deliver the project on schedule

To-complete performance index (TCPI) Performance required in the future in order to achieve a previously defined objective.

Tool Tangible item used on a process to develop an expected output.

Top-down estimating Perceives the project from a high-level perspective and comes up with a total cost (or duration) estimate that later can be decomposed in smaller components.

Total quality management (TQM) Management system that guides the team on the continuous improvement of the product and process quality.

Transfer risk Threat response strategy that transfers the ownership and impact of the risk to another entity.

Trend reports Report that analyzes time-phased results and identifies trends.

Triple constraint Term used to describe three concurrent project constraints that must be simultaneously accomplished, namely, scope, time, and costs.

Tuckman team development model Team development model that establishes several development phases: forming, storming, norming, performing, and adjourning.

Unknown-unknowns Risks that were not or could not be identified on the project.

Value analysis Technique focused on reducing the cost of developing the product without changing the scope.

Value engineering Systematic and quantitative method that examines the product's high-level requirements, looking for alternatives to increase the product's value.

Variable costs Costs that depend on the size of the activity or project.

Variable sampling A measurement is classified on a continuous numerical scale that rates the degree of conformance or nonconformance.

Variance Measures the statistical dispersion from the average. It is calculated as the square of the standard deviation.

Variance analysis Variance between actual performance and a baseline.

Variance at completion (VAC) Difference between the budget at completion and the estimate at completion.

Variance report Report that compares actual values with the baseline.

Vendor, supplier, or contractor A supplier of material or services working under a contract.

Vendor bid analysis Estimates costs based on vendors' proposals.

Verbal communication Oral communication such as meetings, conversations, and phone calls.

Verifiable No ambiguity while validating the requirements.

Virtual team Team members cooperate remotely using communication technology.

Waiver Buyer's voluntary surrender of a contract privilege.

Walkthrough Type of inspection technique that simulates actual execution but bypasses risky or expensive operations.

War room Location used as project command center to improve communication.

Warranty Contractual guarantee provided during a period of time, ensuring that the products and services will be delivered according to the quality requirements.

Weak matrix organization   Type of matrix organization where most of the authority over the project belongs to the functional manager.

Weighted milestones rule   Work performance is assessed by assigning specific percentages when meeting previously defined milestones.

Weighting system   Proposal evaluation technique that enables the organization to select a single supplier or rank suppliers for a future negotiation process.

Withdraw from conflict   Conflict resolution technique that avoids the conflict, or delays its resolution.

Work authorization system   System used to authorize, formally and in writing, the start of work packages or activities.

Work breakdown structure (WBS)   Deliverable-oriented treelike representation of all the work required to achieve the project objectives.

Work breakdown structure dictionary   Document that stores additional information regarding each work package.

Work packages   Elements at the lowest level of the WBS, used to facilitate estimation, assign responsibility to individuals or "work centers," and improve performance control.

Work performance data   Data that were not processed by the project management team, such as activity physical progress, actual dates, planned start and finish dates, technical performance assessments, resource utilization, and actual costs.

Work performance information   Data that were processed by the project management team while performing the control activities, such as forecasts for completion, earned value metrics, and information regarding the deliverables' status.

Work performance reports   Documented project control information used to report performance to relevant stakeholders.

Workaround   Unplanned response for an accepted risk or to a risk that was not previously identified by the team.

Workshops   Information gathering technique where stakeholders are gathered to discuss ideas and generate consensus.

Bibliography

Cleland, David, Karen M. Bursic, Richard Puerzer, and A. Yaroslav Vlasak, eds. *Project Management Casebook*. Newtown Square, PA: Project Management Institute, 1998.

Crosby, Philip. *Quality Is Free: The Art of Making Quality Certain: How to Manage Quality—So That It Becomes a Source of Profit for Your Business*, 1st ed. New York: Mentor, 1979.

Fleming, Quentin W., and Joel M. Koppelman. *Earned Value Project Management*. Newtown Square, PA: Project Management Institute, 2005.

French, J. P. R., Jr., and B. Raven. "The Bases of Social Power." In *Studies in Social Power*. Dorwin Cartwright, ed. Ann Arbor, MI: University of Michigan Press, 1959.

Kendrick, Tom. *Identifying and Managing Project Risk: Essential Tools for Failure-Proofing Your Project*, 2nd ed. New York: AMACOM, 2009.

Kerzner, Harold. *Project Management: A Systems Approach to Planning, Scheduling, and Controlling*, 10th ed. New York: Wiley, 2009.

Kliem, Ralph. *Effective Communication for Project Management*. New York: Auerbach Publications, 2008.

Langford, John W. *Logistics: Principles and Applications*, 2nd ed. SOLE Press Series. New York: McGraw-Hill, 2007.

Lewis, James P. *Fundamentals of Project Management*, 4th ed. New York: AMACOM, 2011.

Meredith, Jack R., and Samuel J. Mantel, Jr. *Project Management: A Managerial Approach*, 8th ed. New York: Wiley, 2011.

Moura, H. *How to Deal with Troubled Projects*, PMI Global Congress 2012—EMEA, Proceedings. Newtown Square, PA: Project Management Institute, 2012.

Moura, H. *PMP Sem Segredos*. Rio de Janeiro: Elsevier, 2013.

Project Management Institute. *A Guide to the Project Management Body of Knowledge*, 5th ed. (*PMBOK Guide*). Newtown Square, PA: Project Management Institute, 2012.

Project Management Institute. *Practice Standard for Project Risk Management*. Newtown Square, PA: Project Management Institute, 2009.

Project Management Institute. *Project Management Professional (PMP) Examination Specification*. Newtown Square, PA: Project Management Institute, 2006.

Verma, Vijay K. *Human Resource Skills for the Project Manager*. Newtown Square, PA: Project Management Institute, 1996.

Wysocki, Robert, and Rudd McGary. *Effective Project Management: Traditional, Adaptive, Extreme*, 3rd ed. New York: John Wiley & Sons, 2003.